THE DEVELOPING POETIC PHILOSOPHY OF PEDRO SALINAS

A Study in Twentieth Century Spanish Poetry

"La reconquista de la entereza del hombre"

Lorna Shaughnessy

Mellen University Press
Lewiston/Queenston/Lampeter

Library of Congress Cataloging-in-Publication Data

Shaughnessy, Lorna, 1961-
    The developing poetic philosophy of Pedro Salinas : a study in
twentieth century Spanish poetry : "la reconquista de la entereza
del hombre" / Lorna Shaughnessy.
        p.   cm.
    English and Spanish.
    Includes bibliographical references (p.   ) and index.
    ISBN 0-7734-9012-4
    1. Salinas, Pedro, 1892-1951--Criticism and interpretation.
I. Title.
PQ6635.A32Z82   1995
861'.62--dc20   94-48872
                                                                    CIP

A CIP catalog record for this book is available from the British Library.

Copyright © 1995 The Edwin Mellen Press

The Edwin Mellen Press   The Edwin Mellen Press
        Box 450   Box 67
Lewiston, New York   Queenston, Ontario
    USA 14092-0450   CANADA L0S 1L0

                    The Edwin Mellen Press, Ltd.
                        Lampeter, Dyfed, Wales
                    UNITED KINGDOM SA48 7DY

            Printed in the United States of America

For my parents

Table of Contents

Preface

Pedro Salinas' poetic trajectory implies, both in its overall outline and in its detail, an impulse towards wholeness. The generally accepted three successive phases of his verse, taken together, present a broadly symmetrical chronological development: three collections of work essentially from the 1920s, three from the 1930s, and three largely from the 1940s. His first book, by its very title *Presagios*, stands on the brink or verge of what is to come (an anticipatory attitude reflected in the title of his first prose volume *Víspera de gozo*, also poised on the threshold of imminent experience). Given this forward-looking perspective, it is no surprise that both the initial and concluding poems of *Presagios* contain the word *mañana*. A mirror-image of this feeling of prelude is detectable in the valedictory tone of his last verse collection *Confianza*. While Lorna Shaughnessy rightly emphasizes the open-ended quality of Salinas's philosophy of life, nevertheless, the final volume of his poetic corpus conveys an awareness of lyrical consummation, since phrases such as "hay algo que se completa" or "Ya está el poema, / aquí, completo" imply the culminating fruit of past experience.

Within the general context of this comprehensive framing device, moreover, a remarkable degree of unity is noticeable too at each major stage in Salinas's evolution as a poet. Thus Crispin sees in the titles of the early-period works three progressive steps in the formulation of an aesthetic: from *Presagios* (primary contacts with reality hint at deeper meanings), via *Seguro azar* (chance discovery provides fresh insight) to *Fábula y signo* (the transformation of external reality into myth). As for the middle-period works of the love cycle, it is arguable that not only do they represent the core of Salinas's achievement in verse but that, by virtue of their thematic interconnectedness as a trilogy, *La voz a ti debida*, *Razón de amor*, and *Largo lamento* constitute the most integrated group in his output. Here the tendency towards organic unity is significantly highlighted in the case of *La voz a ti debida* by the subtitle *poema* which indicates the latent capacity for the volume's seventy sections to combine into a single massive whole. Even his late works, which at first glance appear the most disparate, can be seen to complement one another in a coherent synthesis: hence the crisis of contemporary social values in *Todo más claro* is flanked by two collections that take comfort in the timeless consolations of nature. One of these, *El Contemplado*, is particularly apt for there the sea (whose fluidity engenders in the observer a flow of associations) becomes an all-embracing symbol that embodies the notion of *entereza* by evoking an infinite variety of analogies. The richness of this experience, in turn, has an equally relevant healing effect on the poet, making him whole, and reminding him, here as elsewhere, that he is part of a whole sum of past and future human experience.

Salinas's incisively witty and ebullient, avant-garde verse treatments of city life and its artefacts from the 1920s have worn far better than his much more discursive handling of metropolitan malaise in the 1940s. Actually a subtle thread of modern urban reality survives even in works like *La voz a ti debida* and *El Contemplado* where it supplies a discreet but effective counterpoint to the texts' transcendental concerns. But, ironically, the fact that of these examples *Todo más claro* alone now seems dated may be attributable to the special circumstances in which it was written. Although Salinas' years of exile in America were undoubtedly his most prolific and multifaceted as he diversified into drama, narrative fiction, literary criticism and essays, an uncharitable commentator might deduce that, by cultivating such a diverse range of genres in his quest for wholeness, he over-extended himself and dissipated his creative energies, channelling them in too many directions so that the poems lose some of their edge as the distinction between lyricism and prose polemic becomes blurred.

Salinas once wrote that "Al hablar de la poesía de la realidad, tenemos que concebirla como siendo cada vez más integradora y abarcadora". The appropriateness of such a goal in the context of *entereza* is obvious and its relevance to the Spaniard's own practice is not difficult to illustrate. His wide-ranging expansiveness manifested itself in an embrace that reached beyond the confines of his native culture while simultaneously accommodating the entire Spanish tradition of the past. Aged almost thirty-three when his first volume of poems appeared in 1924, he had been composing verse for more than a decade and had even considered publishing a collection as early as 1913. Right from the start, however, his aesthetic horizons were wide. Here the influence of his friend and francophile Enrique Díez-Canedo was decisive both in stimulating his interest in French poetry and in encouraging him to obtain a teaching-post at the Sorbonne from 1914 to 1917. Solita Salinas has written of her father's cosmopolitanism, "Le parecía importantísimo, para él y para España, el contacto con el mundo europeo". Between the turn of the century and the diaspora of the Civil War, among his older and younger contemporaries, Machado, Jiménez, Guillén and Cernuda also lived for a time in France, and Aleixandre, though unable to do likewise for health reasons, was at least as well read as any of them in French literature. Similarly, Jiménez, Salinas, Guillén and Lorca had all spent significant periods either in England or America by 1930. Such exposure to other cultures may help explain the extraordinary blossoming of Spanish poetry during these years. In Salinas's case attention has been drawn to his translations of Proust and their possible influence on his own evolution. Yet how, we might wonder, would the Spanish poet's rendering of reality have developed without Malarmé's even more fundamental injunction to "Peindre, non la chose, mais l'effet qu'elle produit?" Dehennin, Morris and others have examined the debt that this generation of poets, Salinas included, owed to the Spanish literary tradition. Guillén neatly sums up the point when he observes of the titles used for the three volumes of the love-cycle that they span an entire historical spectrum of creative writing, since *Razón de amor*, taken from a thirteenth century Spanish poem, is redolent of the medieval epoch, *La voz a ti debida*, borrowed from Garcilaso, evokes the Golden Age, and *Largo lamento*, a phrase from Bécquer, recalls nineteenth century Romanticism. For the most part, Dr. Shaughnessy's primary purpose is not the pursuit of complex foreign and Spanish ramifications, a policy which, in practice, the need for clarity justifies. Salinas himself would no doubt have approved, since he remarked that "Mi poesía está explicada por mis poesías". Where better to gloss the text, then, than from the author's own verse? What these cosmopolitan and traditional Spanish resonances indicate here is, therefore, less an interpretive issue than a background confirmation that the impulse towards wholeness in this poet's work is doubly enriched by his breadth of cultural vision.

Salinas's poems were, on his own admission, an attempt to express what he called "este múltiple contenido de mi corazón". Multiple perspective is, of course, a feature of *La voz a ti debida* ("Múltiples, tú y tu vida") and it also accounts for the fact that the poet gives *El Contemplado* the subtitle "Tema con variaciones". Just as the love experience is explored from every angle, so too we receive fourteen versions, as it were, of the speaker's interaction with the sea. Crispin and particularly Havard have persuasively linked this phenomenon to Ortega's perspectivism. Cubism, in both its analytical and synthetic guises, also probably plays a role here since Salinas's years in Paris coincided with that movement's climactic phase. Both involve a desire for comprehensiveness of perception reminiscent of *entereza*. In this context, other features of the Spanish poet's portrayal of experience are also best understood as integrating devices. For instance, what Spitzer calls "chaotic enumerations", the apparently arbitrary lists of nouns characteristic of Salinas's poems, are not as he claims, random recitations where words cease to be meaningful. Rather, what we are dealing with here is a cumulative technique, a synthesizing process whereby disparate verbal elements, charged with meaning, are gathered together, their individual overtones intensified by juxtaposition. Much the same might be said of the paradoxes and conceits that recur in the Spaniard's verse as symptoms of a search for wholeness through the fusion of opposites, more than as an articulation of scepticism or an expression of distancing. When Salinas speaks of "alma de carne o sombra/ de cuerpo" he wants the best of both worlds, a simultaneous enjoyment of bodily and non-physical reality. Conceits too seek to establish unity in dissimilarity. Equally, the Spanish poet's syntactic asides and parentheses become contradictions and inconsistencies of reality as a whole. All of which explains the appropriateness of Lorna Shaughnessy's investigation of *La reconquista de la entereza del hombre* as a unifying theme in Pedro Salinas's collected poems. A number of circumstantial and stylistic factors such as those just outlined point to the key importance of this element in his work. But systematic and detailed analysis of its textual implications has not been undertaken until now. Although more than forty years have elapsed since the Spanish poet's death, and despite the recent celebration in 1991 of the centenary of his birth, Salinas remains, in comparison with other major poets of the first half of this century, relatively under-researched. With the publication of Dr. Shaughnessy's thesis, the total number of book-length works of criticism in English devoted to Salinas amounts to four. Small wonder, then, that while much of his professional and creative life was spent in an English-speaking environment, outside the Hispanic world Salinas's work is little known. Even in Spanish, studies of substance are fairly thin on the ground given the prevailing consensus that he is, perhaps, the most original love poet Spain has produced this century. It may be that his emergence during what has become known as the Second Golden Age of Spanish Verse was a mixed blessing, hindering the assessment of his contribution, as one bright star among a glittering galaxy. This situation makes the appearance in book form of Lorna Shaughnessy's patient and thorough exploration of Pedro Salinas's entire poetic output all the more welcome.

Terence McMullan

Acknowledgments

This book is based on a doctoral thesis submitted to Queen's University Belfast in 1992, supervised by Terence McMullan. I am endebted to the National University of Ireland for their financial support, which has made its publication possible.

Introduction

"Cada loco con su tema", dice el refrán. Así, igualmente, cada gran
poeta con el suyo, el tema vital que desde los adentros preside
misteriosamente sobre los otros temas...

So writes Pedro Salinas in his appraisal of the poetry of Rubén Darío.[1] If we are
to seek a 'tema vital' in his own work, we will inevitably come face to face with
a constant goal, an ideal that colours all his writing, both poetry and prose: the
ideal state of 'entereza'. The term is never clearly defined by Salinas, a writer
who, in any case, abhors fixed definitions, yet it is a term that emerges and re-
emerges in his work. Despite the absence of a definition from the author, we can
quickly establish that this 'entereza', for Salinas, expresses a philosophy of non-
duality, a striving towards wholeness and fulfilment. It is also an ideal that this
poet aspires to in his poetic expression, as Salinas adopts a linguistically anti-
Cartesian posture, seeking to break down the semantic and philosophical boundaries
that categorise human experience in terms of opposition. However, the ideal of
'entereza' is not only poetic and linguistic, it also represents a goal in terms of
personal development, and as such, shares many characteristics with what Jung has
described as "the individuation process". Accordingly, the different elements of the
psyche, both conscious and unconscious, are welded together so that the individual
achieves the status of wholeness or integration. In other words, the quest for
'entereza' not only has literary, but psychological and ontological resonances.

Returning to the theory that every writer has a 'tema vital', Salinas declares:

> Vive su tema entrañadamente tan uno con su persona que con estar
> siempre viviendo en función suya - aun cuando se le figure que
> atiende otros estímulos o motivaciones - no tiene una conciencia
> acabada, total de él.[2]

The poet's relationship with his own 'tema vital' is evidently perceived as not quite conscious, which may explain the absence of a clear definition of 'entereza' anywhere in Salinas's own work. Nonetheless, his use of the term is persistent, and consistently invoked to denote the presence of, or the desire for, values such as integrity and fulfilment, which are presented as positive and inspiring. One useful example can be found in another essay, this time on Don Quijote, who is held up as the very paragon of these values:

> El, por ser un hombre íntegro, era un integrador. Por su camino de
> aunar creencias y actos, ideas y cosas, se accede el fin más deseable
> de nuestro días: la reconquista de la entereza del hombre.[3]

The desire to be "un hombre íntegro" is reflected in Salinas's joint vocations as poet, teacher and critic, and has quite profound implications for the nature of his poetry, where the realms of external and internal reality, of thought and material phenomena, spirit and flesh, draw ever-closer to each other. His friend and fellow poet Jorge Guillén expressed the view that -

> Pedro Salinas was able to fuse into a single whole his life and his
> career, his vocation, his actions and his written works... Salinas is
> Salinas throughout his entire career; each volume contributes to
> defining the whole, and the whole is the most important aspect of
> a great poet's work.[4]

This view that a poet can only be fairly assessed in the context of his or her total output, is not reflected by most criticism of Salinas's poetry to date: very few commentators have taken a broad approach to his *Poesías completas*, most of them concentrating on the love poems of *La voz a ti debida* and *Razón de amor*, or on the first three volumes of the 1920s and early 1930s, *Presagios*, *Seguro azar*, and *Fábula y signo*. There appears to be a general critical consensus that the later poetry is inferior to the earlier, in particular *Todo más claro*; terms such as "prosaic" abound, and many critics have concluded that the sense of social mission central to these poems is detrimental to their poetic merit.[5] The tone of many of these poems could be described as evangelistic, even moralising, and it is this tone which has alienated many critics who, with some justification, hold the opinion that Salinas's message is better expressed in his essays of this period. Once established, this critical attitude seems to have been passed down from one generation of critics to the next, so that serious analysis of Salinas's poetry of the 1940s is rare, and comprehensive assessments of his collected poems even rarer. The attractions of the early works are self-evident: *Presagios*, *Seguro azar* and *Fábula y signo* are very much the product of their time, fascinating because they reflect the pace of social and aesthetic change in Europe in the 1920s. The "love cycle" that followed (*La voz a ti debida*, *Razón de amor* and *Largo lamento*) is frequently described as Salinas's highest poetic achievement. Here, emotional intensity is married to a deceptive lightness of touch; conceptual adroitness combines with a real sensuousness, making these volumes an impressive addition to the rich tradition of the Spanish love-lyric. These works indisputably merit the critical attention they have received. However, the widespread critical resistance to Salinas's later poetry has given rise to a rather fragmented picture of his work. It is not easy to appraise all Salinas's poetry - there is so much of it, and its sheer variety makes it difficult to reach meaningful conclusions that do not dissipate into generalisations. Yet it is worth bearing in mind that Salinas's own approach as literary critic was to seek out the 'tema vital' that binds together the overall production of any author. As a literary critic he endeavoured not to treat individual works as though they were written in a vacuum, but to somehow penetrate the core values therein, what he called - "la visión del creador entero y verdadero".[6] Of course this kind of criticism pre-supposes the presence of a core truth - a constant and unchanging meaning or theme in the collected works of the author in question. This is a supposition that is hotly refuted by Marxist and deconstructionist schools of criticism.[7] While bearing in mind the perils of over-simplification implied by Salinas's own theory of a 'tema vital', the study of his collected poems, and their central impulse or theme of 'entereza', can serve as a means of counterbalancing the critical bias to date that concerns itself mainly with the "estilística" of individual volumes of poetry.

The concept of 'entereza', has varied and far-reaching thematic ramifications. If we are to examine its central importance in Salinas's work, we must begin with the fundamental question of human consciousness itself. Individual consciousness is frequently evoked by the modern poet as an awareness of separation, and consequently as a source of considerable anguish. Much of this reflects the undeniable influence on modern aesthetics of Freud's theory of the Ego, which distinguishes the self from the world. And so we encounter repeated evocations of consciousness as a fall from the primordial and paradisiacal state of wholeness, or 'entereza'. In his volume of essays, *Reality and the Poet in Spanish Poetry*, Salinas describes the narrative epic, one of the earliest forms of written literature, as "the paradisiacal period of man's unity. The unity of reality and the inner world" (p.163).[8] This imitative form of art represents a state of absolute conformity and identification with the empirical world. But literary self-consciousness has eroded this degree of union between internal and external realities: unity has given way to division, and Salinas concludes that, "Modern man, this new man, is man divided in the highest degree" ("The Revolt Against Reality", p.163). The modern artist, therefore, experiences a yearning for the one-ness of this pre-conscious state, and Salinas sets out to heal the Cartesian divisions between internal and external consciousness, defying inherited models of thought. His chosen method for breaching the gap is by reaching out to embrace 'otherness', defined in *Reality and the Poet in Spanish Poetry* as "all that lives outside the poet, the material world which surrounds him, things, society, beings, all of life from a blade of grass to a moral doctrine.." (p.3). In keeping with this impulse to reach outwards, the phrase "más allá" acquires the status of a thematic refrain in Salinas's work, embodying his frustration with the limitations of inner, subjective experience, and the desire to fuse thought and world, "ideas y cosas". This need to establish relationships with 'otherness' echoes the writing of Antonio Machado, whose literary persona, Abel Martín, spells out the fact that without knowledge of 'otherness', there can be no self-knowledge. Martín stresses the importance of the erotic impulse that draws the individual compulsively to the 'other' in the form of the beloved, the object of his biological and ontological desires for union:

> Sólo después que el anhelo erótico ha creado las formas de la objetividad - puede el hombre llegar a la visión real de la conciencia, reintegrando a la pura unidad heterogénea las citadas formas o reversos del ser, a verse, a vivirse, a serse en plena y fecunda intimidad.[9]

The love experience, more than any other, dissolves the boundaries that separate self from 'other', and for Salinas, love represents the highest expression of 'entereza'. In one poem from *Razón de amor* the poet-lover describes how love instils the sensation of at-one-ness:

> Una conformidad de mundo y ser,
> de afán y tiempo, inverosímil tregua,
> se entraba en mí...   (ll.24-26, Raz., p.367)[10]

Salinas's love-cycle is firmly rooted in the Neo-Platonic tradition, acknowledging the existence of two kinds of love, one of the spirit or psyche, the other of the flesh. But his poems reject the Platonic hierarchy that places spirit over flesh: love, for Salinas, must be felt in both "alma" and "cuerpo", for without either it is incomplete. The physical presence of 'otherness' is therefore indispensable to the sensation of 'entereza', and so, in Salinas's love-cycle, the absence of the beloved becomes a nagging preoccupation. This poet is alert to the danger that without physical presence, reality is too easily conceptualised; no reality, in Salinas's poetry, can live in the mind alone.

Salinas's quest for 'entereza' is initially concerned with aspirations for personal fulfilment, as he broadens his knowledge of the self through contact with 'otherness', whether in the material world of phenomena, or in the presence of the beloved. As his work progresses, however, this ideal transcends personal and aesthetic ambitions, and Salinas, like Don Quijote before him, begins to champion 'entereza' as a model for society as well as the individual. It is evident in his later works, notably the poems of *Todo más claro* and the essays of *El defensor*, that Salinas is increasingly conscious of himself as an intrinsically 'social animal'. In striving for personal realisation and individual 'entereza', this facet of personal development - the relationship between self and society - gains thematic importance in this poet's work. In *El defensor*, Salinas quotes the sociologist Simmel, saying:

> Cree el sociólogo Simmel que el hombre se halla comprendido en la sociedad y a la vez frente a ella. Pero estas dos caracterizaciones no se dan separadas, aisladas, forman una unidad, y lo propiamente humano es el ser elemento de la sociedad y producto de la sociedad al mismo tiempo...[11]

In Salinas's pre-1936 poetry emphasis is given to isolated, individual relationships between the poet and "las cosas" of the physical world, or between the poet and the beloved. In exile however, after 1936, his awareness of the self as a social entity is probably heightened by the experience of social, cultural and linguistic alienation in the United States of America. The desirability of social integration and the basic human need for group-identification are recurring preoccupations in *Todo más claro* and *El defensor*. Apart from his personal experience of isolation in exile in the late 1930s and early 1940s, Salinas observes in his new home, the United States, an urban environment that is essentially alienating, where the absence of communication with 'others' and 'otherness' limits personal growth, disempowers the individual, and produces the highly vulnerable "Hombre en la orilla". This anonymous urban citizen who lacks any sense of identity - social or personal - represents for Salinas the aimlessness of a society that has lost sight of the need for 'entereza'. The ramifications of a breakdown in communication between self and 'other' are even more drastic when read in the context of the Second World War. Reading the poem "Cero" and many of the essays collected in *El defensor*, there can be little doubt that in Salinas's mind there was a strong association between the depersonalised, anonymous society he saw in North America at this time, and the dehumanising aggression of one state against another. In order to be 'in touch' with the self, the individual must engage in constant dialogue with 'others' and 'otherness'. We witness this practice in *all* Salinas's poetry, as the most fundamental expression of the quest for 'entereza'. Given that Salinas's consciousness of the self embraces the notion of social integration, then his ideal of "la reconquista de la entereza del hombre" must inevitably have social implications.

At this stage in his life, and in this North American setting, Salinas casts a cold eye on the position of the individual who is in danger of becoming locked into his own consciousness; now more than ever, contact with 'otherness' is necessary, but urban alienation makes human contact increasingly difficult. This new urban reality also impedes any sense of contact with the past, and this is another source of concern in Salinas's later works: the termination of the cultural continuum which has linked and enriched Western philosophy and art from the Hellenic to the Modernist. Gradually, the concept of termination or completion comes to represent the antithesis of 'entereza'; the "cero" to its "suma". Salinas's later work insists more and more vehemently on the importance of idealism, and the necessity of aspiration - not only as a means of self-realisation, but as a universal life-force. The poet's motto becomes "vivir, seguir, querer seguir viviendo" (l.156, "Pasajero en museo", *Todo*, p.707). Life is equated with the desire for continuation, and the individual's quest for 'entereza' becomes a vital motivating factor in collective self-perpetuation because it nurtures human communication. The pursuit of unity and synthesis, either as an individual or as part of a collective, is the 'tema vital', the overriding and unifying theme of this poet.

In the course of examining Salinas's *Poesías completas* questions of influence inevitably arise. There is no doubt that French writers of the first two decades of this century influenced Salinas's work, especially his early poetry. We know that his knowledge of French was good: Salinas received his primary education in the "Colegio hispano-francés" (1897-1903); he visited Paris for several months in 1912 and spent three years there between 1914 and 1917; we also know that in the initial years of his courtship with Margarita Bonmatí, the couple communicated through French. There is ample evidence that Salinas was in close contact with French literature written during the late nineteenth and early twentieth centuries; in 1913 he collaborated with Díez-Canedo and Fernando Fortún in the preparation of an anthology entitled "La poesía francesa moderna".[12] Salinas translated poems for this collection by Emile Despax, Charles Guérin, Léo Larguier, Henri de Réguier and Albert Samain. Further evidence of this ongoing interest is his translation of Proust's "En busca del tiempo perdido" (Volumes one and two), published in 1927. In addition to Salinas's knowledge of contemporary French poetry, he shared an interest in the French Symbolist movement with other Spanish poets of his generation. The highly self-conscious nature of much Spanish poetry of the 1920s reflects the preoccupation with the poetic process demonstrated by French Symbolist poets from Baudelaire to Mallarmé. It is also worth noting that Apollinaire greatly influenced the thematic and stylistic development of the Ultraísta and Creacionista movements in Spain in the 1920s.[13] His use of modern technology as the subject-matter of his playful, humorous poems, and his manipulation of startling and novel images, reverberates in much of the poetry written in Spain throughout this decade. While acknowledging the significance of these influences, this study is more concerned with surveying Salinas's poetry within the Spanish literary tradition, whose influence is manifest not only in his early poems, but in his life's work as both poet and academic. The extent to which this twentieth-century poet draws on his Hispanic literary heritage has received little critical attention to date. Salinas's poetry echoes voices as distant as the Cancionero's; he invokes the metaphysical tone of muse poetry of the sixteenth and seventeenth centuries; the *intimismo* of Bécquer pervades his love-poetry, as does the pruned lyricism of Juan Ramón; and perhaps the most striking contemporary influence throughout this poet's career is that of his close friend Jorge Guillén. Arguably, Juan Ramón Jiménez was Salinas's most direct source of symbolist aesthetics: he was the young poet's mentor throughout the 1920s, even publishing his first collection in 1924.

There is little concrete evidence of significant influence by Anglo-American literature, despite the fact that Salinas resided in an English-speaking environment for over twenty years. During his brief sojourn in Cambridge (1922-3), Salinas corresponded with Jorge Guillén, expressing an interest in the English Romantic poets, and regret at his own lack of proficiency in the language. Keats was a favourite, and in a later poem "Pasajero en museo" Salinas ponders the questions raised by the Romantic on the nature of mortality in his "Ode on a Grecian Urn". Despite Salinas's growing linguistic competence in English in his years of exile in North America, there is nothing specific in his poetry of the 1940s to indicate direct influence by contemporary English or North-American poetry. One poet who captured his imagination, however, was Edgar Allan Poe, whose memory is celebrated in the short story "La gloria y la niebla", published in *El desnudo impecable* in 1951. Salinas took up his teaching post in John Hopkins University, Baltimore, in 1940, and it would appear that the story was inspired by a statue erected in Poe's memory in the city's public park. What conclusions, if any, can we draw from this apparent absence of influence on Salinas by contemporary North-American writing? It appears that the experience of exile thrust the poet into an ever more profound development of his ties with Spanish literary tradition. As former 'Catedrático de filología española' in Seville, and now as an ambassador for Spanish literature abroad, Salinas became more and more appreciative of his own cultural inheritance. The sheer volume of critical material he produced in this period suggests that this poet, although exiled bodily from Spain, intellectually, aesthetically and spiritually inhabited a literary homeland of Hispanic letters.

Salinas's departure from Spain in 1936 was to have a profound effect on his inner life. In letters to friends such as Guillermo de Torre and Dámaso Alonso throughout the 1940s, Salinas expresses a painful sense of isolation and social displacement, which undoubtedly contributed to his growing need to explore the relationship between the individual and society in his poetry and essays at this time. Apart from Salinas's personal circumstances as an exile, the fact that he was living in North America during the Second World War seems also to have affected him considerably. Spanish intellectual life had been relatively unscathed by the First World War, and Salinas had left Spain in time to escape witnessing civil war at first hand. While the Second World War was not fought on North American territory, this was the first time Salinas had lived in a country that was actually at war. The experience coloured some of his poetry of the 1940s: "Cero", and other poems from *Todo más claro* voice the poet's fear for the survival of European civilisation. The poet speaks through these poems in a public voice, in sharp contrast with the love poems of the 1930s. This is not to say that Salinas was untouched by social and political issues prior to the 1940s, but rather that where their presence is explicit in the later works, in the earlier volumes it is implied. Indeed, the conspicuous absence of social realities in Spanish poetry of the 1920s can be read as an implicit statement on the political regime of the time. The systematic political marginalisation of the intelligentsia under Primo de Rivera was an important contributory factor in the emergence of the extremely self-conscious poetry of the so-called "Generation of '27". Spanish poetry of this period is frequently described as being aesthetically obsessive at the expense of reflecting the harsh social realities of the day.[14]

From the early 1930s onwards, however, the sheer pressure and immediacy of political changes and events excites a response from artists and intellectuals in Spain. Aestheticism dissipates, as intellectual life proves not to be immune to the political climate. We know that Salinas was committed to the social and educational policies of the Second Republic. Most of the information at our disposal regarding his role as policy-maker for the new regime (the most famous of his projects being to establish an International Summer School in the Palacio Magdalena), comes from letters written to Guillén in the early 1930s.[15] Yet nothing of Salinas's participation in developments by the new Republic is reflected in his poetry of the 1930s, which instead is dedicated exclusively to an exploration of the nature of human love. This apparent disparity between Salinas's poetry of the 1930s and his concurrent socio-political role is just one example of the complexity of the relationship between biographical fact and individual creativity. In this instance, a direct chain of cause and effect is difficult to justify. While biographical data can enhance our appreciation of the emotional and/or socio-political conditions in which these poems were written, it should never be allowed to eclipse or oversimplify the complexities present in the poetry itself.

The approach taken by many commentators of Salinas's work is to deal exclusively with a particular period in the poet's life. This critical perspective can give the rather simplistic impression that Salinas's poetry is divisible into three thematically and chronologically self-contained groups: 1923-31, 1931-39, and the 1940s, with corresponding clear-cut philosophical positions. In reality, Salinas's thinking is rich in paradoxes and contradictions which cannot be ignored, and are confronted wherever necessary throughout the course of this study. To deny the presence of these paradoxes is to deny the complexity of Salinas's poetry, which at times seems to revel in contradictory attitudes and ambivalent statements, reminding us that ideas are rarely fixed, but evolve and change in the course of a life's work. The nine volumes that make up Salinas's *Poesías completas* do not add up to an infallible philosophical system, and the many shifts of emphasis and perspective made by Salinas as he works towards the personal and poetic ideal of 'entereza', are addressed in this study. By reading each volume of poems in the overall context of the *Poesías completas*, a greater degree of thematic unity comes to light than rigidly imposed chronological divisions might indicate. In order to stress the inter-relatedness of each of Salinas's nine volumes of poetry, the material examined in each Chapter is determined by theme, rather than strict adherence to chronology. Despite the disruptive rift that occurred in his life in 1936, and the radical geographic and cultural changes involved in his removal from Spain to the United States of America, what emerges from the collected poems is the presence of an all-encompassing poetic ideal - personal, social and poetic 'entereza'.

The ideal of 'entereza' has important implications for Salinas's somewhat idiosyncratic attitude to language. While the poet's relationship with all 'otherness' - "all that lives outside of the poet" - is constantly changing, one common denominator is his subversion of inherited meaning. The idea that a quest for totality of expression underlies this poetry does help to explain its peculiar semantic fluidity. The ideal of one all-embracing vision and expression of reality presents a linguistic quandary: how to express true union with a linguistic structure built on the foundations of separation. His deliberate destabilising of semantic order is consistent in that it tends to synthesis and fusion, as he sets about dismantling the distinctions between binary opposites. New realms of experience open up when old thought-patterns and semantic boundaries are discarded. This explains the rather other-worldly, and even mystical aura that surrounds some of Salinas's love poetry, undeniably influenced by the *Cántico espiritual* of John of the Cross.

When the poet-lover is forced to confront the beloved's absence in these poems, we see how the thrust towards semantic fusion operates. In order to alleviate the anxiety caused by absence, it is redefined as a mere signifier of past or future presence, and binary opposites cease to oppose in the all-embracing 'entereza' of the love experience.

In this sense, it could justifiably be argued that Salinas's poetry anticipates many of Jacques Derrida's theories of the nature of meaning, and the unconscious invocation by each value of its opposite.[16] Like Derrida, Salinas appreciates that meaning is always in a state of flux. The only way in which we can fix meaning is to represent something as singular, definitive, authoritative. This, for Salinas, as for Derrida, would amount to a misrepresentation, for it would silence and deny the opposite or different meanings we measure against. Pedro Salinas consciously and stubbornly resists fixed meaning in his poetry, manipulating the symbiotic relationship that exists between opposites. We encounter much conceptual play with binary opposites in his work: his semantic manipulation of shadow and substance, absence and presence, waking and dreaming consciousness, is frequently described by critics as paradoxical. In effect, Salinas's use of the conceit expresses a much broader cognitive reality than the dualistic Cartesian model allows. Binary opposites engage in an elaborate dance in these poems: they change places, to-ing and fro-ing, now reified, now abstracted, ignoring pre-defined categories of experience. And so, the features of Salinas's work most often referred to as semantic inconsistencies, are actually the most consistent expression of his central theme; the total expression of total experience.

Learning from his predecessor Bécquer, who lamented the failure of language to capture the ineffable, Salinas does not even attempt to contain meaning or experience. Instead, he deploys language in such a way that it anticipates experience: no longer seeking to mimic or define, it now creates. Consequently, as Robert Havard stresses, a primordial attitude to language pervades much of

Salinas's work.[17] Language has the power to invent, to surprise even the poet who becomes in a sense, its medium. When Salinas rhetorically addresses his beloved with the question "¿Tú sabes lo que eres de mí?", he answers himself with the following statement -

> Yo no lo sé; lo digo,
> se me asoma a los labios
> como una aurora virgen
> de la que no soy dueño.   (ll.11-14, *Raz.*, p.353)

Ultimately, Salinas's relationship with language is characterised by the degree of autonomy it seems to exercise. There is an underlying irony here, as this very appearance of autonomy is produced by the poet's ability to exercise considerable influence on linguistic structures. In *El defensor*, Salinas claims that "El poeta acrece las posibilidades de lenguaje vivo en grado sumo".[18] By aspiring to linguistic 'entereza', Salinas goes a long way to flexing and expanding the boundaries of poetic expression.

Notes

Introduction

1. See Pedro Salinas, *La poesía de Rubén Darío*, ed. Solita Salinas and Jaime Salinas, Seix Barral (Barcelona, 1975), p.47.

2. As in Note 1.

3. Pedro Salinas, "Don Quijote en presente", *Ensayos completos, Vol. III*, ed. Solita Salinas de Marichal, Taurus (Madrid, 1983). Hereafter referred to in the text as *Ensayos III*.

4. Jorge Guillén, Introduction to Salinas's *Reality and the poet in Spanish Poetry*, John Hopkins Press (Baltimore, 1966), pp.xvi and xxiii. Hereafter referred to in the text as *Reality*.

5. See Howard T. Young, "Pedro Salinas y los Estados Unidos, o la nada y las máquinas", *Cuadernos Hispanoamericanos*, No.145 (January 1962), pp.5-13.

6. To quote Salinas's own comments on Rubén Darío -

> Se me figura la función más deseable del estudio de un poeta la delicada discriminación de su tema, su cuidadosa separación de los temas segundos o subtemas; el precisar el curso que sigue, a través de la obra, resolver las contradicciones aparentes que velan su presencia, llegando por fin a la visión del creador entero y verdadero, salvada de mutilaciones y limpia de desenfoques. (As in Note 1).

7. According to Frederic Jameson, modern literary criticism is still locked into a system of ethics, whereby a text is judged by whether or not it lives up to certain (usually unstated) values. In his book, *The Political Unconscious. Narrative as a socially symbolic act*, Methuen (Cornell University, 1981) p.60, Jameson argues that the moral sensibilities of the past have simply been replaced in critical thinking by a new set of values, drawn from psychoanalysis:

> Here, notions of personal identity, myths of reunification of the psyche, and the mirage of some Jungian self or ego, stand in for the

16

older themes of moral sensibility and ethical awareness, and reconfirm the aptness of that other contemporary continental theme which... turns upon the critique of the 'centre' and the 'centred self'.

8. As in Note 4.

9. Antonio Machado, "De un cancionero apócrifo", *Poesías completas*, CLXVII, ed. Manuel Alvar, Austral (Madrid, 1982), p.318.

10. The edition referred to throughout this work is Pedro Salinas's *Poesías Completas,* ed. Soledad Salinas de Marichal, Seix Barral (Barcelona, 1981).

11. Pedro Salinas, *El defensor*, Alianza Tres (Madrid, 1984), pp.218.

12. Renacimiento (Madrid, 1913).

13. Apollinaire's poetry came to the attention of many Spanish poets through the exposure it received from contemporary literary journals, among them "Grecia" which published some of his work in 1919.

14. Ramiro de Maeztu, essayist, journalist and diplomat, questioned the apparent immunity of writers at this time to the reality of Spanish society, making comparisons with English authors such as Chesterton, Shaw and Wells, whose works reverberated with the social ambiance in which they lived. For Maeztu and others this final stage of symbolist and modernist influence widened the gap between artists and 'mass' society. See "Las letras y la vida" in *El Sol* (17.8.26).

15. A selection of these letters appeared in Christopher Maurer's, "Sobre 'joven literatura' y politica: cartas de Pedro Salinas y de Federico Garcia Lorca (1930-35)" in *Estelas, laberintos, nuevas sendas, Unamuno, Valle-Inclan, García Lorca, la Guerra Civil,* Co. Ord. Angel G. Loureiro, Anthropos (Barcelona, 1988), pp.297-319. The complete correspondence was subsequently published as *Correspondencia: Pedro Salinas, Jorge Guillén (1923-51),* Ed. Andrés Soria Olmedo, Tusquets (Barcelona, 1992).

16. See Jacques Derrida "Structure, Sign and Play in the Discourses of the Human Sciences", (1966), in *Writing and Difference*, Routledge (London, 1978).

17. See Robert Havard, "Meaning and Metaphor of Syntax in Bécquer, Guillén and Salinas", *Iberoromania*, No.19 (1984), pp.66-81.

18. Pedro Salinas, "Defensa de la minoría literaria", *El defensor*, Alianza Tres (Madrid, 1984), p.220.

Chapter I

Ideas y cosas

Objects and Objectivity.

Salinas's aspiration to a state of ontological and poetic wholeness, the quest for 'entereza', is most immediately apparent in the comprehensiveness of his subject-matter, which is no less than "reality", intuited as the vital starting point of all creative activity. This intuition forms the basis of Salinas's critical writings as well as his poetry, typified by the essays collected in *Reality and the Poet in Spanish Poetry*. Chapter One, "The Reproduction of Reality", opens with the by now familiar statement that - "I propose to discuss, in these lectures, the attitude of the poet toward reality throughout Spanish poetry...". This is not to say, however, that the source of poetic inspiration lies solely in the empirically observable world. Salinas's conception of reality is not so narrow, as he clarifies in the following definition:

> ...by it I mean all that lives outside of the poet, the material world
> which surrounds him, things, society, beings, all of life from a blade
> of grass to a moral doctrine elaborated over the centuries... [1]

"Reality" then, not only comprises things as particular, tangible and unique as a blade of grass, but also ideas - conceptual entities such as society, or a moral doctrine. The breadth of this definition reflects the all-inclusive and non-hierarchical nature of the subject-matter of Salinas's poems, which embrace all aspects of human experience, from love to a walk down a city street, from the transcendental to the mundane. It is also true that many of these realities that "live" outside the poet also live within him: concepts such as "society" or "a moral doctrine" exist, equally, within the individual consciousness. A failure to recognise Salinas's acknowledgement of certain experiences as being both internal and external, has led some critics to assume that here is a poet who hovers rather uncertainly between the internal realms of the intellect, and the external realms of matter.[2] It is more likely that the absence of defined boundaries between these two kinds of experience is in fact deliberate, and an indication of the poet's unwillingness to divide up his experience into two mutually exclusive camps: the world of "ideas", and the world of "cosas".[3]

The motif of "ideas y cosas" originates in the essay *"Don Quijote en presente"* where Salinas states: "Vive el ser humano tejiendo su propia existencia en un entrecruzarse de ideas y cosas".[4] The life of the individual is the rich tapestry woven in the warp and weft of abstract and concrete realities. The poet's personal weave is his verse, emerging from the intermeshing of these two, as he relies on both intellectual and sensory stimulus for his work.[5] The categories chosen by Salinas to encompass all reality -"ideas y cosas" - resemble the dual realities of Platonic philosophy. In the broadest terms, Salinas's understanding of "las ideas" as abstract concepts is comparable with the Platonic notion of "noumena". Similarly, Plato's definition of the material, sensorially perceptual world as "phenomena", corresponds approximately to Salinas's view of "las cosas". What is most interesting about this comparison, however, is that in contrast with Platonic philosophy, Salinas does not conceive of "ideas y cosas" in a hierarchical relationship. Rather than seeking to liberate the noumena from its material shackles, his poetry pursues the integration of these realms of experience on one egalitarian level.

Much has been made of Salinas's apparent *conceptista* tendencies, of the abstract, even noetic character of his verse.[6] Certain idealist tendencies must be acknowledged - especially in the context of the love cycle and the poetic treatment of the beloved. Examples of this idealism are not only evident in the love poetry of the 1930s, but in Salinas's love letters to his fiancée Margarita Bonmatí. One such moment of Platonic idealism is recorded in a letter written in 1914: "Por eso amo tanto la música, porque cuando la oigo me olvido de que estamos lejos y tu alma está con la mía, infinitivamente unida, por lazos ideales."[7] And yet, the material world of phenomena is never wholly abandoned by Salinas. The young poet's love letters may exude idealism, but the prose writings of the more mature Salinas are imbued with a profound appreciation of matter. Writing on "La mejor carta de amores en la literatura española", (from Don Quijote to Dulcinea), Salinas has this to say on the relationship between conceived and perceived realities:

> Inmateriales, el querer y el pensar. Mas en cuanto se desee transmitirlos a segunda persona, hay que pedir ayuda a la materia.
> (*Ensayos III*, p.85)

Ultimately, knowledge of reality does not originate either in the intellect or in matter alone, even where a material medium is necessary to communicate experience. Reality makes itself known through the interaction of these two methods of understanding the world - intellectual concept and sense perception - through the marriage of ideas and things.[8]

Salinas's own relationship with reality is never fixed, but rather fluctuates. There are changes of emphasis: he is now more attendant to the inner voice of concept, now to the assault on the senses by external phenomena. The dominant attitude is one of integration, the aspiration to a united, or non-dualistic vision of the world and the self, where internal and external realities merge. While periodic dominance of "ideas" over "cosas" may arise in Salinas's poetic work, in his critical prose writings there is a constant preference for writing that springs from more than one source, that draws on the concrete as well as the abstract. Even in his earliest letters to Margarita, where the expression of personal feeling may have leant towards idealism, Salinas's literary bias clearly leans towards the balancing of abstract concept against physical, perceptual experience. He writes from Madrid in 1914:

> Aquí empieza a iniciarse una tendencia moderna que en poesía se ha de manifestar, creo yo, por el verso-librismo, y que tiene un carácter marcadamente idealista, pero sin perder sus dotes de realidad. (*Cartas* XLI, pp.128-9)[9]

For Salinas, the development of the artist's intellectual and sensual faculties are not mutually exclusive: one of his ambitions as a poet is to capture as fully as possible, the simultaneous presence of these two modes of consciousness.

Etymologically, reality has its roots in the Latin "res" for thing. For all his notoriety as a poet of abstractions and conceptualisms, Salinas is rarely far from the "Suelo" that opens *Presagios*, his first collection of poems. Being sensorially as well as figuratively 'in touch' with people and things, is as essential to the poetic process in Salinas's case, as is the inner life of ideas, and the ability to imagine. His definition of reality as "all that lives outside of the poet" (*Reality*, p.3), is an example of the poet's response to all that is 'other' than himself. The presence of external phenomena creates the poetic impulse - the desire to respond to the circumambient world. Salinas reaches out to form relationships with people, things and ideas; he enters into a poetic discourse with the world.[10] His earliest poetry pays particular attention to the material world of "las cosas", and everyday objects become the subject-matter of his verse.

> Si la poesía no es solamente la creación de varios, sino el modo de responder del hombre a la vida, una forma de expresión frente a las cosas.[11]

The desire to achieve intimacy with the concrete world is reflected by the extensive use of the familiar pronoun "tú" in Salinas's earliest volumes: in *Presagios*, for example, things as diverse as "la cigarra" (No.13), "mano de ciego" (No.3), "columna" (No.70), "el naranjo" (No. 21), and "el libro" (No. 24), are all addressed directly as "tú". In *Seguro azar*, the landscape - so far almost devoid of artefact - alters slightly, to embrace urban realities such as the motorcar in "Navacerrada, abril" (p.116), and the cityscape of "Pasajero apresurado" (p.111). This attraction to artefact and the sensation of a real relationship with the urban environment reaches a climax in *Fábula y signo*, where Salinas opens a dialogue with a miscellany of manmade "cosas": the eponymous statue of "La estatua" (p.170), the shop dummy, symbol of urban sophistication in "París, abril modelo" (p.172), the radiator of the title in "Radiador y fogata" (p.181), and the mundane coin in "Moneda" (p.184). It should be pointed out that this process of dialogue with concrete reality is not limited to artefact, as the personal pronoun "tú" is directed increasingly to the unidentified beloved: in *Seguro azar*, there are nine such poems, and in *Fábula y signo*, there are eleven - a greater quantity than are addressed to individual "cosas". We can deduce, therefore, that Salinas's growing interest in the love theme is already evident in the early 1930s, and that the beloved plays an important role in the poet's relationship with external reality.

Salinas's poetic output of the 1930s is of course dominated by the love cycle; the quest for absolute union with the beloved "tú", and the striving after personal 'entereza' in this union. A lapse in publications occurs in the late 1930s, which can be partially explained by the poet's lack of intimacy with his new environment in the United States, and his inability to conduct discourse with it in an alien tongue. The dialogue recommences in 1943, when, in Puerto Rico, Salinas addresses the empirical world in the form of the sea of San Juan, and begins to compose *El Contemplado*. It is at this point in his poetic development that the relationship with 'all that lives outside of the self', in particular with the physical, perceptual world, finds its most personally fulfilling expression.

The degree of intimacy experienced by the poet in his response to all 'otherness' varies considerably, as his relationships with people, things and society change over the thirty years spanned by his writing. For example, by the time *Todo más claro* is published in 1949, Salinas's attitude to urban life has altered quite radically. The city and its technological trappings are no longer a source of joy and wonder, but manifestations of a materialism grown oppressive through excess. In his early work, however, Salinas's response to his environment - whether urban or natural - displays all the innocence and ingenuousness of a child's. The world view of *Seguro azar* is profoundly animistic; like the small child, Salinas assumes that his relations with the inanimate world closely resemble his relations with people; he assumes that all reality is articulate because he is.[12] This animistic response to the world - the fact that the poet addresses "las cosas" as though they were people, has been confused with an actual bestowing of personality and autonomous being upon them.[13] In fact, the identity of "las cosas" as they are invoked in Salinas's earlier poetry, depends largely on their special relationship with the poet. Rather like the beloved in the love cycle, they represent the "tú" to his "yo", and the new identity they assume at times seems to be conferred by him.

Salinas's approach to reality is comparable with that of the child in another important respect; it is intrinsically non-discriminatory. All reality holds equal value, equal interest: the most mundane and ordinary of objects - a leaf, a mirror or a motorcar - are as valid subject-matter for a poem as the most elevated Platonic ideals.[14] What is not mundane, of course, is the poetic treatment given to these objects when Salinas removes them from their everyday functions and connotations, transporting them to the realms of imagination and fantasy.

But why such an avid interest in "las cosas" at this stage in Salinas's poetic career? Solita Salinas describes *Presagios*, as "despreocupado" in tone, and goes on to explain how the social background against which it was composed provoked:

> ...una nueva relación del poeta con la realidad. Y la realidad de los años veinte es de los "tiempos modernos": el cine, el automóvil.[15]

It is vital to read Salinas's early publications in just such a socio-historical perspective.[16] The momentous changes in the appearance and pace of urban life at this time, the novelty and variety of products now readily available to the consumer, technological innovation and production, had all contributed to a splendid, aesthetic rehabilitation of matter to modern life. The spirit of the industrial revolution reached a climax of optimistic materialism in the 1920s in Europe and North America. Salinas himself observes -

> Creo firmemente que el mundo exterior nunca ha sido tan imperialmente hermoso, tan rico y variado en cantidad y en calidad de cosas, de obras humanas, como lo es hoy. Esta fase de la realidad es novísima. Está cargada con una cantidad de potencialidades poéticas imposible de calcular. Y la poesía tiene que sentirse fatalmente seducida antes o después, por el aspecto del mundo que tiene tanto derecho a ser tema estético como la rosa, la gacela o el sentimiento de la muerte.[17]

In other words, the manufactured object has taken its place in the poetic order of things. This desire to incorporate the spirit of invention - and indeed actual inventions - into his poetry, creates an impression of near-infatuation with artefact in the works of the 1920s and early 1930s. For example, in "París, abril, modelo", (*Fábula y signo*), the shop dummy is eulogised as follows:

> Tú, tú eres la primera.
> Ni en rosa ni en azul
> confiada, nunca en Venus
> buscaste forma, tú,
> inventora de formas,
> modelo,

estatua de ti misma.   (ll.36-42, p.173)

Decked out in the first of the haute couture spring collections, the shop dummy becomes the harbinger of spring, in a very new poetic setting. In this somewhat modernist celebration of human invention, Salinas appears to place artefact above even natural creativity.[18] The colours borrowed from nature are not what lend the mannequin its charm - a point that contrasts very starkly with Salinas's later assessment of the cerulean "azul" of *El Contemplado*, which for the mature poet, cannot be equalled by canvas and brush nor by the pen. Its sublime blue surpasses all artificial imitation. Of course the earlier poem is composed in a playful frame of mind, as is so often the case in these early works when Salinas obliquely alludes to the poetic process.[19]

Salinas's enthusiasm for his urban environments - whether Madrid, Paris or Seville, is evident in "Nivel preferido" (*Seguro azar*, pp.146-7), where the smart city girl is transformed into a mythical creature against the painted backdrop of an artificial bacchanalia:[20]

> coronas para tus sienes,
> ninfa de tacones altos,
> desmelenada, tú, anécdota,
> negándote por teléfono
> a la cita que te di
> en la bacanal, pintada,
> del museo, de once a doce.   (ll.47-53)

The poem traces new outlines for what is notionally 'poetic', which embrace both classical and contemporary motifs.

The machines that so enraptured the Italian Futurists and the Spanish Ultraístas were obviously attractive to the child in Salinas. However his poetic treatment of "las máquinas" differs from that of either movement. While Salinas loved the speed and excitement of the automobile and other mechanical inventions, he did not incorporate these objects into his work for the purpose of glorifying their technological prowess or efficacy.[21] Salinas's treatment of the high-velocity capacity of the modern automobile is much more frivolous and playful than that of the Ultraístas. For example, in "Rapto a primavera" (*Fábula y signo*), the autumn leaves on the bonnet of the car, while seeming to rush to their deaths, are in fact transported to a new lease of life. The car's breakneck speed carries them to another hemisphere where Spring and new growth are imminent:

> Hojas. Otoño. Aquí.
> ¡Corre! Quieren salvarse
> A ochenta, a ciento, a mil,
> sobre los mares, sobre los records,
> a llevarlas
> al otro mundo, a la otra
> mitad donde están brotando. (ll.4-10, p.180)

Although quite taken by the marvels of twentieth century invention, Salinas's imagination is never overtaken by his enthusiasm for the numerous mechanical playthings of urban life. While drinking in the wonders of everyday concrete existence, the life of the mind - the world of ideas - is never swamped by "las cosas", but only further stimulated. The "Rapto" in the title of this poem not only refers to the rapturous, exhiliating sensation of moving at great speed, but also hints at an additional poetic "rapto" - a possible abduction of the concrete world of objects by the poet's imagination. In the 1920s, popular conceptions of the automobile conjured up phenomenal velocities. This state of technological innocence is parodied in "Rapto a primavera", where the actual speed is exaggerated in the awe-struck mind of the viewer: (l.6) "a ochenta, a ciento, a mil," and remains in Salinas's poems something utterly unreal, something fabulous. Indeed, a distinct air of imaginative fantasy surrounds the trappings of modern, urban life in the early volumes, captured by the title of *Fábula y signo*.

In Salinas's early work we witness his fascination with the proliferation of new artefacts and gadgets available on the booming consumer market of the 1920s.

These products of a new industrial age were appropriated in a poetic sense, as they became the focus of some of Salinas's best-known poems of this period. His delight in novelty and invention invariably goes hand in hand with a childlike sense of wonder and a passion for the new. The advent of so many new realities required new linguistic definitions, in a period when industrial invention was rivalled only by the poet's ability to exploit new poetic resources. The literary movement which best captured the rapid changes in Spanish society at this time, the momentum of industrial production and consumerism, was Creacionismo, which placed special emphasis on the denominative powers of language. The use of startling, novel images was encouraged, seen as a foil to the tired and spent rhetoric of the Postromantics. This emphasis on the Adamic role of the poet as rival creator to God, is evident in the glorification of invention and the act of creation in many poems of this period.[22] Such Adamic verse is exemplified by Salinas's "Cuartilla", which opens the collection *Seguro azar* with a blank page awaiting the poet's first penstroke, the creative act. While the tone is playful, a striking Creacionista comparison is drawn between the poet's ability to create, and "The Creation" as told by the book of Genesis. Salinas introduces a mischievous note of rivalry in ll.15 - "¿Vencer, quién vencerá?" The poet's inner reality, conceived in the mind, or the concrete external reality he perceives around him?

> Y la que vence es
> rosa, azul, sol, el alba:
> punto de acero, pluma
> contra lo blanco, en blanco,
> inicial, tú, palabra.   (ll.22-6, p.107)

Potential conflict between these two realities is resolved in Salinas's metaphoric use of "el alba" to equate light and poetry. This dawn brings a new kind of poetry, as the poet's vision of the world is primordial, fresh, pristine. Just as the sun shone upon the world in Genesis, revealing its hidden colours and shapes, so the poet's pen brings new realities to light. Salinas takes up the role of Creator-poet when he puts pen to paper, conjuring up new worlds (ll.24-6).

The Creacionista aversion to the blank expanses of the void is transposed onto the white space of the vacant cinema-screen in "Cinematógrafo", also in *Seguro azar*: "Al principio nada fue" (l.1, p.133). Soon, projected images fill the blank screen, and "máquinas maravillosas" (l.38), the offspring of human genius, contrive to fill the empty air, banishing silence. "La palabra" now takes up its rightful place alongside visual projections of reality -

> Y el primer día de la creación
> se levantó de su rincón
> y vino a asomarse a la tela... (ll.50-2, p.134)

The word becomes incarnate in speaking pictures; again light and language are married as cinema and poetry speak in response to the modern world.

Salinas's interest in "las cosas" in the 1920s is not limited to the advent of new artefacts in his immediate urban environment. While lightbulbs, radiators, typewriters and motorcars may feature in his first three volumes of poetry, they are by no means the dominant subject-matter. All concrete reality holds a fascination for this poet, which is evident throughout his poetic career. However, Salinas is highly conscious that routine consumes familiar objects, the home, the paraphernalia of everyday existence - even the beloved. Novelty is a much-sought and highly valued experience, if by definition shortlived, and Salinas strives to preserve its effects through the constant renovation of the familiar. The real attraction of the Creacionista movement for Salinas was its cult of the new - its poetic exploitation of novelty. The innate strangeness of "all that lives outside of the poet" is what entices the imagination to reach out and enter into dialogue with the world; "las cosas", in this sense act as a direct inspiration for "las ideas". In order to sustain this dialogue, it is necessary to make still stranger that which is already alien to the poet - alien in the sense best captured by the Spanish 'ajeno'.

But how should he de-familiarise the familiar? Can the known be un-known? By providing new perspectives on "las cosas", Salinas reinforces the enigmatic 'otherness' of all inanimate reality.[23] One example of such renovating perspectives is "Madrid, calle de..." (*Seguro azar*, p.132), where a mirror is plucked from its dull, utilitarian existence and liberated when it is carried down a busy city street. No longer passively observed, the mirror is now an active observer, acting out a new role -

> ...Nadie
> vino a mirarse en él. El, sí que mira
> hoy, por vez primera es ojos.   (ll.9-11)

This new role requires new linguistic expression. The mirror is metaphorically transformed into eyes, soaking in reality instead of reflecting it outwards. The ultimate visual coup of this poem is to transform the flat, polished surface of the mirror into the three-dimensional volume of a lake, which simultaneously reflects and is penetrated by the skies above -

> Y le surcan
> - de alas, de plumas, peces -
> crepusculares golondrinas secas. (ll.20-2, p.132)

This poem exemplifies Salinas's ability to open up new perspectives on "las cosas" in these early poems. The mirror, itself acquiring a new perspective on the concrete world when it is removed from its usual context, is transformed in the reader's eyes from a rather mundane household object, to a shimmering lake of hidden depths. The disadvantage of mass industrial production from this poet's point of view, was the process of standardisation it involved, which replaced the love and tenderness once bestowed on objects which were unique and handcrafted. Salinas manages to renew the unique quality of the man-object relationship in another poem from *Seguro azar*, "Navacerrada, abril" (p.116) by painting a romantic setting which he and his car share with the intimacy of lovers: "los dos solos" (l.1), "Y de pronto mi mano / que te oprime, y tú, yo..." (ll.14-15). An anti-utilitarian approach to "las cosas" is evident here. To resuscitate our feelings of intellectual wonder at the 'otherness' and novelty of things, they must be taken out of a tired, routine context.[24] Salinas positively delights in the uselessness of some objects - such as the "Reló pintado" of *Fábula y signo*. "!Qué bien está esa hora / boba, suelta, volando / por los limbos del tiempo!" (ll.6-8, p.166).

Occasionally Salinas's all-pervading interest in the given, observable world is momentarily eclipsed by his desire to possess and transform "las cosas" through his poetic interpretation of them. The poems which best exemplify this process are also those whose subjects are the technological trappings of modern life: "Radiador y fogata", "Underwood girls", and "35 bujías". Despite their relative scarcity, these poems are frequently quoted as most representative of Salinas's early work - presumably because they incorporate elements of the new concrete environment of the 1920s-30s, and illustrate the transforming powers of the rich poetic imagination exercised by the younger Salinas. Yet the workings of this imagination on "las cosas" in these poems, perhaps surprisingly, undermines their 'otherness' rather than accentuating it. They are effectively overshadowed by the poet's conceptual interpretation, which transforms "cosa" into "idea", myth, or archetype. The result, is that a radiator is portrayed as a -

> ...Nueva
> criatura deliciosa
> hija del agua, sirena
> callada de los inviernos
> que va por los radiadores
> sin ruido...   (ll.25-30, *Fáb.*, p.181)

The mythical siren, here "sirena callada", long associated with sea and song, is undeniably a very contrived metaphor for the radiator, presumably inspired by the silent circulation of water, whose heat lures him ever closer. Clearly, the poet's focus is not on the external, concrete reality of "las cosas" at this point, as the radiator serves a purely metaphorical function: it is now a concrete expression of the archetypal siren, albeit silenced. Consequently, the reader's attention and interest is not directed towards the thing itself, the radiator, so much as the poet's idea, his interpretation of it. This is no longer a case of renovating "las cosas" through novel perspectives or de-contextualisation, but one of poetic annexation.[25]

In a similar process to the transformation of radiator into siren, typewriter keys become "treinta eternas ninfas" (l.27) in "Underwood Girls" (*Fábula y signo*, p.203-4). Once transformed by this metaphor, they possess not mechanical, but magical powers -"Entre todas / sostienen el mundo" (ll.2-3). Like oracles, they hold the key to - "destinos de trueno y rayo / destinos de lluvia lenta..." (ll.8-9). Nimble fingers may awaken them and invoke these mysterious powers of creation. However, when the poet sits at his typewiter to compose, he appropriates their potential creativity. Effectively, he relegates these "ninfas" to a role that is purely functional: like the radiator-siren of "Radiador y fogata", they are instrumental to *his* metaphoric expression.

> Tú alócate
> bien los dedos, y las
> raptas y las lanzas,
> a las treinta, eternas ninfas
> contra el gran mundo vacío
> blanco en blanco.   (ll.24-9, p.203)

Again the deployment of the verb "raptar" is significant, as the realm of "las ideas" can be seen to usurp momentarily the physical reality of "las cosas".

It is ironic that in these early poems whose subject-matter is ostensibly the new "cosas" of a rapidly-changing world, Salinas's focus is less on the concrete reality of "las cosas" themselves, than on their potential as referents on which to construct his metaphors. The poetic process whereby these objects are transformed, is the true thematic concern of this group of poems: "Radiador y fogata", "Underwood girls", and "35 bujías". The use of mythological creatures such as nymphs and sirens as metaphoric representations of mundane artefacts, appears, at first, to raise the everyday to a poetic significance rivalling that of the Classics. Indeed, it exemplifies what Salinas elsewhere calls the "exaltation of reality" taken to a metaphorical extreme by Góngora, whose work underwent a profound rediscovery and evaluation by the "Generation of '27", culminating in the tercentenary celebration of his work in that year.[26] Alternatively, the mythologising of contemporary phenomena can be read as evidence of a deep-rooted lack of faith in their poetic value. Classical allusions can be deployed to bolster up what the poet essentially believes to be the ephemeral trappings of modern existence, they can denote a hierarchical value-system which places all that is temporally distant above that which is actual or new. While Salinas's enthusiasm for novelty remains steadfast, these particular poems do seem to challenge the otherwise democratic nature of his subject-matter. Is the poet here dependent on classical mythology, to lend depth and profundity to the objects that are seemingly the subjects of these poems? The references to mythological types undeniably emit resounding echoes through the reader's literary consciouness which would not be triggered by the direct evocation of modern technology. While we may marvel at the efficiency and convenience of the domestic supply of electricity, it is the archetype of the siren, and not the electric radiator, that exudes overtones of seduction. Lurking behind these "radical metaphors" is a question as to the nature of reader-response.[27] Does Salinas's use of mythology open up another dimension in our relationship with these objects? The answer must be affirmative, but is restricted to the boundaries of intellectual appreciation. Through the 'exalting' influence of classical literary tradition, Salinas transforms our relationship with "las cosas" from one which is both sensory and conceptual (we apprehend the object through the senses: we conceive its purpose and function), to something that is purely abstract and conceptualised. The inherent poetry of "las cosas" in these early poems is no longer freestanding or self-justifying; it is not even entirely contemporary, but largely dependent on literary tradition to somehow sanction its meaningfulness in the present.

Modern technology elicits a poetic response in both "Underwood girls" and "35 bujías". But this is not the classic Romantic response where the poet reflects upon perceptions gleaned through the senses, thereby formulating ideas and abstractions. Salinas's poetic response to these objects does not, in fact, grow from sense perception, but from a highly conceptual understanding of their function. The choice of objects is significant: the typewriter has obvious associations with poetry, and the 35 candle-power light-bulb inspires the electric light/enlightenment conceit that transforms it into a muse.[28] The lightbulb is only switched on during the solitary nocturnal hours that the poet associates with creative activity:

> En el cuarto ella y yo no más, amantes
> eternas, ella mi iluminadora
> musa dócil...   (ll.15-17, p.136)[29]

The essential adjective here is "dócil" - subject to his whim, passive. Any autonomous reality is pre-empted by the muse's poetic function; she serves the poet; with her aid he will produce his poems -

> descifraremos formas leves, signos
> perseguidos en mares de blancura
>
> por mí, por ella, artificial princesa,
> amada eléctrica.   (ll.20-3)

These lines clinch the lightbulb's secondary metaphoric function: not only is it the poet's muse, but also his fairytale princess, the answer to his dreams. He jealously guards her by day - captive in her crystal palace - releasing her only at night-time, to illuminate his solitude.

> Yo la veo en su claro
> castillo de cristal, y la vigilan
> - cien mil lanzas - los rayos

- cien mil rayos - del sol.   (ll.4-7, *Seg.*, p.136)

Like classical myth, the fairytale is a rich source of archetype.[30] By drawing on
these genres for metaphor, Salinas effectively de-particularises concrete objects.
As the archetypal reality of fairy-tale princess or muse becomes more and more
apparent in the poet's metaphoric presentation of the lightbulb for example, the
concrete nature of the "cosa" itself fades in the reader's mind, dwindling to an idea,
a concept.

What these poems typify is a tendency in Salinas's early work to arrogate
"las cosas" for his own poetic purposes: specific phenomena are de-particularised
through metaphor, interpretation, or archetype.   Antonio Blanch rather misses the
point when he suggests that Salinas is striving to communicate the intrinsic
materiality of matter.[31] The poems cited by Blanch as evidence of the habitation
of matter by the poet are "El árbol menos" in *Seguro azar*, and "La estatua",
Fábula y signo. In the former, burning wood brings sensations of the forest
flooding into the poet's consciousness.   But this is not to say that the poet
experiences what Blanch terms as "su ser vegetal". Sense perceptions may invade
the poet's inner reality, but they are still emanating from outside the self:

> Ciprés:
> largas sombras azules
> en un muro encalado,
> veo.
> El ruiseñor cimero
> cantarín del antojo,
> oigo.
> Por su masa secreta,
> índice vertical
> del paisaje seguro,
> sé.   (ll.4-14, p.153)

In true 'tree-consciousness', if such a state can be apprehended by the poet,
"paisaje" would not be perceived as the third person indicated by the "su" of l.11.

The presence of the verb "saber" as opposed to "ser" in l.14 is also significant. There is a world of difference between knowing and being, and while the poet perceives the tree's woody world, he is not part of it; he does not enter into its reality in the manner suggested by Blanch. Similarly in "La estatua", although Salinas makes an overt comparison between himself and the statue (both are moulded from clay), he remains outside its material substance:

> a ser lo primero, tierra,
> lo primero que tú eras,
> lo primero...   (ll.15-17)
> que fui yo.   (l.19, p.170)

Salinas aspires to the poetic fusion of "ideas y cosas", abstract and concrete realities, but he is pragmatic enough to be aware of the limitations of the individual consciousness: contrary to Blanch's assertion, he cannot experience the very materiality of matter, and even if he could, this may not be poetically desirable, as he would effectively lose the realm of "las cosas" as a reference point of 'otherness'.

Salinas, in his early work at least, draws on the stimulating physical presence of this 'otherness' as manifest in the novel inventions of the time, or indeed by re-creating the familiar so as to restore its novelty and 'otherness'. He does this by imposing new semantic definitions onto material phenomena, and then presenting them as discoveries, as a source of revelation. In order to sustain the experience of novelty, "las cosas" must be presented from increasingly unexpected perspectives. Ironically, one potential side-effect of this process is that they cease to be "cosas" to become the poet's "idea". This conversion of "cosas" into "ideas" in Salinas's early work, despite the obvious attractions of phenomena, is not representative of all his poetry. There appears to be a distinct Platonic hunger for permanence in these early poems: not only are we made aware that the novelty of "las cosas" is shortlived, but constantly reminded that matter itself is irrevocably perishable. Writing on the works of Jorge Carrera Andrade, Salinas observes how another poet responds to this dilemma:

> Y ahora confiesa que el polvo devora la presencia de las cosas. El dilema abre su tragedia. Una de dos: o el mundo se derrumba aquí ante nosotros, ya era solo presencia... o había algo más que la presencia de las cosas, sus ausencias, sus imágenes, sus ideas.[32]

A similar need for 'something more than physical presence' characterises Salinas's work up to his departure from Spain in 1936. Perhaps it is the sheer force of absence - the absence of material evidence of home, patria, his native culture, that somehow causes this Platonic yearning to diminish in his later work. Salinas's poetry of the 1940s is firmly rooted in concrete reality, with which the mind interacts, but does not seek to surpass. The critical writings of the 1940s also demonstrate an awareness of the need for equilibrium between external and internal realities. To exclude one or other from his poetic range of vision would impede any possibility of achieving wholeness, or 'entereza' of expression. Salinas did not need to be reminded of the dangers of over-conceptualisation. All of his poetry, even the early poems which thematically seem to subject "las cosas" to the rigours of "las ideas", demonstrate a movement towards the semantic integration of concrete and abstract expression. Manipulated by Salinas, ideas become less abstract, more readily intuited at the surface of material reality. Simultaneously, the essential 'otherness' of "las cosas" seems increasingly open to perception by the mind's eye. The poet's inner life and external reality live in a constant and mutually-influencing condition of interrelatedness.

The interaction of "ideas y cosas", that "entrecruzarse" envisioned by Salinas, permeates many more levels of his work than its basic subject-matter. Such interaction extends beyond the use of phenomena as a stimulus for the germination of new ideas. Nor is this relationship limited to the intellectual superimposition of archetypes onto particular concrete objects. Salinas's poetry demonstrates a reluctance to impose rigid semantic distinctions - even in areas as clearly defined in the Western consciousness as mind and body, or abstract and concrete experience. A semantic metamorphosis takes place in this poetry which is far more radical than any radiator-siren metaphor, and which ultimately generates a striking impression of the interchangeability of abstract and concrete realities.[33] This reciprocal semantic approximation of abstract and concrete is enacted through the parallel and interrelated processes of the reification of ideas, and the abstraction of matter. The former could be described as a 'concrete abstraction', because it renders palpable that which is intrinsically conceptual. The earliest example of this in Salinas's published poetry is in *Presagios*, where he describes his poetic aspirations as an "eterna ambición de asir lo / inasidero" (ll.20-1, p.55). The inherent paradox of this statement is echoed much later in *Razón de amor*, when the poet-lover asks of "la salvación" (l.1) -"¿Se la coge a puñados como al mar?" (l.3, p.339). The impossibility of catching up a concept in handfuls is rendered more concrete by the "salvación-mar" simile. Like the sea, salvation appears to be tenable, but like the sea, which is matter and not thought, it eludes the closed fist, slipping through our fingers. The simile illustrates the equally elusive nature of abstract and concrete realities, despite the palpable appearance of the latter.

In other instances it is the quality of adjectives accompanying abstract nouns that contributes to the lingering impression of their tangibility; even the void has a texture -"el fondo / duro y seco de la nada" (ll.22-23, *Fáb.*, p.165). An emotional response, a positive or negative ambience (not generally conceived of as concrete experience), is invoked with violent physicality:

> Los síes -¡qué golpetazos
> de querer en el silencio!
> las últimas negativas
> a la noche le quebraban.
> (ll.12-15, Respuesta a la luz, *Fáb.*, p.179)

Equally violent and palpable are the concepts of good and evil: "el puñal del bien y el mal / que nosotros hemos de clavar en el pecho", (ll.11-12, *Pres.*, p.101). These 'concrete abstractions' tend to have an effect of reinforcing the semantic weight of a concept, of giving emphasis to an idea. At times the effect of this device can be rather tongue-in-cheek: one example is where Salinas takes a rather incongruous and original approach to the emotional tangle of farewells and literally tries to, "Desenredar esa madeja / del adiós redondo" (ll.12-13, *Fáb.*, p.205).

Another technique commonly deployed by Salinas in his reification of ideas, is the 'chromatic concept'. For example, the multi-variable nature of farewells is stressed by their description in terms of colour: "adioses negros, blancos; / adiós riendo, adiós llorando" (ll.18-19, Los adioses, *Fáb.*, p.205). And again, in "El teléfono" from the same volume, the conceptual substance of distance acquires its own hue: "tan de color de distancia" (l.31, *Fáb.*, p.200). Even memory has a colour, as does sorrow: "su gran color de pena" (l.37, *Raz.*, p.342). It is no accident that these nouns, qualified by colour, constitute a semantic unit in Salinas's poetry: farewells, distance, memory and pain - all indicate absence, and in the examples cited, refer specifically to the absence of the beloved. Salinas's conceptions of absence and presence are as semantically fluid as his approach to "ideas y cosas", as physically absent realities manifest the visually evident characteristic of colour. Such exploitation of sensory perception in the evocation of abstract realities facilitates the semantic approximation of "ideas y cosas", while undermining inherited philosophical definitions of these realms of experience as mutually exclusive.

Another common form of reification found extensively in Salinas's work is anthropomorphism, or what Jorge Guillén calls "la vivificación", where concepts not only become sensible, but even acquire the physical attributes of human form.[34] One example of this is "Mirar lo invisible", where evening mists blur the concrete world, rendering it ephemeral and enticing the poet to enter into a state of creative *ensueño*. But the poetic imagination requires more than abstract imponderables; it too seeks inspiration from matter, and accordingly, projects physical limb and human gesture onto the amorphous evening.

> La tarde me está ofreciendo
> en la palma de su mano,
> hecha de enero y de niebla,
> vagos mundos desmedidos...
> (ll.1-4, Mirar lo invisible, *Seg.*, p.145)

Similarly, "la tarde" takes on the attributes of a living organism in "Afán", from *Fábula y signo*, - "se estira, vibra, tiembla / no puede más" (ll.29-30, p.197). The evening seascape represents a "suma de la belleza / el mundo" (ll.16-17), as the natural world is stretched to its absolute limits of breathtaking beauty. The physical symptoms it displays, such as trembling, are evidence of an empirical world that is emotionally-charged, humanised, "vivificado". Concepts are entified - literally embodied, in many of Salinas's poems. Even silence is unmasked to reveal a human face in "Triunfo suyo", from *Seguro azar*, "su rostro de sin remedio / eternidad, él, silencio" (ll.21-2, p.162). One noun, "silencio", whose oppressive nature is experienced sensorily as well as intellectually, embraces both the concrete and abstract realities of "rostro" and "eternidad".

Not only do ideas take on physical characteristics, they also display emotion and motivation, the attributes of autonomous personality.[35] Where this arises the tone tends to be ludic, as in "La tarde libre", from *Fábula y signo*, where the lovers plot to 'steal' an evening from their weekly working routine, and dedicate it to themselves.

> La semana de abril
> de pronto se sintió
> una ausencia en el pecho:
> jueves, su corazón. (ll.1-4, p.185)

The temporal entity of a week in April 'feels' all the figurative emotional associations implied by the possession of a human breast. The fact that reification operates at two levels becomes especially evident when dealing with some of the poems in the love cycle. In *Razón de amor*, for example, "un no" is firstly transformed from a negative response into a substantive, or identifiable "cosa", it is then personified, granted the psychological and emotional ability to acquire its own motivations and behavioural patterns: "A veces un no niega / más de lo que quería" (ll.1-2, p.355).

Complementary to this process of reification in Salinas's work is the parallel process of abstraction. Once again, the poet's artistic and philosophical end is to stress the simultaneity and interconnectedness of abstract and concrete experience; to strive for 'entereza' of perception. At times, the relationship between "ideas y cosas" echoes the Romantic's understanding of thought as the residue of sensory experience. One example of just such a poetic progression from the concrete and particular to abstract thought, is a poem from *Confianza* bearing the very apt title of "Las cosas", where we are taken from purely sensual appreciation -

> Al principio, ¡qué sencillo,
> allí delante, qué claro!
> No era nada, era una rosa
> haciendo feliz a un tallo...   (ll.1-4)

- to the realms of Platonic idealism:

> Hay otra cosa mejor,
> hay un algo,
> un puro querer cerniéndose
> por aires ya sobrehumanos   (ll.23-6)
> que puede más, y más allá.   (l.28, p.659-60)

But how typical is this transition from "cosa" to "idea" of Salinas's work? And what of his vision of a total reality? The weight of evidence suggests that despite the "radical metaphors" of some early poems, reification is in fact a more common tendency in his poetry than abstraction.

One tendency that is often mistaken for abstraction is the poet's attempt to grasp the essence of a given experience. For example, when Salinas describes the upward motion of a fountain, and the downward curve of a palm in the geometric terms of "Dos líneas" (l.5), "pura geometría" (l.20), in "Fecha cualquiera", he is choosing to evoke its essence in visual terms, rather than conceptual abstraction. Here, purity of line is concretely descriptive of physical form. However, there is conceivably a hint of the influence of 'poesía pura' at work here: apart from the visual attractions of geometric form, Salinas draws a conceptual analogy between geometry and intellectual lucidity. The qualities of 'pureza' and 'claridad' were aspired to by many Spanish poets in the 1920s, and the poem, "Fecha cualquiera" is essentially a visual appreciation of geometric form, whose linear essence is analogous to the poetic aspirations of 'poesía pura'. [36] As the poem's title suggests, geometry is omnipresent in the empirical physically perceptible world, and the final lines serve to reinforce this point: "La pura geometría / dime, / ¿Quién se lo quita a la tarde?", (ll.20-22, *Seg.*, p.114). Geometry is so intrinsic a part of sensible reality that it should not be mistaken for abstraction. The geometry of this poem is 'pura' precisely because it is so intrinsic to life; it is not decorative or ornamental, but an essential expression of concrete reality.

In his Introduction to *Reality and the Poet in Spanish Poetry*, Jorge Guillén highlights the quest for essence as a driving force behind all Salinas's critical writings, suggesting that in the very act of literary criticism, he is "searching out the work's essential characteristic, and 'essence' means unity", (*Reality*, p.19). This equation is most revealing. If we follow Guillén's line of argument, then the quest for essence in Salinas's poetry does not necessitate a rejection of matter in favour of abstract concept, but requires a fusion or unification of the two. The essence of any experience, for Salinas, must capture it entirety or 'entereza'. In his pursuit of a total perception of reality, Salinas was perfectly conscious of the perils of over-conceptualisation. In his essay, "El poeta y las fases de la realidad" he warns that "el fabuloso aumento de realidades, materiales y espirituales" (and in Salinas's mind, the two cannot be separated), presents the poet with two distinct dangers. The first is the temptation to write poetry that simply reproduces the extraordinary wealth and variety of external reality; a temptation succumbed to by many Futurists and Ultraístas. The second is more subtle: that in response to this proliferation of externals, the poet may feel overwhelmed by the world of phenomena, and turn inwards, producing a purely abstract poetry fed only by the intellect; a "forma delirante del individualismo".[37] Salinas's awareness of the undesirability of excessive abstraction is evident as early as *Fábula y signo* where, in a poem entitled "Mar distante", the reality of the faraway sea is abstracted in stages that progress from "imagen" 1.1) to "estampa" (1.2), to "nombre" (1.7), until finally we learn that -"si no es el mar, sí es su idea / de fuego, insondable, limpia" (ll.12-13, p.169). Without physical presence, reality is too easily conceptualised. If the insertion of the adjective "limpia" is another allusion to the pruned, stark verse advocated by the 'puristas', then "Mar distante" may convey a warning as to the danger of over-emphasising the essence of experience, and departing utterly from the present, physical reality of the here and now. The poem concludes with a vision of drowning, "y yo, ahogándome en ella" (ll.14-15, p.169), and it is significant that the poet drowns - not in the sea's swell - but in the quagmire of his own ideas.

In order to reach a vision of a reality that is non-discriminatory, concrete and abstract experiences must cease to be perceived as antagonistic. To this end, Salinas entifies "ideas" and conceptualises "cosas" to a point where semantic boundaries blur. This is particularly true of the denominative function of language, where abstract nouns frequently replace concrete. Where this occurs, the superficial normality of syntactic structures is subverted by their unexpected semantic content. There is obvious incongruity in the substitution of an abstract value for a concrete object: in an early poem the reader is surprised to find that the iron of a breastplate, so impenetrably solid, dissolves into the abstractions of eternity, in "Coraza hecha con el acero de lo eterno" (1.2, *Pres.*, p.101).

The fusion of "ideas y cosas" that is brought about by both reification and abstraction, sometimes occurs as a two-way process in the same poem - as for example in "Placer, a las once": "Del hombro cuelga la aljiba / toda llena de alfabetos" (ll.6-7, *Seg.*, p.128). The alphabet suddenly ceases to be a conceptual, generic term for a compendium of letters, becoming instead something physically tangible with volume and weight, that can fill a quiver, and presumably is as sharp as the arrows we expect to find there. A similar example of this systematic substitution of abtract for concrete nouns occurs later in the same poem, where "El niño blande su espada" (1.17), "toda afilada de quieros" (1.19). Desires, enthusiasm, the child's lust for life are as keen as a sword-edge; the simile is compressed by the insertion of "quieros". Juxtaposed with these examples of reification, or 'vivificación', is the abstract noun, "caprichos", which now acquires a physical form with which to leap, and a benign, smiling disposition in the lines - "Caprichos salteadores / risueñamente..." (ll.26-7). Finally, in lines 29-31, a "secreto" provides us with a perfect example of a sensorially perceptible, concrete abstraction:

> El secreto, cascabel,
> suena, la solución perfecta,
> suena la alegría dentro.   (p.128)

Through the repeated replacement of concrete nouns by abstract, Salinas successfully subverts the denominative function of substantives. This is one aspect of linguistic manipulation in Salinas's work that Robert Havard would class as a "counter-language" technique, that is, working against the norms of inherited linguistic structures.[38]

More radical than the examples of displaced abstractions cited above, is Salinas's frequent use of listing devices, and the apparently random juxtaposition of concrete and abstract nouns, often referred to in critical commentaries as 'enumeración'.[39] Abstract and concrete nouns placed side by side in deliberate juxtaposition inevitably exert a degree of semantic influence on one another, so forging a new semantic context that embraces the 'entereza' of human experience, and reflects Salinas's unified vision of a reality that ceases to make dualistic distinctions. Far from presenting a world that is fragmented and chaotic, as Spitzer suggests, Salinas presents here a world view that fully integrates internal and external forces. Spitzer's own definition of this listing technique is that of an "enumeración caótica", where "las palabras abstractas se codean con las concretas" in a "bazar confuso".[40] And in an extraordinarily subjective evaluation of this tendency, he describes this "desorden enumerativo" as an example of "asíndeton despectivo", transferring his own very conservative prejudices as to the 'correct' subject-matter and form of verse, onto the poet:

> ...el desorden enumerativo es manifestación del disgusto que siente
> el poeta frente a la realidad de nuestra vida, radicalmente
> desordenada: un caos... [41]

It is interesting to contrast Spitzer's evaluation of the undifferentiated enumeration of concrete and abstract nouns as an expression of a chaotic vision of the universe, with J. F. Cirre's assessment that -

> Pudiera pensarse que esta técnica enumerativa se aproxima a la de
> los surrealistas en lo que de aspecto caótico ofrece... no hay afán
> desintegrante, como en el surrealismo, sino, por el contrario, una
> integración.[42]

This is precisely the effect sought by Salinas's deployment of enumerated nouns: not to express a reality that is disintegrated, but rather to integrate abstract and concrete experience.

What at first glance appear to be arbitrarily enumerated nouns, on a closer examination generally reveal - not chaos - but order, an inner logic of contiguity. Their juxtaposition is never truly random, and can be categorised in many cases as a clear example of lexical cohesion, as each noun is semantically connected through mental association and context. Sometimes emotional content will provide the key to the relationship between abstract and concrete realities - as in "Aquí", *Fábula y signo*, where the poet is unwilling to leave the idyllic setting he shares with the beloved in the here and now implied by the title. This emotional ambience - his reluctance to be separated from this place and person by either space or time - is evoked by the enumeration of varied nouns:

> Nunca me iré de ti
> por el viento, en las velas,
> por el alma, cantando,
> ni por los trenes, no.   (ll.21-4, p.176)

The contextual associations between these nouns are fairly transparent: lovers are separated by water, the wind is a driving force behind the boats that transport them, here evoked through the metonym of "velas". Trains, like boats, are a means of transport and therefore, in this emotional framework, are closely tied to the poet's dread of separation. The rogue noun here is "alma", more abstract than concrete, but which is syntactically enumerated as though it too, were a means of transport, akin to boats and trains - which it could prove to be, were the poet not utterly present with the beloved in soul as well as in body. But no. His soul, we are assured, is completely attendant, and will never provide the means of their separation.

Where tension arises between lovers, the same technique can evoke quite a different emotional atmosphere: enumerated nouns now reveal the potential negativity of the lovers' silence in "Ruptura sin palabras": "amarguras, polvo / sañas y sequía", (ll.45-6, *Fáb.*, p.192). Dust, the most concrete of these nouns, is the inevitable product of, and a metonym for drought ("sequía"): both serve as physical manifestations of the sterile feelings of rage and bitterness ("sañas" and "amarguras"). The juxtaposition of one abstract and one concrete noun in each line is quite deliberate and facilitates the expression of an emotional experience which is 'felt', both in the body and the mind.

The "enumeración" of abstract and concrete realities is especially prevalent in the love-cycle, an indication of a progressively integrated view of reality in Salinas's work. The love experience heightens the individual's awareness of the inseparable nature of inner and exterior realities, so accelerating their poetic fusion. Union with the beloved opens the poet's eyes to the possibility of union with "all that lives outside of the poet".[43] As he awaits the arrival of the beloved, the poet is aware that in order to recognise her, he must be open to new kinds of experience that will not comply with old patterns of thought. If we wish to embrace 'otherness' in our lives, he warns the reader that we must be receptive to mystery:

No, no dejéis cerradas
las puertas de la noche,
del viento, del relámpago,
de lo nunca visto.   (ll.1-4, p.221)

We must leave ajar the metaphoric doors of human consciousness to "lo nunca visto", the unknown. All that lies outside the self, all mystery, is metonymically represented by the darkness of the night in which we cannot see, and the wildness of the elements, over which we have no control. When the beloved finally arrives, all that is known and familiar will come tumbling down - "murallas, nombres, tiempos, / se quebrarían todos" (ll.36-7, *La voz*, p.222). Concrete "murallas" in ruins serve as a reminder of and metonym for the futility of clinging to past times ("tiempos"), and previous notions of identity ("nombres"). When we come face to face with 'otherness', new definitions are required; chronological order is turned on its head; the past bears no logical relation to the present. The same is true of language: in love, inherited meanings are cast off as the lovers seek out their own means of expressing the integrated reality of the "trasmundo". Love overturns all inherited orders, all existence prior to itself. Perhaps it is because Salinas deploys the enumeration of "ideas y cosas" so extensively in the love cycle to convey love's anarchic and dramatic effects, that the device is so frequently associated by commentators with depictions of chaos. In fact it conveys a new, unified reality discovered through the love experience. Old laws are no longer relevant - even the laws of gravity are not borne out by lovers, who are buoyed up "en aires, en ausencias / en papeles, en nada" (ll.5-6, *La voz*, p.320). "Aires" are obviously ineffable and weightless; "ausencias" serve as a metonym for empty space, and thus are closely linked to "aires"; "nada" is the ultimate expression of the void. Amidst these imponderables is planted particularised matter: "papeles" in received semantics would be categorised as "cosas", material objects. Yet, from our reading of earlier poems such as "Cuartilla" and "Underwood girls", we are aware that in Salinas's personal symbol-system, "papeles" tend to represent blank pages, and can also serve as a metaphor for emptiness.[44] The equation of "nada" and "papel", concept and thing, recurs in *Razón de amor*, when love -still latent in the poet - struggles to emerge from the realms of inner experience to participate in the world of "las cosas".

> Tantea a un lado y a otro:
> se tropieza con el cielo,
> con un papel, o con nada.
> (ll.6-8, Torpemente el amor busca, p.344)

A variation on the listing of various concrete and abstract nouns is the juxtaposition of just one of each: this use of apposition has a levelling effect that edges towards metaphor more than metonym. Having already encountered the semantic contiguity of time with ruins in various cases of enumerated nouns, this association is now compressed to a metaphor, so that "columnas" *are* "tiempos":" Un gran horror a techos / quiebra columnas, tiempos..." (ll.3-4, Amor, amor, catástrofe, *La voz*, p.248). [45] In creating such metaphors, Salinas draws concrete and abstract experience still closer.[46] Sometimes he overtly explains his own metaphors, as in "Una sortija, una promesa, son lo mismo" (l.7). However the connection between the idea of promise and the ring-object, is not in this case the expected metonymic relation where the ring acts as a token - a manifestation of the prometido's pledge. The ring-promise metaphor is drawn from the physical form of the object, and not its symbolic function; they are similar because "inspiran la ilusión, por ser redondos / de que no tienen fin" (ll.8-9, *Largo*, p.498).

Abstract and concrete nouns are so semantically inter-related in Salinas's poetic scheme, that their metaphoric equivalence can be sealed by the simple insertion of an "o" -

> ¿te acompaña
> ese inmenso querer estar contigo
> que se llama el amor o el telegrama?
> (ll.15-17, ¿Acompañan las almas?, *Raz.*, p.352)

Love, in Salinas's work, is characterised by a gnawing impatience to be with the object of one's desires: the telegram is the means of sustaining contact between separated lovers, or of announcing an imminent arrival. Here, the two are presented as interchangeable, as their standard significances merge in the poet's own definition of love as the all-consuming desire to be in the presence of the beloved.

The undifferentiated value given to all substantives in Salinas's poetry undoubtedly subverts any preconceptions of an 'objective' semantic system. But does his assault on the distinctions between abstract and concrete really indicate, as Spitzer suggests, the poet's disapproval of a chaotic and fragmented world? Perhaps the best response to this assertion is to be found in one of Salinas's earlier poems, which describes an infant's reactions to the overwhelming variety of experience she encounters every day in the physical world. Everything, from "las sopas" (l.3) to "el tren" (l.6), "montaña" (l.7) and "mar" (l.8) - everything, is encapsulated by the denominations "Tatá, dadá" (l.1). The adult's analysis of this situation is that "todo lo confunde" (l.10). But there is no hint of disapproval in this evaluation of the child's world view. On the contrary, her ingenuous perception of the world as a toy, a "bola", is appealing to Salinas's own poetic spirit of discovery. In his own way, he too paints the world as "todo / hecho una bola confusa" (ll.18-19, *Pres.*, p.56).[47] This striving after fusion, the blurring of dualistic philosophical and lexical definitions, expresses a new awareness of reality and the self that is all-embracing, "entero".

The enumeration of "ideas y cosas", far from being random and arbitrary in Salinas's work, is a reflection of the infinitely varied, but ultimately unified nature of reality as he perceives it. By juxtaposing and equating these two forms of perception, intellectual and sensory, Salinas presents us with an alternative vision of reality where concepts and objects no longer relate to one another on a chronological basis. For former poets, the Romantics in particular, the perception of the empirical inspired a subsequent conception of ideas, and these two means of apprehending the world were related sequentially. Now, however, ideas and things are temporally interrelated and must be apprehended simultaneously. The linguistic result of this is very similar to that of collage, where apparently unlike realities are apprehended visually and intuitively in one, unified, spatial and temporal context.

A quantitative assessment of Salinas's verse reveals that the enumeration of concrete and abstract nouns is most prevalent in the modern, urban setting of the early poems and in the love cycle. The fact that this device is scarcely evident in *Todo más claro*, for example, may indicate that the feelings of well-being, and 'entereza' of the love relationship, have given way to a sense of fragmentation or isolation. Or may be due to the fact that the poet derives less pleasure from urban life than he did in the 1920s when it represented his "Nivel preferido":

> Y abajo, allí, a media hora
> accidentes, dimensiones,
> ruidosas delicias, números,
> estaban ellas, mis gracias.
> (ll.21-4, *Seg.*, p.146)

In later works, the modernist metropolis is perceived as increasingly anti-poetic. Far from offering a vision of reality that embraces every possible level of experience, the city is now perceived as mono-dimensional. The glorious confusion of event and abstract realities, - "accidentes, dimensiones" - and the city's cacophony in "Nivel preferido" are succeeded by the cult of singularity and razor-sharp precision in "Civitas Dei": "Lo exacto triunfa de lo incalculable" (l.47, *El Cont.*, p.642).

Any attempt to quantify the frequency with which abstract and concrete nouns occur in Salinas's use of the poetic device of enumeration, is greatly facilitated by Almela Pérez's computer-assisted breakdown of various grammatical units in his poetry.[48] Because the nature of this evidence is statistical, it fails to take specific context and meaning into account. Nonetheless, Almela's wordlists demonstrate some interesting lexical preferences in Salinas's work, from which we can draw some tentative conclusions.[49] If we consult Almela's data on the specific nature of the nouns enumerated in Salinas's work, (as opposed to those used in any other context), we find that throughout his poetic career the enumeration of "cosas" consistently outweighs that of "ideas". In addition, it becomes evident that of the phenomena listed in this literary device, the vast majority are drawn from nature. In *Presagios*, *Seguro azar*, and *Fábula y signo*, the elemental substantives "vientos", "cielos", "estrellas", "luz", "olas" and "tierras" dominate such cases of enumeration. Almela's computer-lists also reveal the recurring, though considerably less frequent incidence of the following ideas:

"años", "alegrías", "tiempos", "números", and "dimensiones".[50] This purely quantitative assessment can only demonstrate the relative dominance of material reality over abstract concept in a specific denominative context. A more qualitative reading is necessary to reveal the significant metonymic relationships between these two categories of nouns. Despite the amount of critical emphasis given them, very few artefacts or modern technological inventions, figure among the substantives in this device of enumeration: in the early volumes only "trenes" and "cajas de lápices" appear - the latter only once. A similar pattern emerges in the love cycle, where the most frequently listed nouns are, again, drawn from the natural world: "viento", "luz", "estrella", "astro", "flor", "ola", "mar", and "piedra". The most common ideas are, as in the case of the earlier poems, "tiempos", "historia", órdenes", "números", and "nombres".[51] Perhaps surprisingly, artefacts and man-made objects are more common here than previously, reflecting the multi-faceted character of the love relationship. Most of these "cosas" bear a distinctly metonymic relationship to the ideas with which they are juxtaposed: the equating of "tiempos" and "historias" with "ruinas", "palacios", and "murallas" is just one example. Added to these are the "cosas" associated with the beloved - metonymic expressions of her external reality: "espejos", "trajes", and "retratos". While physical manifestations of the natural world are still dominant, an increasing interest in time ("tiempo"), and the question of personal identity ("nombre"), is evident in the context of the love relationship, where the lovers aspire to an eternal love, and discover the true nature of the self in knowledge of the other.

Natural elements are not as prevalent in *Todo más claro* as in either the pre-1936 works, or *El Contemplado*. This is probably due to the fact that a substantial number of the poems collected in *Todo más claro* were written before 1943, when Salinas's sojourn in Puerto Rico commenced, and with it, the intuition of a new relationship with nature. *Todo más claro* is characterised by an urban landscape of disenchantment: yet despite the distinct urban ambience of this work, references to artefacts are scarce, and many of the poems are reflective and introverted, dominated by the in-scape of the mind. The most frequently cited ideas are (not surprisingly), "amor", "destino", "palabra", "idioma" and "sueño", encapsulating the atmosphere of urban alienation that permeates the collection: the absence of love, the need for dreams and a "seguro azar"; and not least, the poet's persistent striving for communication.

Although differing utterly in mood, as the title suggests, *Confianza*, like *Todo más claro*, is almost entirely devoid of "enumeraciones", which no longer feature as one of Salinas's favourite methods of expressing his vision of a total reality. On the few occasions where they do arise, the nouns are without exception concrete, and are all derived from nature. Although they were not published until 1954, many of these poems were written between 1943 and 1944 during Salinas's stay in Puerto Rico, far from the mighty metropolis, and surrounded by the great natural beauty of the island. One example of this is the poem "Redondez", where: "Al corazón oceano / mirlo, chopo, alondra, llegan" (ll.33-4, p.824). Verbs are much more frequently listed than nouns in *Confianza*, indicating a growing perception of reality as process rather than product: "Alas van, ondas fluyen, suenan hojas, / brillan abejas" (ll.3-4, p.806). Natural processes are perceived as dynamic and emotionally positive -

¿Trabaja el sol? No trabaja,
sale, luce, esplende, alegra.   (ll.51-2)
¡activo todo, y sin ansia!   (l.65, Regalo, pp.801-2)

Not surprisingly, the substantive content of *El Contemplado* has more in common with *Confianza* than with *Todo más claro*. Given the subject-matter, (the sea of San Juan, Puerto Rico), a high incidence of elemental substantives is to be expected: "espumas", "olas", "luz" "vientos" and "sombras". Again, there are few artefacts: "velas" is perhaps the only example to figure with any consistency, and bears a largely metonymic relationship to "mar" and "viento". But most interesting of all is the conspicuous absence of "ideas", or abstract nouns, suggesting that Salinas's poetic focus has moved still further away from the idealism of some of his earlier work.[52]

In Salinas's ever-evolving relationship between internal and external realities, and his poetic quest for absolute perception, an unavoidable question is raised by the poems of *El Contemplado* - namely, whether "el contemplado" itself is "idea" or "cosa"? Is what we read here a description of an 'objective', empirically observable reality? Has "el contemplado" a 'real' existence that is wholly independent of the poet? Or is this another example of subjectivism, which transmits only the poet's conceptualised version of matter, and where, by inference, concrete reality is only knowable in the mind? Indeed, are the "Variaciones" presented here less those of the infinitely-changing sea, and more those of the poet's own psyche?

The title of the volume is already one stage removed from the material reality of the sea of San Juan, for which reason the sea, ostensibly the subject of these poems, could be read as the passive object of the poet's musings. These reflections or 'contemplations' are further filtered by language, so that two levels of interpretation are at play, distancing the reader from the original subject-matter, and suggesting that what is communicated in the pages of *El Contemplado* is not so much the sea itself, as the poet's idea of it. The title gives cause for reflection in more than one of the "Variaciones" that make up the piece, as Salinas ruminates on the denominative powers of language and on the act of naming (or re-naming) experience. This "Tema" opens the collection with what appears to be a classic example of subjectivism -

De mirarte tanto y tanto..　　　(l.1)
te he dado nombre, los ojos
te lo encontraron, mirándote.　　(ll.6-7, p.611)

- where the poet's observations seem to determine the identity and definition of "tú". Another line, "mis ojos te estrenaron" (l.21), sounds suspiciously akin to the kind of Creacionista appropriation of matter already encountered in some earlier poems. This statement comes close to denying the sea its historical existence prior to the poet's encounter with it. However, an alternative reading of this critical act of naming would concentrate less on the act of contemplation as an intellectual exercise, and more on the physical act of sense perception. The aforementioned lines - "te he dado nombre, los ojos / te lo encontraron, mirándote" (ll.6-7, p.611) - can be read quite differently. Is this really a case of intellectually conceived definition superimposed onto concrete reality? The above lines specify that the name, "El contemplado" comes primarily through the eyes, and it is significant that in Almela's computer data, "ojo" is cited as occurring 32 times in the text.[53] Furthermore, the dominant verbal expressions in *El Contemplado* are those of sense perception, ("mirar" emerges 28 times; "ver" 15), while those of intellectual conception are few and far between, ("contemplar" occurs on only 4 occasions in the text, and "pensar", on 2). It is as though the sea were merely using the poet's gaze as a medium through which it suggests its own name. The act of naming is thus transformed from a highly self-conscious projection of the self onto external reality, to an almost unconscious response to stimulus from the 'other'.[54]

> Por las noches
> soñando que te miraba,
> el abrigo de los párpados
> maduró, sin yo saberlo,
> este nombre tan redondo
> que hoy me descendió a los labios. (ll.8-13, Var. I, p.611)

The sea invades the poet's subconscious, permeates his dreams, and in this way directs his waking conscious thoughts. Clearly, such disclaimers of authorial responsibility are not to be taken literally. What is significant is the emphasis that Salinas chooses to place on the active role of concrete reality in the poetic process.

The inherent poetic potential of observable matter, previously obscured by Salinas's "radical metaphors" in his early work, is now restored to "las cosas" in *El Contemplado*.

The Creacionista sentiments of some of the earlier poems raise an interesting question as to whether it is the actual phenomena of modern life that exude poetry, or, as Vicente Cabrera suggests, the words that name these realities:

> Si para Salinas la palabra 'máquina' es tan poética como 'beso', lo que sucede es que para él la palabra, sí, en general la palabra, es medio de expresión poética. En este sentido se puede decir que Salinas no tiene un lenguaje poético especial; su lenguaje poético, es la lengua en su totalidad.[55]

There is more than a grain of truth in Cabrera's argument: in the Creacionista poems it is particularly difficult to judge whether the source of poetic inspiration lies in the "cosas" themselves or in the poet's interpretative treatment of them; whether the actual poetry stems from the referent or the metaphor. In *El Contemplado*, however, the presence of poetry in empirical reality, in "las cosas" themselves, is irrefutable.

How should the poet respond to this poetic potential? Is the naming of concrete reality, the denominative function so beloved by the Creacionistas, the only possible point of contact between the poetic imagination and the manifest poetry of matter? It becomes increasingly evident in *El Contemplado* that the physical world no longer represents for Salinas a blank page onto which he should project his internally conceived realities. The denominative function of language is the central theme of another poem, suggestively titled "Dulcenombre" (No.3, p.616). Again there is ambiguity in Salinas's description of the act of definition. This "Variación" opens with the statement - "Desde que te llamo así / por mi nombre..." (ll.1-2) - but is "mi nombre" the name for the sea, thought up by the poet? Or is it his own name? The same deliberate ambivalence emerges from the lines: "Pero tengo aquí en el alma / tu nombre, mío" (ll.9-10), which can be read as either a declaration of possession or of integration. Rupert Allen's analysis of some very ambiguous statements in this section of *El Contemplado* is very persuasive.[56]   Referring to the lines - "Si te nombro, soy tu amo / de un segundo..." (ll.15-16) - he concludes that the act of naming merely represents a momentary possession of the sea, as the poet's internal concept and the external reality gel in his mind, before that external reality re-possesses itself, outside the poet. Such moments of artistic arrogance, where Salinas claims to be master or even creator of concrete reality, should be read with an appreciation of his capacity for provocative irony. This kind of feigned omnipotence is very often a feature of Salinas's self-parody. A good example of this tongue-in-cheek tone is "Tú, mía", in *Fábula y signo*, (pp.194-5). where the poet's posturing is so extreme that any serious consideration of it is pre-empted.

Quieta
estás, elevada en el sitio
donde te dejé de ver.
No darás un paso más.

Nunca cumplirás más años   (ll.10-14)
Tu eres ya una fecha sola.   (l.23)

The reader is perfectly aware that not even poetic prowess can stop time in this way. Everyone - poet and reader alike - knows that the beloved's existence is subject to, and the product of, the external realities of time and space. We assume that the poet does not believe his own claims of omnipotence either - and so a complicit relationship is established between poet and reader.

In the case of "Dulcenombre" poet and object, observer and observed are intimately related by the sharing of a single identity. As Rupert Allan so concisely comments: "The One Contemplated is simultaneously the ocean and the poet".[57] For this reason - "ya nunca me eres extraño" (l.3); their identities are now inextricably linked; the sea forms part of the poet, and vice-versa; the subject-matter of *El Contemplado* is both sea and poet. But the poetic urge to define the sea of San Juan does not stop at the act of naming. Much as we have seen already in earlier poems, there is a desire to find the essential qualities of physical experience. This hankering after essence finds particularly conceptual expression in statements such as "te busqué el azul verdad" (l.11, p.162), and the sensory evidence of the sea's blueness does not seem to satisfy the poet: he needs to apprehend it mentally as well as sensorially. The fact that he applies the adjective "verdad" to a conceptual version of colour, implies that only an intellectual grasp of it is authentic; that its physical manifestation is somehow counterfeit. This is not, however, a case of Platonic idealism, and Salinas goes on to demonstrate the inevitable frustration of such idealism when applied to the physical world of phenomena. No abstract concept of a colour, no imagined blue, can ever out-blue the colour of "el contemplado". And so he answers his own rhetorical question - "¿Eras cómo te pensaba?" (l.17), with a negative:

> Más azul. Se queda pálido
> el color del pensamiento
> frente al que miran los ojos
> en más azul extasiados. (ll.18-21, Var. I, Azules, pp.612)

Physical reality is not ever what it is thought to be: the quest for a purely intellectual 'essence' will never capture the true nature of phenomena, for the simple reason that it cannot encompass the very materiality of matter.[58] Juan Ramón's plea to the intellect "Que mi palabra sea / la cosa misma..." is an unachievable goal; a linguistic and material impossibility.[59]

As it happens, the sea of San Juan reveals its own essence: there is no need for the poet to plumb the depths of a conceptualised sea. *El Contemplado*, unlike the artefacts of earlier works, does not owe its poetry to the poet's metaphors. Its poetry is innate, as essential to its physical reality as its blueness. Realising this,

Salinas makes no attempt to interpret or transform its autonomous and self-sufficient reality:

> Lo azul nadie te lo da,
> gracia es indivisa,
>
> belleza a nadie negada,
> a nadie ofrecida.
>
> No quiere la luz, por dueña,
> ninguna pupila;
> (ll.47-52, Var. IX, Tiempo de isla, p.631)

Observed, but not passively objectivised, *El Contemplado* represents a new phase in Salinas's evolving relationship with the external reality of "las cosas". Regardless of its new name, the reality of this sea is not bestowed upon it by "ninguna pupila" of the mind's eye. The function of the poet's eyes here is to absorb, soak in, rather than project inner visions onto the external world. Ironically, he finds his role transformed in much the same way as did the mirror in "Madrid, calle de" (*Seguro azar*, p.132), which, when extracted from its customary role of reflecting outwards, became a pool that contained whole skies in its depths, rather than glancing them off its surface. All that is required is to observe - to live through the eyes in the here and now. In words that could apply to the tendency in Salinas's earlier work to obliterate the here-and-now, material reality of "las cosas", transforming them through myth and archetype, he continues:

> El presente, que tanto se ha negado,
> hoy, aquí, ya, se entrega.
> (ll.19-20, Var. VIII, Renacimiento de Venus, p.627)

At this point it is surely quite reasonable to conclude that "el contemplado" is not solely an ideal, or poetic conception, but a wholly autonomous reality that is other than the poet, who can now celebrate the very 'otherness' of matter that he previously strove to arrogate. While Salinas's presence is always felt in these poems, it is not a jealous, possessive presence, but it is, rather, attentive. There are moments in this collection that are strikingly reminiscent of Jorge Guillén's *Cántico*.[60] In many ways, *El Contemplado* is Salinas's *Cántico*. There is no hint of superimposed, archetypal vision in the lines,

> Obediencia. A la luz. Pura obediencia;
> ella, en su cenit, manda.
> (ll.37-8, Var. II, Primavera diaria, pp.615)

- but rather submission on the poet's part to what his eyes witness. The presence of luminous perception, the revelatory experience that enters the mind through the eye, striking like sunlight, is particularly reminiscent of Guillén:

> La mañana, que asciende hacia su colmo
> - esplendor - paso a paso,
>
> en contornos se goza y en perfiles,
> rechaza lo enigmático.
> (ll.7-10, Var. VI, Todo se aclara, p.622)[61]

The poet's own elation, finding himself not only in the presence of, but highly attuned to this 'otherness', finds formal expression in the highly-charged exclamations of Variación IV, "Por alegrías", such as "¡Tesón, en la dicha!" (l.18, p.617), again echoing Guillén's celebratory *Cántico*.

A turning-point occurs in this poem, around l.21: through total submersion in the other, Salinas enters into explicit self-analysis, questioning his own response to the "alegría" that the sea expresses: "Entonces, ¿por qué estoy yo / con mano en mejilla?" (ll.21-22). By answering his own question, he arrives at the conclusion that the sea's joy is his; that they are in fact inseparable; that observer and observed have fused -

> ¿Suyas, mías, qué más da,
> si están a la vista...? (ll.23-4)
>
> ¿Si todos los gozos suyos,

todos, me los brinda...? (ll.27-8)

Y aquí en los ojos, las suyas
se vuelven las mías. (ll.37-8, Por alegrías, p.618)

Rather than the poet superimposing his own frame of mind onto the landscape, we
see here how it is the sea that infectiously transmits its dynamism, or "alegrías" to
him.

Even by attempting to define Salinas's "contemplado" as exclusively "idea"
or "cosa", we fall into the trap of dualistic thought which the poet strives to resist,
as it does not allow for the kind of relationship with "all reality" he aspires to. In
El Contemplado, Salinas presents an ideal relationship between self and external
reality, where he is open to the nature of the physical world, and this world is
receptive to his vision. There is no question of supremacy by one or the other;
they co-exist in a relationship of constant interaction. The sea of San Juan, is
simultaneously 'other' than the poet, and part of him, part of his experience; but
is never wholly possessed by him. The interaction of noumenal and phenomenal
realities is effected through artistic creation, where the mind fuses with the
empirical world: thinker and thing, observer and observed, poet and sea - both find
expression in the poem.[62] While the poet's sources stem from both "ideas y
cosas", the poetic act constitutes a new relationship between the two. The creation
of a poem involves the mind and the senses: the poem itself is both concept and
artefact. With his verse, the poet hopes to participate in the sea's 'sea-ness', just
as something of the sea is absorbed by his imagination and becomes part of him.

El Contemplado represents a climax in the co-operation between "ideas y
cosas" in Salinas's poetry: internal and external realities have merged to such an
extent that the sea is presented as a conscious, thinking substance -

feliz, de idea en idea
de cresta en cresta, corriendo,
tan blanca como la espuma

> trabaja tu pensamiento.
>> (ll.100-103, Var. XI, El poeta, p.638)

It is interesting, too, that the "poeta" of Variación XI is the sea, and not Salinas. And in Variación V, the sea, now characterised as a pícaro, 'steals' the poet's perceptions, making them its own, encapsulated in the seascape. In this way a full circle of reciprocal expression between "contemplado" and "contemplador", closes, as the sea becomes a visual poem of sunset, cloud and foam:

> Tú, Lazarillo de ojos,
> llévate a estos míos;
> por la aurora, con espumas,
> con nubes, por los ocasos...
>> (ll.27-30, Var. V, Pareja muy desigual, p.619)

"¿Vivo en ella, o ella en mí?", the poet asks, as observer and observed reach an unprecedented degree of fusion, a new joint identity.[63] By entering into the sea's being, participating in it, the poet's sense of the self is enhanced, not diminished.

> Poseído voluntario
> de esta fuerza que me invade,
> mayor soy, porque me siento
> yo mismo, y enajenado.
>> (ll.14-17, Var. XIII, Presagio, p.647)[64]

It is in this new sensation of being simultaneously self and 'other', that Salinas achieves a feeling of personal wholeness, of 'entereza'. *El Contemplado* celebrates the 'otherness' of material reality, and represents a new phase in Salinas's poetic relationship with the perceptual world, a phase that is characterised by the creative integration of self and 'other'. It is neither a straightforward example of subjectivist thought, nor a case of the poetic sublimation of an idealised, internally conceived reality. Salinas's aim in this collection is to find a poetry that comes equally and simultaneously from within and without, drawn from both the inner consciousness and the external world of phenomena: "the contact between external reality and his own, spiritual reality" (Reality, p.3).

This is a considerably different poetic approach to that of Salinas's earlier work, where the temptation to superimpose inner vision onto external phenomena was often too strong to resist. It also represents a departure from the poetic processes of the love-cycle, where the striving for total union with the 'other' resides, rather uneasily, alongside a tendency to idealise the beloved, rendering her more archetype than flesh and blood woman. *El Contemplado* can be seen as a sea-change in this respect. Where previously the world was defined according to the measures of the mind, so that concrete phenomena became a metaphor for the poet's inner life, the act of definition is now reciprocal: if Salinas names the sea "el contemplado", then he too is defined by his relationship with it, as "contemplador", an active participant in the world of phenomena. In this way the autonomy of matter - its essential being and inherent poetry - is restored. The unfathomable sea of San Juan teaches the poet that the external world of 'las cosas' cannot be reduced by the individual consciousness to a purely metaphorical status.

Again, Salinas's commentary on the work of another poet casts some light on his own poetic practices. We can apply his critique of the use of metaphor in the poetry of Jorge Carrera Andrade to the early examples of "radical metaphor" in *Seguro azar* and *Fábula y signo*. Metaphor, Salinas suggests, helps the poet to discover a 'nueva realidad':

> ...la nueva realidad inventada por el poeta. Es el descubrimiento. Pero, ¿a qué cosa se hace tal descubrir? El precio ha sido la disfiguración de las cosas reales y distintas. La metáfora es una falta de respeto a la pura realidad objetiva de esos dos elementos de donde nace.[65];

Where two "cosas" are linked metaphorically, warns Salinas, they lose something of their original identity, and become primarily instrumental to the poet's idea of them - the unifying idea that yokes them together, and in a sense, denies their essential separateness. In *El Contemplado*, metaphor is replaced by observation: fulfilled by material reality as it stands, the poetic imagination is less inclined to transform, interpret or denote, in terms of objective correlatives.

> Quisiera más que nada, más que sueño,
> ver lo que veo.
>
> No buscar hondos signos por celestes
> mundos supremos.
>> (ll.1-4, Ver lo que veo, *Confianza*, p.837)

Contemporaneous with the composition of *El Contemplado*, this poem, collected in *Confianza*, captures the tone of Salinas's 'cántico' in praise of the sea of San Juan. The candid openness of the sea makes its entire being evident, manifest; there is no need to seek profound or transcendental truths.

However, to suggest that Salinas's poetry can be readily categorised into chronological blocks, representing clear-cut philosophical stances, is as misleading as it is artificial.[66] There is evidence as early as *Presagios* that Salinas was perfectly aware of the need to counter-balance the urge to idealise, transform, metamorphose, with a rooted appreciation of the inescapable reality and 'otherness' of matter. The opening lines of his first published collection are, after all,

> Suelo. Nada más.
> Suelo. Nada menos.
> Y que te baste con eso. (l.1-3, *Pres.*, p.53)

Even where the inner realm of ideas appears to dominate some earlier poems, this does not always indicate an aggressive intellect that seeks to appropriate the otherness of external things. The seemingly transparent dissatisfaction with the sea's blueness in "Afán" (*Fábula y signo*) -

> No, no me basta, no.
> Ni ese azul en delirio
> celeste sobre mí,
> cúspide de lo azul   (ll.1-4, p.197)

- is not, in fact, a declaration of the imminent eclipse of matter by imagination. Its tone and philosophy are much closer to that of *El Contemplado* than may at first appear. What frustrates here, is not the sea's blueness, which is after all the "cúspide de lo azul"; neither is it the impossibility of defining its essence; but a desire to participate in that otherness, in the sea's sea-ness. The poem concludes with the challenge: "Tú, ya no más; yo más" (1.36). There is nothing more the inspiring landscape can do to make itself accessible to the observer. The challenge faced by the poet is not how to assimilate the world into a private, inner vision - but how to encourage the inner realms of the mind to participate in, and not subjugate, the outer material world. In order to harness these two realms of experience, the poet must at once absorb empirical reality, and be absorbed by it. There is, therefore, no risk of a loss of self, but only the promise of an enhanced, enriched understanding of the self and the circumambient world.

The evolution of a harmonious relationship between internal and external realities in *El Contemplado* is made possible by abandoning any attempts to arrogate observed phenomena, and by channelling imaginative energy into the act of contemplation, so that the profound observation that produces the poems of *El Contemplado* eventually becomes synonymous with the poetic process: "Sí. Ver lo que se ve. Ya está el poema / aquí, completo" (ll.71-2, Ver lo que veo, *Confianza*, p.839). The transition from the first person singular of the title, "veo", to the impersonal use of the reflexive "se ve", in these, the poem's closing lines, demonstrates the parallel movement of emphasis in Salinas's poetic approach - from highly personalised interpretations of phenomena, to what is both personally and universally perceptible. The fusion of internal and external realities is now complete, and is only made possible by the poet's attentiveness to both: he must look and envision, in the act of observation. Similarly, he must attune to both the inner voice and the outer -

¿Quién me llama por la voz

de un ave que pía?
(ll.1-2, Var. IX, Tiempo de isla, *El Cont.*, p.629)

There is not only a lesson in observation between the lines of *El Contemplado*, but equally important, a lesson in listening. Casting back to *Presagios*, we can read a marked progression in Salinas's receptivity to outer voices: "Estos dulces vocablos con que me estás hablando / no las entiendo paisaje" (ll.1-2, No.20, p.74). While the language of natural phenomena is uncomprehended in this instance, the poet nonetheless derives pleasure from its mystery -"Pero es tan dulce el son de ese tu no aprendido / lenguaje", (ll.11-12). Nature's language is instinctive, unlearned by nature itself, and therefore cannot be consciously learned by the hearer: "Y me lleves a la claridad de lo incognoscible / paisaje dulce, por vocablos desconocidos" (ll.18-19, *Pres.*, p.74). In other words, the author of *Presagios* sees nature's language and his own as entirely separate and mutually incomprehensible. While he can appreciate its 'otherness', its unsayable and unlearnable essence, he sees no place for his own art in its poetic process.

In a later poem from *Fábula y signo*, he encounters nature's voice once again: "Si no es el mar, sí es su voz delgada" (l.3). Failing to comprehend the sea's language, its self-expression, he tries to conceptualise its essence or identity, by naming it:

Si no es el mar, sí es su nombre
en un idioma sin labios
sin pueblo,
sin más palabra que ésta:
mar.   (ll.7-11, Mar distante, p.169)

Despite all Salinas's claims for this new, previously unspoken tongue, we know that the language in which this name is conceived is none other than the language of ideas, the intellect, the 'lipless' voice that speaks is the inner voice of the psyche.

In *El Contemplado*, a new auditory sensibility opens the poet's ears to nature's language. Perhaps it is worth reiterating that these poems were composed in the Hispanic linguistic environment of Puerto Rico, after several years of exile in North America. Also, that *El Contemplado* is Salinas's poetic response to the dazzling and sonorous presence of the Sea of San Juan.

> y ese cantar que me buscan
> las horas, sin encontrarlo,
> de la mañana a la noche,
> con blanquísimo estribillo,
> tus olas lo van cantando. (ll.7-11, Var. V, Pareja muy desigual, p.619)

More than simply listening, this constitutes a realisation that he too can participate in nature's poetry; that the music of the spheres is audible all around, and beckons the poet to add his voice to that of all material reality. The final stage in this approximation of inner poetic reality to external reality is the coincidence of nature and poetry in *Confianza*:[67]

> Flores acaban en rimas
> versos que empezaron tallos.
> Hasta en el jardín más quedo
> todo va diciendo algo.   (ll.30-3, Extraños, p.827)

This is not to be confused with neo-pastoral prescriptions that all art should derive from nature, but is the logical culmination of a consistently animistic view of the world in Salinas's poetry. What closer affinity could there be between poet and matter, than for both to produce poetry? What is more, the poetry of matter is not confined to nature. Despite Salinas's disillusionment with urban life in *Todo más claro*, the sheer comprehensiveness of his poetic sources persists, and he continues to interact with technology as well as with nature - evidence of a continuing inclusivity and 'entereza' of vision. All matter has its song, even the clanking of machinery has a poetry to those whose approach to reality is truly open and non-discriminatory; from "El motor del avión" (l.34) to the "máquinas terreras" (l.40) -

"sueños recitan, mecánicos" (l.43, "Extraños", *Confianza*). The voice of matter is always "extraño", alien to the individual's consciousness: it is the voice of external reality, of "all that lives outside of the poet".

> ¡Cuánto decir nos rodea,
> lo oigamos o no lo oigamos!
> Voces y voces y voces,
> gritos y susurros, clamores,
> navegantes del espacio.
> ¡Todos extraños!   (ll.1-6, *Confianza*, p.826)

Poetry cannot be extracted from matter like the essence of a perfume from the flower: a poem does not grow from extracted, abstracted essences, but in conjunction with concrete reality; it is the result of the confluence of inner and outer voices. This point of fusion is what distinguishes Salinas's world view from the dualistic thinking of Cartesian philosophy. Poetry, for this poet, encapsulates "ideas" and "cosas", and renders them uni-dimensional -

> For me, poetry is nothing but the aggregate of relations between the
> psychological reality, strange and abnormal, the poetic soul, so
> exceptional and clairvoyant, and external reality, usual and ordinary,
> the reality of the outside world. (*Reality*, p.4)

Salinas's own definition of poetry is a formula that involves "ideas", (psychological reality); "cosas", (external reality); and the mysterious workings of the poetic process, (what Salinas calls the poetic soul).[68]

One of the earliest illustrations of this formula can be found in *Presagios*, where the poet's shadow provides a perfect image of how the coincidence of internal and external conditions can produce a new entity, a new reality:

> La criatura extraña
> que entre el sol de septiembre y yo creamos,
> sabe cosas de mí que yo no sé.   (ll.4-6, p.85)

Like his poetry, the shadow is at once part of the poet's self, and a participant in the world outside him; it is him, but it is also more than he is.

The very act of perception instils a degree of tension between intellect and matter, but nowhere more than in the creative process where the very act of selecting a subject can be seen as a form of subjectivism. Salinas becomes increasingly aware of this tension as his poetry develops, turning it to his advantage in the highly self-conscious exploration of the relationship between the poet and his subject-matter in *El Contemplado*, exposing the inherent tension between the poetic appreciation of object, and its potential objectivisation. In Salinas's quest for 'entereza' of perception, language is an ally, which, like the shadow of his early poem, is constant, although constantly alterable. Accordingly, his poetic expression reflects the infinitely alterable states of 'objective' and 'subjective' experience, compounding "ideas y cosas", and giving voice to both inner and outer realities.

Notes

Chapter I

1. Pedro Salinas, *Reality and the Poet in Spanish Poetry*, The John Hopkins Press (Baltimore, 1966), p.3.

2. The absence of clearly drawn boundaries between external and internal experience is frequently read as evidence of confusion and disorientation in the poet's own mind as to the nature of each. For example, when comparing Salinas's approach to reality to that of Cernuda, Derek Harris has the following to say:

> La preocupación central de los poemas de Salinas - la incapacidad de distinguir entre la realidad interior de la mente y la realidad tangible del mundo exterior - es algo muy distinto a la temática de *Perfil del aire*. Salinas no sabe decidir entre una y otra realidad.

Derek Harris, Introduction to *Perfil del aire*, Tamesis Books (London, 1971), p.70.

3. Nonetheless, in *Reality and the Poet in Spanish Poetry*, Salinas sets about defining separate external and internal realities, saying -

> What I intend to consider here is a problem which I think should be the first to be examined in connection with every poet: the relation between his poetic world and the real world, the contact between external reality and his own spiritual reality. *Reality*, p.3.

The definition is not terribly helpful, and confusion mounts as the material world becomes somehow "real" while the internal world of the poetic imagination is "spiritual". The more Salinas expands on the nature of reality in this instance, the more clouded by value-laden adjectives his definition becomes. And yet, there is a phrase here which may assist us in appraising his own poetic response to this reality - "the relation between his poetic world and the real world" - because the notion of relationship lies at the very heart of the poetic process for this poet. The sources of his verse are not to be found in one camp or the other, but in the relationship between internal and external experience.

4. Pedro Salinas, *Ensayos completos, Vol. III*, ed. Solita Salinas de Marichal, Taurus (Madrid, 1983), p.75.

5. Robert Havard quite rightly points to the influence of Ortega y Gasset on Salinas's understanding of "reality", glossing Ortega's *Meditaciones* -

> In Ortega's view, then, reality, 'the definitive being of the world', is found neither in external objects nor in man, but in what effectively is an interrelationship between the two, the perspective.

Robert Havard, *From Romanticism to Surrealism. Seven Spanish Poets*, University of Wales Press (Cardiff, 1988).

6. Most notably, Leo Spitzer's article, "El conceptismo interior de Pedro Salinas", *Revista Hispánica Moderna*, Vol. VII (1941), pp.33-69, presents us with a picture of Salinas as a poet interested only in the realms of abstraction and intellectually conceived realities. This interpetation is refuted by J. F. Cirre, who argues that the sources of Salinas's poetic invention are not all abstract: "La complicación conceptual que los poemas ofrecen ha dado origen al mito del intelectualismo a ultranza de Salinas". See J. F. Cirre, "Pedro Salinas y su poética", in *Homenaje a Rodríguez Moniño*, Editorial Castalia (Madrid, 1966), p.93.

7. *Cartas de amor a Margarita, 1912-15*, ed. Solita Salinas de Marichal, Alianza Tres (Madrid, 1984), p.127. Hereafter referred to in the text as *Cartas*.

8. In his Introduction to a selection of Salinas's poetry, David Stixrude acknowledges the vital contributions made by both "ideas" and "cosas", to Salinas's poetry, describing it as "...an ideologically complex and problematical whole right from the beginning - complex because the human being is complex and has varying needs (eg. the senses yearn for objects, the spirit for ideals)...". See Pedro Salinas, *Poemas escogidos*, Austral (Madrid, 1982).

9. In his Introduction to *Reality and the Poet in Spanish Poetry* Jorge Guillén outlines something of an empiricist philosophy in his friend's work, which seems to refute received notions of his work as predominantly idealistic and abstract.

> Salinas is always involved in relationships of love or friendship with things and people, always ready to discover in them their value, their transcendence, their inner meaning. Their vital meaning is understood and felt only when it is well fixed and rooted in a concrete particular. (p.23) As in Note 1.

10. The underlying parallels between Salinas's poetry and dialogue have been exhaustively examined by Alma de Zubizarreta in *Pedro Salinas: el diálogo creador*, Gredos (Madrid, 1969). In Chapter I (p.87) she describes Salinas's special relationships with "las cosas" in his early poetic work as:

> Un trato directo con las cosas es la nota que mejor definiría su primera etapas poética, de *Presagios* hasta el límite de *La voz a ti debida*, Salinas canta a las cosas estableciendo con ellas un diálogo.

11. Pedro Salinas, "Una metáfora en tres tiempos", in *Ensayos completos, Vol. III*, Taurus (Madrid, 1983), pp.124-5.

12. This animistic tendency in Salinas's work is true to the classic tenets of child psychology. See, for example, a summary of Jean Piaget's theories in J. H. Flavell, *The developmental psychology of Jean Piaget*, Van Nostrand (Princeton, 1963). C. B. Morris comments on this childlike sense of discovery in Salinas's early works:

> The excitement found in things that generally thrill and amuse children was due to his ingenuous ability to marvel and admire, which Guillén called 'that faculty of the child-poet'.

C. B. Morris, *A Generation of Spanish Poets, 1920-36*, Cambridge University Press (Cambridge, 1969), p.113.

13. See Alma de Zubizarreta's assessment of this poet-cosa relationship: "Es evidente que Salinas separa las cosas de la totalidad del mundo, individualizándolas hasta conferirles una personalidad y existencia propias." *Pedro Salinas: el diálogo creador*, Gredos (Madrid, 1969), p.88.

14. In his sensitivity to the poetry of the everyday, Solita Salinas discerns the influence on her father of the French poet, Jules Laforgue:

> Salinas siente gran afinidad con su mensaje poético, y cita sus versos "Ah, que la vie est quotidienne!" ...Y poco tiempo después de citar estos versos, Salinas escribe un poema que empieza así: "¡Que nuestra vida sea un himno cotidiano!". Solita Salinas de Marichal, "El primer Salinas", in *Boletín de la fundación F. G. Lorca*, No.3 (June 1988), p.24.

The poem whose opening line is reproduced above was written in a letter to Margarita Bonmatí from Madrid in 1913, and appears in *Cartas de amor a Margarita, 1912-15*, ed. Solita Salinas, Alianza Tres (Madrid, 1984).

15. *Boletín de la fundación F. G. Lorca*, No.3, "Homenaje a Pedro Salinas" (June 1988), p.25.

16. One can only conclude that David Stixrude overlooks the spirit of 'the roaring twenties', and seems to ignore the latent poetic potential of technological invention at this time, when he writes - "One can explain what the technological poems mean with reference to the mainstream of the poet's language, ideas, intuitions, but it should be very difficult to say why precisely such a theme attracted him in the first place". See David Stixrude, *The Early Poetry of Pedro Salinas*, Editorial Castalia (Princeton/Madrid, 1975), p.94.

17. Pedro Salinas, "El poeta y las fases de la realidad", in *Insula*, No.146, XIV (January 1959), pp.3-11.

18. This connection between the shop dummy and Venus is reminiscent of Darío's elevation of Paris, the capital of couture and modernist aesthetics, to Olympian heights. In fact, in his book on Rubén Darío, Salinas draws a similar analogy when he alludes to - "Venus, vestida por Worth, va por la rue de la Paix seguida por un millionario viejo verde". See Pedro Salinas, *La poesía de Rubén Darío*, Editorial Losada (Buenos Aires, 1968), p.37.

19. Other examples of this ironic presentation of the creative act are "Cinematógrafo" (*Seguro azar*, pp.133-5), and "Underwood girls" (*Fábula y signo*, pp.203-4).

20. In her Introduction to *Cartas de amor a Margarita, 1912-15*, Solita Salinas alludes to Salinas's reading of Belgian poet Verhaeren's "Les Villes Tentaculaires", as evidence of his enthusiasm for urban poetic settings in this period.

> ...el tema tratado en el libro atraería la atención de Salinas. Verhaeren canta la ciudad moderna, la de las grandes fábricas y las nuevas multitudes. Sabe captar el ritmo rápido de los tiempos modernos, las pulsaciones de las máquinas. (p.17) As in Note 7.

21. Salinas was apparently a notoriously fast and reckless driver: Alberti reminisces - "In his Fiat A - 4.014, Pedro Salinas, every morning, eagerly seeks death, accompanied by insults, threats, angry glares of police and pedestrians". This quotation is taken from Alberti's "Itinerarios jóvenes de España", *La Gaceta Literaria*, No.49 (January 1929), quoted in translation by C. B. Morris, *A Generation of Spanish Poets 1920-36*, Cambridge University Press (Cambridge, 1969), p.114.

22. According to Vicente Huidobro, whose "Arte Poética" represents a Creacionista manifesto, the poet should strive to create an autonomous poetic world in his writing, that will complement rather than mirror the given world.

> Inventa nuevos mundos y cuida tu palabra;
> el adjetivo, cuando no da vida, mata...
> ¿Por qué cantáis la rosa, oh poetas?
> ¡Hacedla florecer en el poema!
> Sólo para vosotros
> viven todas las cosas bajo el sol.
> El poeta es un pequeño Dios.

Vicente Huidobro, "Arte Poética" published in "El espejo y el agua" (Madrid,1918).

23. In May 1934, a welcoming party was thrown for F. G. Lorca in the Florida Hotel, Madrid, to celebrate his triumphant return from theatrical acclaim in Buenos Aires. A more intimate dinner was held in Salinas's home after the event, attended, among others, by Carlos Morla, who recalls Salinas's fascination with collecting miscellaneous objects, saying "Pedro coleccionaba con fervor "cosas feas" que, en su casa, se transforman en motivos tan bonitos como decorativos". He even records Salinas's unique perspective on the aesthetic potential of the most ordinary artefacts - "...no hay objetos feos en la vida, que todo depende de cómo y dónde se los coloca y luego de cómo se les mira". See Carlos Morla, *En España con F.G. Lorca*, Aguilar (Madrid, 1958), pp.383-4.

24. This deliberate process of defamiliarising everyday objects may owe something to developments in the visual arts between 1900 and the 1930s. As early as 1917, Marcel Duchamp, exhibiting under the pseudonym of R. Mutt, subverted utilitarian attitudes to everyday objects with his 'ready-mades', revealing the renovating and transforming role of context in visual perceptions. One of Duchamp's exhibits was the apparatus for holding milk bottles in the manufacturing process, transformed in human perception by its removal from an industrial context, and its deliberate re-location in a Gallery - a space associated with aesthetic appreciation, not utilitarian function.

25. Perhaps this poem best illustrates C. B. Morris's criticism of contrivance in Salinas's early poems when he comments that "Salinas inflated things with a grandiloquence that at times ennobles and enhances his subject, and at others appears gratingly contrived". See C. B. Morris, *A Generation of Spanish Poets 1920-36*, Cambridge University Press (Cambridge, 1969), p.115.

26. In Chapter Five of *Reality and the Poet in Spanish Poetry*, "The Exaltation of Reality", Salinas writes of Góngora's vision of the concrete world:

> Reality must be transformed into another kind of poetic reality, material, sonorous, plastic, but not idealized; the artist must operate on it with the magic power of word, metaphor, image... (p.140)

But Salinas recognises the inevitable change in the poet's relationship with the concrete world of "cosas" in the course of achieving this "exaltation".

> Reality, by dint of being exalted, raised to aesthetic value, disappears, is pulverised, is lost. (p.145) As in Note 1.

These comments could be applied with equal relevance to Salinas's treatment of certain "cosas" in his early work.

27. The term "radical metaphors" is taken from Vicente Cabrera's *Tres poetas a la luz de la metáfora: Salinas, Aleixandre, Guillén*, Gredos (Madrid, 1975), p.29.

28. Salinas's choice of the lightbulb as a poetic subject, and his portrayal of it as a feminine entity, has precedents in the visual arts as pointed out by Dawn Ades in her book, *Photomontage*, World of Art Series, Thames and Hudson (London, 1986), p.30.

> The New York issue of Picabia's "391" (1917), had contained photographs of plain, mass-produced objects suggestively labelled, like the electric lightbulb titled "Américaine".

Apart from the poetic potential of the lightbulb as an analogy of the enlightening presence of the muse, the advent of domestic electricity was indeed a source of wonder and awe all over the world. From Europe, the USA was seen as epitomising modernity, as it led the field in the early part of the century in so many areas of industry.

29. There may be a less abstract (indeed, a directly biographical) source for the fusion of lightbulb and muse in this poem. While working and studying in Paris (1914-17), Salinas spent many solitary nocturnal hours engrossed in his work, and composing letters to his 'novia' in Algeria. Extracts from some of his letters written prior to their marriage in 1915, make a very explicit connection between the electric light, by which Salinas writes, and his awareness of Margarita's presence, despite the distances separating them. On buying a frame for her photograph and placing it on his desk, he writes -

Vida, eran las cuatro y media, aún había luz del día: pero en seguida
he encendido mi lámpara y se ha puesto sobre ti esta luz nuestra,
esta luz de mi lámpara, a la cual te escribo, y que ahora alumbra....
estas hojas blancas, y tu figura. (Carta LXVII, Paris 1914), *Cartas
de amor a Margarita, 1912-15*, Alianza Tres (Madrid, 1984), p.205.

The beloved's presence and the "luz" from the lightbulb are subconsciously equated
in the muse of the later poem, "35 bujías". These letters also reveal the possible
origins of another 'light metaphor' which is developed in the love cycle,
culminating in the shared "luz de dos" of "Estabas, pero no se te veía" of *Razón
de amor* (l.25, pp.346-7).

30. Rupert Allen sees the lightbulb as representative of Jungian archetype. He goes
on to draw parallels with fairy-tales such as the brothers Grimm's "The Glass
Coffin", where the princess is rescued from a glass castle:

The reader will note that the story of the glass coffin is a classical
example of the anima motif, the activation of the feminine
unconscious, and that it corresponds closely to the poem, "35
bujías"....

Rupert Allen, *Symbolic Experience: A Study of Poems by Pedro Salinas*, "The
anima figure as helpmate", The University of Alabama Press (Alabama, 1982),
pp.70-1.

31. Antonio Blanch, "Pedro Salinas y Paul Válery", in *La poesía pura española*,
Gredos (Madrid, 1976), pp.280-83.

32. Pedro Salinas, "Registro de Jorge Carrera Andrade," *Ensayos de literatura
hispánica*, ed. Juan Marichal, Aguilar (Madrid, 1966), p.387.

33. Robert Havard astutely points out that, "Salinas is sceptical about the reality of
all kinds of words, hardly discriminating between concrete and abstract
denominatives". Robert Havard, "The Reality of Words in the Poetry of Pedro
Salinas", *Bulletin of Hispanic Studies*, LI (1974), p.37.

34. Summarising Salinas's animistic approach to all reality - both concrete and
abstract - Guillén describes the process enacted by his friend's work as a
"vivificación del mundo". See Jorge Guillén, Prologue to *Poesías completas*, Seix
Barral (Barcelona, 1981), p.1.

35. The injection of emotion and consciousness into these already materialised concepts is glossed by Inés Marichalar as a "...doble conversión: la concreción de lo abstracto, y su vivificación: son frecuentes los diálogos con las realidades abstractas ya seres vivos". See Inés Marichalar, "El proceso de comunicación en Pedro Salinas," *Prohemio*, No.4 (1973), pp.379-403.

36. The term "poesía pura" came to be associated with the poetic ideal of purity of language, and the banishment of linguistic imprecision and ornamentation. The practice of pruning postromantic verse of its sentimental and rhetorical excesses was referred to by F. G. Lorca in 1922, as a shared vocation of his generation:

> ...todos los poetas que actualmente nos ocupamos, en más o menos escala, en la poda y cuidado del demasiado frondoso árbol lírico que nos dejaron los románticos y los posrománticos.

F. G. Lorca, "El cante jondo (primitivo canto andaluz)", 19.2.22., in *Obras completas*, Aguilar (Madrid, 1969), p.45.

37. Salinas outlines the potential dangers of an increasingly rich empirical environment in the following extract:

> Dos peligros saltan a la vista como los más temibles en mi opinión. El primero es que la mente poética se deje dominar por ese imperialismo de la realidad externa. Es tan proteica y deslumbrante la faz del mundo en una de esas condensaciones de fuerzas vitales que llamamos ciudades o naciones, que el poeta puede sentirse tentado a creer que la vida no es nada más que eso y hacer una poesía de reproducción. El segundo peligro consiste en rechazar el dominio de la realidad externa ya sea mediante una concepción intelectualista y abstracta del universo que el hombre puede erigir dentro de su cabeza o en las minas de lo subconsciente, forma delirante del individualismo.

Pedro Salinas, "El poeta y las fases de la realidad", *Insula*, No.146, XIV (15.1.59), pp.3 & 11.

38. See Robert Havard, *From Romanticism to Surrealism. Seven Spanish Poets*, "Pedro Salinas. The Poetics of Motion", University of Wales Press (Cardiff, 1988), p.181.

39. In the same text, (see Note 38), Havard elucidates: "...This system of random recitation denies the nouns a proper connotative context and virtually destroys them

as denominatives, as Spitzer noted by describing them as words which 'cease to be words'" (p.181).

40. Leo Spitzer, *El conceptismo interior de Pedro Salinas*, *Revista Hispánica Moderna*, Vol. VII (1941), pp.41-44.

41. Leo Spitzer, "La enumeración en la poesía moderna", in *Lingüística e historia literaria*, Gredos (Madrid, 1955), p.340.

42. J. F. Cirre, *El mundo lírico de Pedro Salinas*, Don Quijote (Granada, 1982), pp.72-3.

43. *Reality and the Poet in Spanish Poetry*, p.3. As in Note 1.

44. The virgin "blancura" of the blank sheet of paper represents a challenging void for the poet in both these poems: when he takes pen to paper it is to fill this vacuum: "punta de acero, pluma / contra lo blanco, en blanco" (ll.24-5, Cuartilla, *Seg.*, p.107). Likewise, in the act of typing, the keys become: "eternas ninfas/ contra el gran mundo, vacío, / blanco en blanco"(ll.27-9, Underwood Girls, *Fáb.*, p.203).

45. One example previously cited is the poem "No, no dejéis cerradas...", from *La voz a ti debida*: "murallas, nombres, tiempos / se quebrarán todos" (ll.36-7, p.222).

46. If we apply Salinas's theories on the nature of metaphor to his own poetry, we can conclude that metaphor assists the poetic realisation of a reality that transcends dualistic philosophies.

> Una metáfora es como la expresión de lo que el poeta piensa del mundo y de las cosas.... La metáfora es un acto intuitivo por el cual el poeta se apodera de una realidad nueva, en la cual quedan absorbidas las dos realidades anteriores... De manera que la metáfora, como poesía, para mí es una creación de nuevas realidades.

Pedro Salinas, "La metáfora en tres tiempos", in *Ensayos completos, Vol. III*, Taurus (Madrid, 1983), pp.121-132.

47. The 'semantic confusion' that allows Salinas to perceive reality as one, single plane, is described by Darmangeat as - "...la profunda unidad psíquica de las categorías del universo, elaboradas por el poeta". See Pierre Darmangeat, *Machado, Salinas, Guillén*, Insula (Madrid, 1969), p.174.

48. Ramón Almela Pérez, *Hacia un análisis lingüístico-cuantativo de la poesía de Pedro Salinas*, Universidad de Murcia (Murcia, 1982).

49. Almela makes the following cuantitative assessment of substantives in Salinas's poetic works in general:

> ¿A qué realidades presta atención la poesía de Salinas? Al dominio de lo animado: casi la mitad de las ocurrencias de los sustantivos le pertenecen. Es cierto que los temas de su poesía son fundamentalmente amorosos, no naturalistas. Sin embargo, su léxico sustantivado es rico en designaciones cósmicas: mundo, tierra, flor... Síntoma indiscutible de que Salinas toma de la realidad externa, y para su poesía, lo que apoya sus sentimientos y de que desecha lo que los impurifica, es la ausencia total de léxico económico y político. (As in Note 48, pp.185-6).

50. Ramón Almela Pérez computes the incidence of these concrete substantives in Salinas's first three volumes as follows: cielos 39; estrellas 15; luz 34; tierra 30. The abstract nouns most frequently enumerated in these works are calculated as follows: años 11; dimensiones 3; números 6; tiempos 21, (Part 111, "Datos", pp.251-292, as in Note 48).

51. The incidence of these substantives in the love cycle, as computed by Almela, gives the following figures:
Cosas (concrete nouns): astro 10; estrella 40; flor 32; luz 152; mar 61; ola 18; piedra 20; viento 28.
Ideas (abstract nouns): historia 7; órden 18; nombre 56; número 17; tiempo 66, ("Datos", pp.292-360, as in Note 48).

52. Again, using Almela's quantitative assessment of substantives as a means of measuring Salinas's relative preoccupation with "ideas" or "cosas", we find that while concrete nouns with specific relevance to the sea pervade the text, (espuma 24; mar 18; ola 25; playa 10), abstract nouns are very scarce; the only two figuring with any frequency being amor (8) and tiempo (18). ("Datos", pp.360-374, as in Note 48).

53. As in Note 48, pp.360-374.

54. It is interesting to contrast the naming process as described in *El Contemplado*, where the name grows from the flooding of the senses and the subconscious by external reality, with the process described in Salinas's earliest published work, *Presagios*.

Posesión de tu nombre,
sola que tú permites
felicidad, alma sin cuerpo.
Dentro de mí te llevo
porque digo tu nombre,
felicidad, dentro del pecho. (ll.1-6, p.57)

The poet sets out to possess the beloved through the act of enunciating her name. The element of permission in ll.2, a hint of some participation on her part, is entirely discredited by the lines to follow, as her 'reality' is appropriated, usurped by the poet's internally conceived definitions of her, "dentro de mí".

55. Vicente Cabrera, *Tres poetas a la luz de la metáfora: Salinas, Aleixandre, Guillén*, Gredos (Madrid, 1975), p.106.

56. Rupert Allen, *Symbolic Experience: A Study of Poems by Pedro Salinas*, "The experience of unity", The University of Alabama Press (Alabama, 1982), pp.129-131.

57. As in Note 56, p.129.

58. Carlos Feal Deibe sums up this realisation rather neatly in the statement that for Salinas, as for Guillén, "lo esencial es algo real, no ideal". Carlos Feal Deibe, *La poesía de Pedro Salinas*, Gredos (Madrid, 1971), p.231.

59. Juan Ramón Jiménez, "Eternidades", *Segunda Antolojía*, ed. Leopoldo de Luis, Austral (Madrid, 1983), p.236.

60. Jorge Guillén's *Cántico* declares a 'credo' of the wholly autonomous and independent existence of "las cosas". Their 'otherness' helps him to define his own place in the material world. "Las cosas" are -

Irreductibles, pero
largos, anchos, profundos
Enigmas - en sus masas.
Yo los toco, los uso.   (Más allá III, ll.85-8, p.82)

¡Oh perfección: dependo
Del total más allá
Dependo de las cosas!
¡Sin mí son y ya están!   (VI, ll.141-4, p.84)

Jorge Guillén, *Cántico '36*, ed. José Manuel Blecua, Labor (Barcelona, 1970).

61. These lines recall Guillén's poem "Más allá", where daylight quite literally 'reveals the world' to the poet, and in so doing, awakens his consciousness of self in relation to otherness:

> Mientras van presentándose
> Todas las consistencias
> Que al disponerse en cosas
> Me limitan, me centran.   (ll.13-16, p.79)

In Guillén's *Cántico*, daylight banishes all visual haziness and obscurity: it is analogous to the experience of mental illumination; the equivalent of banishing doubt. Thus, in a poem that appeared in *Cántico '28*, "Desnudo", the emergence of form effectively (as paraphrased by Salinas in *El Contemplado*), "rechaza lo enigmático".

> Claridad aguzada entre perfiles
> De tan puros tranquilos,
> Que cortan y aniquilan con sus filos
> Las confusiones viles.   (ll.9-12, Desnudo, p.211)

Jorge Guillén, *Cántico '36*, ed. José Manuel Blecua, Labor (Barcelona, 1970).

62. Salinas's poetic solution to the depiction of 'objective' reality owes something to Antonio Machado. Speaking through the persona of Abel Martín, in "De un cancionero apócrifo", Machado confronts the problem of how to preserve the integrity of the 'other' in the process of composing verse.

> - ¿Y cómo no intentar - dice Martín - devolver a *lo que es* su propia intimidad?... Esta empresa fue iniciada por Leibniz - filósofo del porvenir, añade Martín -; pero sólo puede ser consumada por la poesía, que define Martín como conciencia integral. El poeta, como tal, no renuncia a nada, ni pretende degradar ninguna apariencia.

A more accurate and perceptive poetic credo for *El Contemplado* could not have been written by Salinas himself. He firstly acknowledges and embraces the fully autonomous 'otherness' of the sea of San Juan, then rather than attempting to poeticise either the thing itself (an impossible task), or his conceptualisation of it, he makes poetry of the interaction between the two, where the autonomy of both poet and matter, inner and outer realities, is captured and preserved by a new "conciencia integral". See Antonio Machado, *Poesías completas*, CLXVII, ed. Manual Alvar, Austral (Madrid, 1982), p.320.

63. The rhetorical questioning of whether the poet inhabits the sea or vice-versa, echoes a poem by Juan Ramón Jiménez in *Diario de un poeta recién-casado*, where syntax enacts the entwining of the two:

No sé si el mar es, hoy
- adornado su azul de innumerables
espumas -
mi corazón; si mi corazón, hoy
- adornada su grana de incontables
espumas -,
es el mar.
      Entran, salen
uno de otro, plenos e infinitos,
como dos todos únicos.

J. R. Jiménez, *Segunda Antolojía poética*, p.233. As in Note 59.

64. This idea, that by participating in something bigger than the self, the self is augmented, is another possible example of Jorge Guillén's influence. In "Viento saltado", first published in *Cántico '28*, the interaction between wind and poet creates the same sensation for Guillén as that of poet and sea for Salinas.

¡Cuerpo en el viento y con cuerpo la gloria!
¡Soy
Del viento, soy a través de la tarde más viento,
Soy más que yo!

Jorge Guillén, *Cántico*, p.216, as in Note 61.

65. See Pedro Salinas, "Registro de Jorge Carrera Andrade", in *Ensayos de literatura hispánica*, ed. Juan Marichal, Aguilar (Madrid, 1966), p.381.

66. It is for this reason among others, that I have chosen not to examine the poem "Civitas Dei" in this Chapter. As already stated in the Introduction, the selection of material for each Chapter of this thesis has been made on thematic grounds, in keeping with the overall thematic thrust of the piece. While "Civitas Dei" ostensibly inhabits the sea-scape of *El Contemplado*, the poem's thematic content bears little relationship to the poet's relationship with the sea of San Juan, as explored in the other 14 "Variaciones" of the collection. Instead, it offers an allegorical presentation of an emerging hiercharchy of values in Salinas's later work. Nature figures increasingly as a source of inspiration to the poet, and a model of 'entereza'. The natural world also serves as a foil to the new ascendency

of the modern metropolis - the new order of measured materialism. In "Civitas Dei" the 'Holy City' is found in the water, as though in the act of reflection the sea performs a baptismal restoration of modern civilisation to a state of pre-lapsarian innocence. In contrast with the self-conscious exploration of the poetic relationship between poet and matter in the other "Variaciones", the thematic key to "Civitas Dei" is social rather than aesthetic, and has considerably more in common with the poems of *Todo más claro*. Its inclusion at the end of *El Contemplado* detracts from this collection's unity of theme and tone. In Chapter Four, "Civitas Dei" is examined alongside the poems of *Todo más claro* in the context of Salinas's overtly expressed social concerns, and his exploration of the self as part of a collective, social entity.

67. Robert Havard makes special reference to nature's voice which he describes as "the metaphor of articulate phenomena": "Found throughout Salinas's poetry, it is one of his favourite systems of imagery, accentuating the flux between the real and poetic worlds". See Robert Havard, "The Reality of Words in the Poetry of Pedro Salinas" in the *Bulletin of Hispanic Studies*, No.51 (1974), p.46.

68. Philip Silver also comments on Salinas's understanding of reality as a three-way network of relationships between the poet's inner consciousness, the empirical world, and the poetic process.

> De manera que la visión dual de la poesía que Salinas formula en "La realidad y el poeta", dista mucha de dar la clave del mecanismo de su propia poesía. No es, en verdad, ninguna relación dual, ninguna serie de relaciones del tipo fuera/dentro, imaginación/realidad imperiosa, la que genera directamente la poesía de Salinas. Al contrario, lo que sí se plantea... es en realidad una relación triádica entre poeta, mundo y lenguaje poético.

Philip Silver, *La Casa de Anteo, Ensayos de poética hispánica, de Antonio Machado a Claudio Rodríguez*, Taurus (Madrid, 1985), p.135.

Chapter II

Alma y cuerpo

Love's eternal incarnation.

Salinas's love-poetry can be read as an allegory of the quest for 'entereza'. Through the love experience, the individual seeks union with the 'other' in the form of the beloved; this is just one expression of 'entereza'. The very nature of love involves another kind of union, which is the fusion of body and soul, "alma y cuerpo". If physical attraction is consummated in the sexual union of two bodies, then Platonic aspirations are realised in the merging of two psyches or souls. The lyrics contained in Salinas's love-cycle of *La voz a ti debida*, *Razón de amor*, and *Largo lamento*, not only enact the lovers' coming together, but the fusion of these two kinds of human feeling, traditionally defined as erotic and Platonic. We watch, therefore, as anarchic eros overturns the old orders in an orgy of broken columns and ruins, in "Amor, amor, catástrofe". We contemplate ascendant agape rising steadily towards absolute union in poems such as "Empújame, lánzame..." or "¿En dónde está la salvación?". The presence of both these kinds of love in Salinas's poetry, and his conscious striving to integrate them, suggests that he is writing very consciously within the conceptual framework of the Neo-Platonic tradition. At times the poems of the love-cycle are imbued with a sense of existential doubt, recalling the tensions present in some of Quevedo's most celebrated love-sonnets.

The Baroque poet was torn between the service of divine and human love: inspired by love to aspire to eternity, yet condemned to forsake love's physical consummation so as to prolong the ennobling effects of aspiration. The vital difference between his poetry and Salinas's, is that Salinas writes within a secular context, and aspires to an eternal incarnation of love in *this* life: a love that accepts no temporal limitations; a love that defies mortality; a human love that embodies the 'divine' dimension of the soul. Salinas has little difficulty in reconciling the notion of eternity with secular, human love, because the world inhabited by the lovers of his poetry, the "trasmundo", is not bound by the same temporal and spatial constraints as the measurable, empirical world. Strangely, it is at once of this world and beyond it, "más allá", incorporating both the physical and metaphysical characteristics that this poet feels are essential to human love, and to the achievement of 'entereza'. Like his Neo-Platonic forbears, Salinas is acutely aware that because love intensifies human experience - both sensual and spiritual, it concentrates the individual consciousness and raises ontological questions.

The existential dilemmas instilled by intense human feeling may be universal, but what are the particular implications for the poet striving to communicate this experience of love? The lovers' quest for eternal incarnation requires a new kind of language; one that, like love, will defy mortality. The poet-lover's aim is to reach the "trasmundo", a brave new world of love that springs from absolute union with the beloved. Concomitantly, he sets out to forge a new poetic idiom that will reach beyond, "más allá de", the limitations of inherited language. As lover, he is compelled by depth of personal experience to explore the extraordinary nature of human love, which takes the individual beyond all singular boundaries, whether physical or metaphysical, drawing him inexorably towards the 'other'. As poet, he must come to terms with the shortcomings of language in communicating this process. By reaching out to integrate with what lies outside the self, the poet-lover is drawn inward again, to explore the inner depths of the psyche, heightening individual self-awareness. Salinas's love-poetry traces the process whereby love breaks down the boundaries that separate self from 'other', internal from external experience, forging an entirely new conception of identity that is at once singular and dual.

The bringing together of binary opposites, male and female, is necessary to the realisation of 'entereza', in a new, joint entity. Lovers will therefore abandon their "vivir a medias" (1.44) of solitary virginity, in favour of a -

> Mundo, verdad de dos, fruto de dos,
> verdad paradisíaca, agraz manzana
> sólo ganada en su sabor total
> cuando terminan las virginidades.
> (ll.64-7, Verdad de dos, *Raz.*, p.435)

The bitter apple recalls Adam and Eve's sampling of the fruit of the tree of knowledge, here recorded - not as a fall - but as a positive step towards complete consciousness, only realised in its "sabor total" when human love is physically consummated and the lovers fuse. This would seem to echo Jung's emphasis on the interdependence of animus and anima - the need to open to the 'other' and to 'otherness'. In Jung's theory of contrasexual archetypes, the anima corresponds to eros, and to 'feminine' connective qualities, while the animus represents logos, the discriminative, 'masculine' powers of cognition. Both are required to make up the whole human personality.[1] Celibacy confines the individual to the parameters of his/her own body. Lovers experience an urgent need to expand beyond the limits of the self, to explore and know the 'other', and by exploring the 'otherness' of the beloved, each one discovers 'otherness' in the self, again echoing Jungian theories of the presence of both sexual archetypes in the individual personality.[2]

> ¡Cómo nos encontramos con el nuestro
> allí en el otro, por querer huirlo! (ll.129-30, *Raz.*, p.422)

Love is thus evoked by Salinas as a spontaneous reaching out towards the beloved, but equally, it is seen to inspire an inward-reaching reflex, a striving for self-knowledge that is further impelled by knowledge of 'otherness'. Physical fusion with the beloved becomes symptomatic of self-fulfilment, as each of the lovers gains self-knowledge through intimacy with the other. Salinas presents this process as being reassuringly inevitable - even predestined:

> Estaba allí, esperándose, esperándonos:
> un cuerpo es el destino de otro cuerpo
> (ll.131-2, Salvación por el cuerpo, *Raz.*, p.422)

The reflexive pronoun of "esperándose" breaks down boundaries between "él" and "ella", and the "nos" of "esperándonos" seals the lovers' collective entity. One body is the destiny of another: this seems to imply that the discovery of the true self is realised in the flesh, and not in the mind or soul - a point that is highlighted by the title of one of the eight, long poems that conclude the collection *Razón de amor*: the final passage of "Salvación por el cuerpo" celebrates a new incarnation of the self in union with the beloved -

> Encarnación final, y jubiloso
> nacer, por fin, en dos, en la unidad
> radiante de la vida, dos. (ll.142-4, *Raz.*, p.422)

Salinas presents love's consummation as a joyous re-birth, a recognition of the self not only as a singular entity, but as part of the interactive entity of the couple. The inexorable, fatal attraction that draws one body to another is communicated with the same persistence and frequency with which it is felt by the lovers. This irresistible gravitational pull also offers evidence of a consistant trend towards integration, and ultimate 'entereza' in the love experience:

> los minutos que pasan
> por todas las esferas
> nos empujan, seguros,
> un cuerpo hacia otro cuerpo. (ll.42-5, Hora de la cita, *Largo*, p.552)

The fact that the lovers are so frequently depicted as being impelled towards union by the driving force of their passion, does not mean that Salinas sees them as the victims of forces beyond their control. While love appears to impose its will upon the lovers, it is actually dependent upon their co-operation, for without the lovers' bodies, it cannot enact its perpetual process of unification. And so, in another of the long poems from *Razón de amor*, love approaches the lover in the persona of "La felicidad inminente" -

> Viene toda de amiga
> porque soy necesario a su gran ansia
> de ser
> algo más que la idea de su vida.   (ll.97-100, p.447)

No reality in Salinas's poetry - not even the innermost feelings of love - can live in the mind alone, but requires materialisation in the flesh. And so, once the process of incarnation has begun, and "la felicidad" of the poem's title is actual rather than imminent, love will succumb to the will of the lovers - "Rendida en nuestro cuerpo" (l.123, p.447). As the first person plural indicates, they now represent one self-determining body, having won self-knowledge and self-possession in union with the 'other'.

In Salinas's conception of love, not only does one body seek out another, but the soul also finds its ultimate goal of 'entereza' in union with the beloved. Here too, the individual identity is radically redefined as a consequence of the lovers' new 'dos-en-uno' identity:

> El alma dividida
> por fin se unió a sí misma
> uniendo a otra alma.
>   (ll.57-9, Paz, sí, de pronto, *Largo*, p.547)

Significantly, in its pre-love existence, the soul is defined in terms of division, stressing incompleteness and the impossibility of the individual's ever achieving the status of wholeness or 'entereza' in isolation from the 'other'.

Throughout all his poetry, Salinas demonstrates a fascination with the essential nature of material reality. The love experience stimulates this curiosity, as the poet-lover explores the nature of all 'otherness', physically manifest in the beloved and beyond, "más allá". In the love-cycle we observe the lovers as they perpetually seek out new experiences extending beyond the limits of their own physicality: there is even some poetic exploration of the idea that they could inhabit other physical phenomena in "Mira, vamos a salir" (*Largo lamento*, pp.579-81). Reading this suggestion metaphorically rather than literally, we can deduce that the phenomena suggested in the poem are selected by the poet because they share the lovers' tendency to combine and fuse. The poem explores, in turn, the possibility of inhabiting the material reality of trees, with separate trunks, but whose branches seek each other out (ll.16-21); of being waves, whose separate motions harmonise and eventually dissolve together in the sand (ll.22-6); of two silences, so perfectly married that they are only audible as one (ll.28-34); and finally -

> Y si quieres más probemos
> a ser luz,
> tú una llama, yo otra llama,
> tú una mitad, yo la otra
> de esa luz, que para serlo
> a los dos nos necesita
> y nos contiene a los dos.   (ll.35-41, *Largo*, p.580)

The poem traces the poet-lover's quest for metaphors with which to describe the two-in-one phenomenon of love, exploring various possibilities until alighting on the conceit of two flames that emit one light.[3] This extended metaphor also calls to mind the lighting of the nuptial candle with two separate flames in the celebration of marriage.

Salinas constantly points to the necessary presence of 'otherness' as a prerequisite for true unity and 'entereza'. The lovers project their own happy encounter onto their empirical surroundings and conclude that - "Todo querría ser dos / porque somos dos", (ll.34-35, *Raz.*, p.410). At times the lovers themselves are confused by this new and indescribable sense of self. They recognise the futility of attempting to describe their interrelatedness in numerical terms: they cannot be defined as strictly "dos" or "uno" while they exist as both, a point that is reiterated even in Salinas's later love-poems, written between 1936 and 1939, and collected under the title of *Largo lamento*. One example is the ambivalently titled "Pareja, espectro", where the poet assures us that:

> se abolió el gran dolor, la eterna duda
> de saber si es que somos dos o uno;   (ll.113-4)

> Fácilmente comprendo la importancia
> de haber traspuesto el numeral tormento
> perdiéndonos, del todo y para siempre,
> en esa selva virgen tan hermosa:
> la imposibilidad de distinguirse.   (ll.119-23, p.454)

Once unification is realised, the lovers will return to a state of primordial innocence: this is as true for the poems of *Largo lamento* as it was for *La voz a ti debida*. In this prelapsarian state, the soul reputedly enjoys absolute union with matter, and inhabits a "trasmundo" of love that resembles the Garden of Eden before original sin made Adam and Eve conscious of their separateness, both from each other and from their natural environment.

By stressing this sense of unity and the 'entereza' of the couple, many poems from *Largo lamento* seem to undermine strict "narrative" interpretations of the love-cycle: such interpretations usually claim to detect a systematic movement from encounter in *La voz a ti debida*, to disillusionment in *Razón de amor* and despair in *Largo lamento*. However, this is a view that allows no room for the fact that in all three volumes, Salinas's conception of love involves a constant flux between "tú", "yo", and "nosotros", the constantly evolving relationships between poet, beloved, and all 'otherness'. It is by now widely accepted in critical circles that Salinas was involved in an extra-marital relationship in Spain in the 1930s, at the time he was composing the first two volumes of the love-cycle. Indeed it is commonly suggested that his subsequent separation from this woman in 1936 explains the thematic dominance of the beloved's absence in *Largo lamento*; clearly the poet had his reasons for giving the collection its melancholy title. Nonetheless, it is important to distinguish between 'real' sentimental relationships and literary ones. Serious critical readings of *Largo lamento* are very scarce, and the kind of superficial treatment given to these poems in the past has led to many generalisations, and above all, a feeling that the tone of the book is all gloom and despair. While there is a profound sense of isolation in some of these poems, there is in others a continuing expression of faith in the possibility of love.[4] The already-mentioned "Pareja, espectro" is just one example of Salinas's on-going poetic exploration of an intimate yo-tú relationship. Seen in the overall thematic context of the *Poesías completas*, the beloved can be read as just one of the many poetic expressions of 'otherness' in Salinas's work, as he strives to maximise the potential of every relationship between the individual and his circumambient world.

In his love-poetry, Salinas often expresses a sensation of physical unity between the lovers that borders on symbiosis. So profoundly integrated are the first and second person in the 'nosotros', that they begin to appear physiologically interdependent; two organisms breathing and living as one. Such is the lover's intimate knowledge of the beloved, that her flesh feels almost like his own: "es casi como mía / de tanto haberla amado", (ll.28-9, *Todo*, p.723). This is not so much a case of possession as of complete integration as the lovers at once create themselves and one another, nourished by their mutual love:

> Y lentamente vas
> formándote tú misma,
> naciéndote,
> dentro de tu querer,
> de mi querer, confusos...
>   (ll.26-30, ¡Qué probable eres tú!, *La voz*, p.283)

The adjectival "confuso"' is the key to their integration: there is no clear dividing-line between one organism and another. The fact that lovers are depicted as being both biologically and emotionally interdependent is the source of the paradox expressed by Salinas in "Cuando tú me eligiste...", also from *La voz a ti debida*, for if the poet-lover's life is not autonomous, but interdependent with that of the beloved, then how can he die? Can he relinquish a life that is not solely his? By the same token, those who have never loved, have never lived according to the poet-lover, and should therefore have no means of dying: "los que no han muerto / y ya no tienen nada que morirse en la vida", (ll.40-41, p.318).

It would appear that the poet owes not only "la voz" to his beloved and muse, but indeed his entire being. How can this union, this total integration be expressed? Despite the tender nature of the lovers' utterings, language continues to distinguish between first and second person, driving a cruel wedge between them. While Salinas celebrates the familiarity of personal pronouns in *La voz a ti debida*, "¡Qué alegría más alta, vivir en los pronombres!" (p.243), he is also aware of the paradox that they encapsulate. Once intimacy becomes a reality, distinct pronouns are rendered redundant, and even come to represent the anguish of separateness, as Salinas is faced with the task of evoking unity within linguistic structures better equipped to distinguish and discriminate:

todo el dolor de la primera y la segunda
persona, que separa
a dos personas para siempre
en las gramáticas y en el mundo.
(ll.127-30, Pareja, espectro, *Largo*, p.455)

Not satisfied that the lovers be physiologically and sentimentally connected, Salinas develops a kind of poetic symbiosis, where the semantic content of his poetry and its syntax are as interconnected as the lovers themselves. Circular syntactic structures, the repetition of words and phrases, mirroring effects - all help to communicate the degree of union experienced by the lovers.[5] Circularity of syntax is deployed to evoke the irresistible attraction that leads him back to the beloved:

> De ti salgo siempre
> siempre tengo que volver a ti.
> (ll.32-3, Empújame, lánzame.., *La voz*, p.273)[6]

The stressed syllables of the couplet open and close with "ti"; the mirrored repetition of "siempre" closes one clause and opens the next; all these features demonstrate the poet's dependency on the beloved, as the poem syntactically enacts the inevitable process of returning. Elsewhere it is the pain of separation that is incorporated by syntax and rhythm: the classic line-repetition of - "no volvernos a ver: / no volvernos a ver nunca a tu luz..." (ll.38-9, *Raz.*, p.347) drives home the finality of never seeing one another again, through the emphatic repetition of the verb in the negative.

Personal object and possessive pronouns frequently figure in the syntactic patterns of repetition in these poems; they also provide scope for wordplay. For example, in the statement, "Posesión tú me dabas / de mí, al dárteme tú" (ll.24-5, *La voz*, p.317), Salinas subverts the reader's conventional expectation that the lover will possess the beloved. Here instead, she grants him self-possession, self-knowledge, by giving herself to him. In this poem she figures as an active partner, not to be passively pursued and won. The crux of the poem's semantic value lies in the alteration of the emphatic final pronoun in each line, which changes from "mí" (l.24) to "tú" (l.25). Such manipulation of possessive pronouns frequently clinches the poet's meaning, as in -

> No había que buscar,
> tu sueño era mi sueño.
> (ll.51-2, Aquí / en esta orilla.., *Raz.*, p.366)

- where the straightforward repetition of the noun is enhanced by the interchangeable nature of "yo" and "tú", now equated by love so that the lovers share the same dream.

The role of syntax here becomes virtually metaphoric as syntactic patterns enact the lovers' interdependence and new-found 'entereza': another example of this is the combination of various object pronouns with the infinitive, as in -

> el ansia de salvarme, de salvarte,
> de salvarnos los dos, ilusionados
> de estar salvando al mismo que nos salva
>   (ll.28-30, ¿En dónde está la salvación?, *Raz.*, p.339)

The metamorphosis experienced by the lovers, that renders their separate destinies one, is spelt out by the progression from "me" and "te" to "nos", as first and second person identities are replaced by the new collective identity of the couple. The same motion from singular to plural pronouns provides the answer to the question posed by the poem's title line "¿En dónde está la salvación?". Again, in *Razón de amor*, the exclamation, "¡Darme, darte, darnos, darse!" (1.55, p.415), illustrates how "te" and "me" merge into "nos", which is in turn absorbed into the reflexive form of "darse", as love generates its own linguistic momentum.

From the repetition of the infinitive, we move on to observe how Salinas plays on various forms of the verb. Perhaps it is in this trait, more than any other, that the love-cycle echoes the Cancionero tradition. The *Canciones* of Juan del Encina are typical of their genre, and some examples of his use of this device, when quoted alongside Salinas's, reveal an extraordinary syntactic similarity in poems divided temporally by centuries. Perhaps even more similar than their syntax, is the spirit of these love poems, where each poet delights in his own genius, where words are still the instruments of a game, and self-expression is expansive, demonstrating the utter exuberance and buoyancy of the love experience.

Villancico No.61

No quiero tener querer
ni quiero querido ser.
(ll.1-2)
Pues no me quiere querer,
ya no quiero suyo ser.
(ll.36-7)

and *Canción No.16*:

Querría no dessearos
y dessear no quereros,
más si me aparto de veros
tanto me pena dexaros
que me olvido de olvidaros.(ll.1-5)[7]

Lo que queremos nos quiere

Lo que queremos nos quiere
aunque no quiera querernos.
Nos dice que no y que no,
pero hay que seguir
queriéndolo:
porque el no tiene un revés,
quien lo dice no lo sabe
y siguiendo en el querer
los dos se lo encontramos.
(11.1-8, *Raz.*, p.357)

The repetition of the same verb in varied forms, and the conceptual circularity this creates, is as evident in Salinas's poems of the twentieth century as in those of the sixteenth. The modern poet also capitalises on the dynamic potential of verbal expression by rendering love active, (see 1.2): love *will* love, however reluctantly, and the lovers will achieve "este fervor infinito / contra el no querer querer" (ll.34-5, *Raz.*, p.358).

In order to stress the degree of 'entereza' that the lovers have found in their union with the 'other', Salinas avoids using either the first or second person form of the verb, opting instead for the collective "queremos". This evasion of grammatical distinctions between first and second person is a constant reminder to the reader of the reciprocal nature of love. The lovers are not only recipients of love, but active participants, as the to-ing and fro-ing of their caresses demonstrates in "Destino alegre": "dos seres lado a lado / por besarse, besándose, besados" (ll.86-7, *Raz.*, p.432). Their caressing is not a single act, over and complete, but a continuous exchange, as indicated by the present participle "besándose". This vision of love as a self-perpetuating process figures again and again in Salinas's love-poetry:[8]

> Cuando arrojados
> en el pecado que es vivir
> enamorados de vivir, amándose...
> (ll.69-71, Verdad de dos, *Raz*., p.435)

These lovers are not merely the passive victims of life and love, "arrojados", thrust into the world at birth, "enamorados", possessed by love. They aspire to eternal love, a neverending and active process of "amándose", and this desire for further love is felt by both "alma" and "cuerpo". Therefore, when the lovers try to prolong the splendid isolation of their night together by holding back the dawn in the poem "Despertar", they do so in both body and soul: "¡Tardar! grito del alma / ¡Tardar,tardar! nos grita el ser entero" (ll.26-7, *Raz*., p.424). These short lines illustrate how intimacy generates 'entereza' on two levels: there is the 'entereza' of the couple made up of two halves, the "nos" of l.27; and the additional 'entereza' gained by the individual through the experience of love, of self-knowledge through knowing the other, in the "ser entero" of the same line. In this way lovers can enjoy a double sufficiency - both as "dos seres" and as "la pareja". Their meeting has not been purely physical, but the coming together of body and soul: not just, "un choque de materia / y materia" (ll.7-8), but rather a -

> prodigioso pacto
> de tu ser con mi ser
> enteros. (ll.13-15, ¿Fue como beso o llanto?, *Raz*., p.350).

Complete, 'enteros' as individuals, and fully conscious of being made of both "alma y cuerpo", the lovers have assisted each other in their mutual discovery of the true self by coming together. This self-realisation in body and soul through symbiosis is celebrated in a "Canción de la vida total", from *Largo lamento*.

> Por eso vivo
> entero todo,
> dentro de ti.   (ll.87-9, *Largo*, p.570)

In Salinas's conception of love, only when the body is regarded as totally separate from the soul, can two separate kinds of love be considered possible; divine or profane, spiritual or carnal. His evocation of the love experience therefore undermines Cartesian notions of a mind/body split, both conceptually and linguistically, and is closer in spirit to pre-Cartesian, than post-Cartesian philosophy. From Plato to Thomas Aquinas, man was perceived as a body-and-soul composite. For the scholastic philosopher, of course, this raised many theological questions, the most thorny of which was how the soul would survive the separation implied by the body's death? Unlike his predecessors, the twentieth century poet is not daunted by such riddles, and can gravitate to a conception of infinite self-perpetuation in both body and soul. By aspiring to eternal incarnation, Salinas is simply taking a step further what was logically feasible in the Neo-Platonic system that brought together profane and divine love. The coincidence of the philosophies of Renaissance humanism with an increasing aesthetic appreciation of human form in the sixteenth century, raised questions previously unasked by the artist. Reflecting on this, Salinas writes -

> The Renaissance dug up marbles and adored bodies. Which did it prefer, the palpitating perishable body or the statue? Does it choose the marble or the flesh? The Renaissance gives up neither, it is precisely the solution of that dilemma, the desire to eternalise marvellous rosy bodies of mortal flesh in the immaculate whiteness of ideas, white as marble.[9]

Like the Renaissance artist, Salinas strives to eternalise the flesh through the application of his craft, although his medium of language is not as palpable as the sculptor's marble.

An intense awareness of the dual nature of love, at once physical and metaphysical, is a vital part of the whole tradition of love-poetry inherited by Salinas.[10] This is precisely why the love experience serves as such an effective analogy for the quest for 'entereza', which for Salinas, involves self-development both spiritually and physically, "alma y cuerpo". There can be little doubt that this poetry is written within a strong literary tradition, so self-conscious are its echoes of the dominant themes and preoccupations of former love-poets. The Neo-Platonic conception of man as microcosm of the Universe (that is, both human and divine), colours all of Salinas's love-poems, and the occurrence of compound-references to "alma y cuerpo" is so frequent as to constitute a refrain. Salinas draws on many Platonic and Neo-Platonic motifs, and this "alma y cuerpo" epithet appears in various guises. In some poems the corporeal element is indicated by "carnes", as in "¿Quién, quién me puebla el mundo?" (*La voz a ti debida*, p.326), where the poet responds to his own question with the words, "No, ni carnes ni alma" (1.3), neither body nor soul. When the beloved is absent, we are told that the lover feels bereft both physically and metaphysically: "sin huellas de la carne" (1.21), "sin señal de las almas" (1.24). If his memory of the absent beloved fails to conjure up the reality of these two vital components, so too does her anticipated presence in the future - "Mañana... / tan sin alma y sin cuerpo" (ll.1 & 4, p.229). The fact that he anticipates her presence in terms of both body and soul is perhaps more significant than her actual absence; it is further proof that his conception of her "alma y cuerpo" are inseparable.

> ¡Mañana! Qué palabra
> toda vibrante, tensa,
> de alma y carne rosada... (ll.29-31, Mañana, *La voz*, p.229)

There is a degree of ambiguity - probably deliberate - in the syntax of 1.31, where "rosada", although singular, appears to qualify "alma" as much as "carne".

The poet-lover's emotional response to the beloved is inspired by her 'entereza' as both a physical and metaphysical entity. In turn, the 'entereza' of his feelings is apparent in their expression, as he consciously avoids any distinction between Platonic and erotic love. Even in his invocation of the beloved's physical presence, Salinas involves her soul in a rather manipulative example of synecdoche.

Aspects of her person traditionally alluded to and praised in the Courtly love ethos, such as eyes, mouth, and hands, here represent her physicality, but always in conjunction with her spirituality:

> Por eso los amantes
> se prometen los siempres
> con almas y con bocas.
> (ll.38-40, ¡Pasmo de lo distinto!, *Raz.*, p.401)

The juxtaposition of body and soul is a constant feature in the love-cycle, and as it permeates the reader's consciousness, it recalls love-poems of other eras, and is easily assimilated as familiar conceptual territory. To an extent it can be said to conform to our subconscious expectations of how love is expressed in poetry, and that for this reason we are not surprised to find that the beloved's soul is presented as an appendage to her body in the lines: "esta gran soledad / bocas solas con sus almas solas" (ll.21-2, *Raz.*, p.386). Body and soul, here, seem to serve the same function. The same can be said of "Mundo de lo prometido", where the poet observes with his soul as well as his eyes -

> y lo busco
> en el agua, con los ojos,
> con el alma, por el agua. (ll.7-9, *Raz.*, p.387)

The eyes act as more than a window to the soul here; their mirrored, syntactic juxtaposition with the soul produces an effect of equation. Eyes and soul seem to reflect one another infinitely: the gazer gazes "por el agua", but cannot escape his own gaze reflected "en el agua".

While Salinas highlights the interdependence of "alma" and "cuerpo" and the lovers' mutual dependency, it is undoubtedly the poet-lover's particular needs that he dwells upon. The "tú" addressed in the poems is both beloved and muse; to her he owes his "voz", his poetic identity; in truly Neo-Platonic terms, she is the source of all life and all goodness. However, Salinas generally stops short of idolising the beloved - this is not, after all, a case of unrequited 'amour lointain' in the Courtly mode. Nonetheless, he repeatedly stresses the beloved's "alteza", and at times presents himself in as undeserving a light as any Courtly suitor, as in the lines: "¡Tú no puedes quererme! / estás alta, ¡qué arriba!" (ll.1-2, *La voz*, p.297). This elevation of the beloved places her on a higher plane than the lover: she is not made of the same crude stuff as sub-lunary beings such as he. The title lines of "No, no puedo creer / que seas para mí", are just one example of such conventional declarations of inadequacy. The poem continues:

> ¿Amar tú?, ¿Tú, belleza
> que vives por encima, (ll.5-6)
> en la gran altitud,
> donde no se contesta? (ll.9-10, *La voz*, p.300)

The beloved's spiritual superiority is even spelt out in terms of a Platonic scale of ascent, from human to super-human perfection. In these poems Salinas draws on the Platonic conception of love as an ennobling influence: having suffered love's anguish, the beloved is elevated to ever higher *escalas*, until she acquires the status of the sacred: "Cada dolor por mi culpa / te volvía más sagrada" (ll.19-20, *Largo*, p.563). All this seems to imply a distancing of the beloved from the physical, as she ascends higher and higher towards the Platonic ideal of a non-physical love. Nonetheless, as she ascends the Platonic stairway to perfection, she does not forsake the poet-lover, but assists him through the purifying power of her love. Like the Courtly mistress and muse, she inspires her suitor to aspire to new spiritual and emotional heights:

> ...hacia mí te inclinas
> y hasta mi suelo me tiendes
> escala de tu cariño...
> (ll.23-5, Ahora te veo más clara,*Largo*, p.563)

In this poem, Salinas's elevation of the beloved to the rather saintly role of divine intercessor seems to undermine the ethos of 'entereza' which dominates his love-poetry. Elsewhere, the beloved's dual nature is stressed and her presence as flesh and blood is keenly felt. In fact, this extremely conventional depiction of the beloved as spiritual guardian, aiding her suitor in his quest to overcome the baser aspects of his love, and to aspire to a 'purer' Platonic love, is the exception rather than the rule in Salinas's work. The poem implicitly recalls the Neo-Platonic distinction between physical love, "dessear", and Platonic, "amar". However much Salinas absorbs and assimilates literary tradition in his own work, he allows for no Platonic hierarchy of soul over body in his amorous and poetic scheme. In his 'razón de amor' the effects of love are certainly elevating, but the beloved's ascent is more often converted by Salinas from a Platonic *escala* towards union with the divine, into a secular ascent towards self-knowledge and fulfilment:

> subida sobre ti, como te quiero,   (1.16)
> en tensión todo el cuerpo, ya ascendiendo
> de ti a ti misma.
> (ll.19-20, Perdóname por ir así buscándote.., *La voz*, p.285)

The lover is not in awe of her ascent, which significantly, is an ascent *in* the body, as opposed to the Platonic motion which transcends the flesh. The beloved's upward aspiration to self-realisation inspires feelings of love in the poet, but it is a love of equals, and not that of undeserving suitor to inaccessible mistress.

Salinas's presentation of the beloved's ascent is rarely confined to the realm of the soul, and the fact that it is an ascension of the entire self, of both "alma y cuerpo" may owe something to the poet's religious background. Catholic doctrine allows for the conception of such miraculous events as Mary's 'assumption' into heaven in both body and soul, and the eventual resurrection of the faithful, in body and soul, on the day of judgement. The poet resorts to religious terminology to describe the beloved's "alteza", because it is probably the idiom available to him that best suggests 'otherness' and 'other worldliness'. However, the 'other world', for Salinas's lovers, is profoundly rooted in this one: it is the "trasmundo", where the lovers hope to gain immortality in the flesh. For this reason, sexual satiation is described in pseudo-spiritual terms, as for example -

> ¡Cuántas veces mis manos
> se quedaron tranquilas en paz, puras,
> saciadas de su sed por lo infinito,
> tan sólo acariciándote las alas
> que disimulan ciertas formas tuyas!
> (ll.63-7, Volverse sombra, *Largo*, p.474)

Despite her resemblance to some heavenly being, the beloved is very much a flesh and blood presence in these poems. Unlike the Courtly muse, she is not untouchable.

Love is perceived as a means of arriving at the total integration of body and soul, a means of achieving 'entereza'. The degree of interaction between "alma y cuerpo" demonstrated by the lovers is reflected in the expression of their love. Salinas may draw on literary convention and pseudo-religious terminology, but he applies them in a way that is very modern and secular. The lover is 'purified' by their love-making, as the flesh ceases to be inferior to the soul in the Platonic sense, becoming instead a means of achieving spiritual, as well as sexual union. By caressing the contours of the beloved's body, therefore, the poet makes contact with her spirit, the "alas" that allow her to soar. His physical desire for the beloved, and the existential desire for immortality are now inseparable - what is more, sexual contact between the lovers expresses both these desires. Similarly, when the beloved returns his caresses, she 'redeems' the poet, enabling him to realise his spiritual, as well as his sexual potential:

> Los besos que me das
> son siempre redenciones:
> tú besas hacia arriba,
> librando algo de mí, (ll.5-9)
> en los fondos oscuros. (l.10, La materia no pesa,*La voz*, p.291)

The above lines need to be read within the literary context of the *a lo divino* genre. Where the mystic poet, Juan de la Cruz, evoked divine love through the allegory of sexual love, many love-poets in turn, have elevated sexual love by evoking it *a lo divino*. Salinas can be seen to draw on the resources of poetry that celebrates both divine and profane love. Solita Salinas, in her "Presentación" of the *Cartas de amor a Margarita, 1912-1915*, writes of her father's particular enthusiasm for Juan de la Cruz's "Cántico espiritual" in the period between 1912 and 1914, a fact which emerges from his love-letters at this time.

> A pesar de que él insiste en el carácter no literario de estas cartas, en ellas hablará larga y detenidamente de sus lecturas, de sus preferencias literarias. En este momento, el poema en lengua española más admirado por él es el Cántico espiritual de San Juan de la Cruz. Lo tiene por modelo de poesía amorosa, y a comentarlo dedica una carta.[11]

There is abundant evidence of a profound influence by the mystic poet on Salinas's conception and expression of love in this formative period of his life. The commentary on the "Cántico espiritual" alluded to by Solita Salinas, can be found in a letter dated 20 August 1913, where Salinas writes:

> Para mí es una de las piezas primeras, si no acaso la primera, en castellano y siempre la he preferido íntimamente... Es todo amor, pero un amor tan humano, tan real, tan limpio, que es un modelo de poesía amorosa.[12]

What attracts Salinas to the mystic's work is undoubtedly the fact that it captures the essence of the love experience as both physical - "humano, real" - and spiritual - "limpio". But the twentieth century love-poet perceives these qualites in a way that is profoundly democratic; spiritual and sexual love for Salinas are absolutely equal and inseparable. Both are expressions of inter-personal relations: the spiritual resides within the individual, and while the poet may seek it outside himself in the beloved, he does not look to the super-human as a spiritual source.

Salinas does not humanise divine love, nor does he deify human love. His poetry acknowledges only one kind of love which is 'entero': physical and metaphysical to equal degrees. It would be naive, therefore, to read a poem such as "¡Pastora de milagros!" (*Razón de amor*, pp.341-3) as a purely formal imitation in the *a lo divino* genre. There is no denying that the language he deploys is overtly religious, even echoing cadences of the "Ave Maria". The very phrasing of the rhetorical question, "¿Lo sobrenatural / nació quizá contigo?" (ll.2-3), seems to hark back to that particular prayer's celebration of Mary as the physical source of the divine, stating as it does, "el señor es contigo". Here, however, the beloved does not give birth to a Saviour, as the prayer recalls. Instead, "lo sobrenatural" is born *with* her - that is to say, the poet-lover discovers his own spirituality in discovering the beloved: "Alto se está contigo, / tú me elevas.." (ll.26-7). She acts as intercessor, guiding him to a higher understanding of life, of love, of himself. The lines - "tan inocentemente, / tan fuera del pecado" (ll.59-60) seem to echo the stipulation in Marian doctrine that the mother of God must, herself, have been conceived without sin, and would in turn conceive without the 'sin' of carnal love. As Salinas's understanding of love excludes any notion of sin - least of all in its sexual expression - we can surmise that the reference is made ironically, as the following lines would seem to verify: "que nos parece un juego / con las cosas más puras" (ll.61-2).

For Salinas there is no original sin, and lovers thrive in a prelapsarian state of innocence, where the body is entirely pure. The purpose of this poem is not so much to compare the beloved to the Virgin Mary, as to compose his own "Ave", a song in praise of human love.[13] Again, secular language breaks down when the poet attempts to describe "lo sobrenatural", that is, any experience that lies outside the realms of rational thought and concrete, empirical reality. Only religious terminology seems to evoke the sense of wonder experienced by the lover, and his desire to praise the woman who has worked these miracles, the "Pastora de milagros" of the poem's title.

Salinas returns to the formulaic expression of prayer in *Largo lamento*, in another celebratory poem, "Canción de la vida total" (pp.568-71), where rhythmic patterns, the repetition of nouns and phrases, and the minimal length of line, are all suggestive of a litany. The beloved grants the poet-lover his sense of being: "Por ti se logra / en mí lo puro" (ll.70-1). The rhythmic and semantic crescendo associated with religious litanies is emulated here by the incidence of certain refrains, indicating 'high points' in the poem: the phrase "por ti" appears in 17 of the poem's 94 lines.[14] Another refrain reminiscent of religious litany is "la vivo en ti", as in the following lines -

Mi vida oscura	
mi vida honda	(ll.1-2)
la vivo en ti.	(l.5)
Mi vida clara	
mi vida alegre	
la vivo en ti.	(ll.35-38)
Mi vida extrema	
mi vida máxima	
la vivo en ti.	(ll.67-9)[15]

- lines which could easily be spoken in prayer by the supplicant, invoking union with his/her God, since the lexicon, particularly in ll.67-9, is resoundingly religious. Salinas has adopted the formula of religious litany in order to draft his own hymn to "la vida total"; to the life of both "alma y cuerpo", and the eventual 'entereza' that this will bring: "Por eso vivo / entero todo..." (ll.87-8). The "yo" of the poem is symbolised by a tree, and it is the development of this symbol that lends the poem its semantic structure. It is through the beloved that the "yo" is nourished, not only physically, but spiritually, in the same way as the tree draws sustenance through its roots from the soil:

tú, mis raíces.
De ti me llega
la porción honda,
de abajo, eterna
de mi existir.   (ll.26-30)

The religious tenor is unmistakable: the beloved "tú" provides not just daily bread, but the spiritual food of eternal life, "la porción honda", and "eterna". In this symbol of the tree, Salinas manages to integrate two important archetypes in the Western literary and religious consciousness. There is the Christian iconography of the tree as representing Christ's crucifixion, and man's redemption: according to this set of symbols the tree in Salinas's poem can be interpreted as the growth of the soul, aided by the intercession of Mary, the Christian icon of feminine purity and perfection. There is also the pre-Christian symbol of the tree of life: the firmly-rooted tree that grows upwards from the fecund Earth towards the stars, spanning both heaven and earth, which also acts as a symbol of spiritual aspiration. In some passages of the poem, the degree of conflation is quite extraordinary, as the beloved seems to intercede with both Mother Earth, and Divine Patriarch:

Ella
por ti me nutre,
por ti recibo
la sangre lenta
la triste sangre
que viene del centro del mundo.
       (ll.10-15, Canción de la vida total, *Largo*, p.568)

"Ella", Mother Earth, nourishes man - but with spilt, sacrificial blood, "triste sangre", reminiscent of Christ's on the cross. In this way, the blood-sacrifice made by the Judaic-Christian father-God, is now drawn up through the matriarchal earth, by the tree's roots. How typical of Salinas to choose such an all-embracing symbol as the tree with which to illustrate "la vida total", the 'entereza' of heaven and earth. The complete individual should, like the tree, reach downwards into the secret depths of this world, and upwards, to the unknown heights of the heavens:[16]

> de arriba a abajo,
> de abajo a arriba:
> flor, florecido;
> trémulo, hoja,
> hondo, raíz.
> (ll.90-94, Canción de la vida total, *Largo*, p.571)

The beloved seems to instil in the poet's mind an association between Nature's regenerative cycle, and the sacrificial cycle of birth, death and new spiritual life. Perhaps intimacy with the feminine, which is 'other' than himself, draws the poet closer to Nature's life-giving processes, and inspires reflection on the cyclical patterns of life and death. A *credo* of love emerges in the same collection, *Largo lamento*, in another poem that is characterised by its prayer-like syntax and tone:

> Por ti creo
> en la vida que está siempre queriendo
> volverse hacia sí misma, hacia la vida.
> Por ti creo
> en la resurrección, más que en la muerte.
> (ll.97-101, ¡Cuántas veces te has vuelto!, *Largo*, p.529)

It is not so much the poet's perception of the beloved that elevates her, as love itself, which Salinas portrays as an enlightening experience. As the lovers aspire to eternal union with one another, their ascent re-enacts the journey of the mystic's soul, upwards, towards union with its creator. There are many instances in these love-poems where Salinas's lines echo closely those of Juan de la Cruz.

> De el alma que se goza de haber llegado al alto estado de la perfección, que es la unión con Dios.[17]

> por fin, sí, la unidad
> en el amor más alto.
> (ll.76-7, Cara a cara te miro, *Largo*, p.586)

Ascension is not the only path to love's fulfilment and 'entereza', and the lovers can also seek self-realisation by descending into the innermost depths of their emotions. A psychological challenge is posed in the image of love as a mine: subterranean and subconscious, it entices the couple to seek out and excavate their own untapped potential. Until the beloved is found, the precious commodity of love is trapped, "como una oscura / fuerza entrañada" (ll.2-3), and cannot emerge "desde su mina a la vida" (l.11, *Raz.*, p.344). The poems repeatedly evoke love's latent potential in terms of an unmined resource. Love is the driving force that urges the lovers to overcome their limitations, to look deeper and deeper within themselves, to the 'entereza' of self-knowledge -

> que vayas
> más allá todavía
> por las minas
> últimas de tu ser...   (ll.33-6, *La voz*, p.280)

The two-way motion of ascending the Platonic *escala* and descending into the mines of the subconscious, is central to this poet's perception of the love experience. The fact that Salinas's use of the Neo-Platonic motif of ascent should have its literary ancestry in the mystic tradition is hardly surprising - we need only glance at the poetry of Fray Luis de León to discern a probable influence. This mystic traces the ascent of the soul, which, inspired by earthly beauty, looks up towards its divine Creator and source. Less predictable, is the fact that Salinas's evocation of a descent into the sensations and revelations of love also stems from the mystic tradition. For Juan de la Cruz, earthly life constitutes less a springboard to the divine than a form of imprisonment; for this mystic, descent is a necessary part of the soul's eventual ascent. He indicates in his "Introducción" to the *Noche oscura del alma* that only by descending into a dark night of the soul, a "negación espiritual", can the mystic transcend the confines of earthly experience.[18]   It is interesting too, that Juan de la Cruz should choose subterranean settings for the encounters of the amada and amado, soul and Creator, in his *Cántico espiritual*:

> En la interior bodega
> de mi amado bebí,   (Verso 18)
>
> Y luego a las subidas
> cavernas de la piedra nos iremos... (Verso 37)[19]

Salinas's comments on the *Cántico espiritual* leave little doubt that his own love-poetry has been influenced by Juan de la Cruz's evocation of divine love. The task of the mystic, he outlines, is to penetrate mysteries:[20]

> His technique is that of immersion or penetration, like that of a diver or miner... The mine of the soul, immeasurably dark and at the same time incomparably luminous, and in whose depths are found beauties far higher than those we touch with our hands of flesh or see with our mortal eyes.
> (*Reality*, pp.121 & 128).

These comments cast as much light on the work of Salinas as that of Juan de la Cruz, as the same motions of ascent and descent serve the modern poet to explore and communicate the love-experience on every level. Like the mystic poet, the lovers' ambition is to be admitted to the mysterious and apparently paradoxical "subidas cavernas" of love; like their literary ancestor, this will be realised via a descent; the "trasmundo" can only be reached 'tras' *this* world. And so a motion that may seem paradoxical -

> ...en descensos alegres,
> se sube, si tú guías,
> la inmensa
> cuesta arriba del mundo.
>   (ll.38-41, ¡Pastora de milagros!, *Raz.*, p.342)

- is sublimely logical in love's terms. Love exalts the poet to heights he has never imagined possible, and plunges him into unimagined depths, so that he now finds himself - "más alto ya que estrellas / o corales" (ll.19-20, Cuando tú me eligiste, *La voz*, p.317). Both celestial heights and submarine depths are embraced by the qualifying adjective "alto", and this lack of semantic distinction is reinforced by the insertion of "o", which renders the stars and corals indistinguishable. It is precisely this functional ambivalence in Salinas's very idiosyncratic use of language that expresses the 'entereza' of his vision: distinctions break down, and apparent opposites are enveloped in an unexpected manner, by a single, unifying adjective.

The poetic principle of 'entereza' which unites opposites and breaks down semantic divisions, governs Salinas's use of the motions of ascent and descent in the love-cycle. In his poetic scheme, these motions cannot be attributed exclusively to the realms of "alma" or "cuerpo" respectively. While the heavenward aspiration of the soul suggests a non-physical, or 'spiritual' interpretation to the motion of ascent, this is not a hard and fast rule. By the same token, the primal impulse to know the beloved physically may be expected to gravitate downward, towards the materiality of the earth: yet this is not to say that the motion of descent is associated solely with physical or erotic love. Salinas deploys a very telling conceit to express the inseparability of these two impulses in the love relationship. He draws an analogy between love and the hawk that hovers before swooping to possess its quarry - " mira, la quiere, cae" (1.17, *Raz., p.373*), but which plummets only to soar again, "con ardor de subir" (1.18), driven by the same primal instinct of desire in both its descent and ascent.

> Por eso no se sabe
> de qué profundidad
> viene el amor, lejana,
> si de honduras de cielos
> o de entrañas de la tierra.   (ll.19-23, *Raz.*, p.373).

That love's effects are profound is not in question: but the source of its depths is ambiguous; whether it comes from above, like a gift of grace from a divine source of love; or from below, from the earth, itself a source of infinitely evolving life, is never clarified. Nor, one suspects, is Salinas interested in making such hard and fast distinctions in a poetry whose thematic context and linguistic expression is based on the notion of fusion. The phrase, "honduras de cielos", points us to Antonio Machado's *Galerías* LXI, where the ever-watchful poet awaits inspiration from both above and below: he watches the sky for signs, but it is a sky of depths as much as heights -

> Poetas, con el alma
> atenta al hondo cielo... (ll.25-6)[21]

Machado's "galerías", like Salinas's understanding of love, are at once ethereal and profound: airy passages that open in the poet's consciousness as the result of delving into the depths of his soul. On a purely psychological level, they can be read as symbolising the enlightenment that comes from exploring the subconscious.[22] Machado's "hondo cielo" motif is elaborated by Salinas in several of these poems, for example -

> bogando por el cielo
> sirenas y corales
> en las nieves perpetuas
> y en el fondo del mar,
> constelaciones...
> (ll.9-13, Extraviadamente, amantes.., *La voz*, p.254)

Again we encounter the sea/sky paradox of "corales o estrellas" already seen in "Cuando tú me eligiste" (*La voz*, pp.317-8). By visually fusing heaven and earth, Salinas subverts the reader's expectations: sirens and corals now navigate the heavens, and divers are lured to their deaths in the sea's depths by the stars. This visual *espejismo* lends the poem another layer of meaning, as the stars' reflection in the water presents a mirage, a chimera, as elusive as the sirens of Greek mythology.

Another example of the influence of Machado's "hondos cielos" may be the recurring motif of the lovers treading on air, as though it were solid ground beneath their feet: "ir pisando / por el suelo del aire" (ll.47-8, *Largo*, p.452). This motif crops up again in the poem "¿En dónde está la salvación?" (*Razón de amor*), where Salinas makes it clear that salvation, for the lovers, constitutes eternal love. But where can it be found? -

> ¿..si pisando los
> cielos que miramos
> o bajo el techo que es la tierra nuestra..?   (ll.8-10, p.339)

Finally, he concludes that love's ultimate goal lies neither in the heavens, nor on earth - "no son ni diamantes ni astros" (l.30, *Raz.*, p.414). Love's realisation is impalpable, and the lovers' reward will be neither precious stones mined from the earth, nor stars plucked from the heavens. Love's reward is still more love, and the quest for eternal love continues in the form of the lovers' ascent and simultaneous descent.

The body is no longer seen as a limitation of any kind: it does not house the lover's captive soul, but together with it, soars and dives. This is Salinas's most dramatic departure from the Platonic tradition, as he refuses to grant the spirit supremacy over the flesh, and both lay equal claim to the right to eternity. Because love is never exclusively of the body or the soul, but is the product of their fusion, the lovers' bodies do not always obey nature's laws.

> Te sentirás hundir
> despacio, hacia lo alto,
> en la vida del aire.
>   (ll.16-18, Los cielos son iguales, *La voz*, p.277)

Ascent and descent are not only simultaneous, therefore, but indistinguishable: psychological exploration and spiritual aspiration fuse in the mysterious, extra-dimensional motion that incorporates heaven and earth, in the "trasmundo". The lovers' bodies inhabit two spheres of experience, the noumenal and the material. It is as though they are subject to not one, but two gravitational forces, which attract them simultaneously upwards and downwards. So inextricably connected are their physical and spiritual aspirations to further love, that their very love-making constitutes a pseudo-Platonic ascent, as they scale the heights of ecstasy:

> ...va ascendiendo
> por escala de tactos,
> de bocas, carne y carne.
>> (ll.9-11, ¡Qué probable eres tú!, *La voz*, p.283)

Deviation from the Platonic hierarchy of soul over body culminates where the Platonic scale is replaced by an erotic *escala* of caresses as the lovers approach sexual union. Their paradise, the goal of an eternally incarnate love, is inseparable from the poet's fundamental quest for 'entereza' because it must incorporate both "alma y cuerpo". Access to this paradise can only be gained by complete immersion in this life, the material life of the body and the senses.

> El paraíso está debajo.   (l.108)
> Y por eso desnudos, voluntarios
> lo vamos a buscar
> sumergiéndonos,
> suicidas alegres hacia arriba.
>> (ll.111-14, Suicidio hacia arriba, *Raz.*, p.443)

Vulnerable, receptive, "desnudos", the lovers will plumb the depths of their physicality, and from this baptism of total immersion rise to "el final acierto" (l.115) of their love.

The poetic quest for eternal love has obvious resonances of the mystic's desire for eternal union with the Godhead. Indeed, the entire tradition of Neo-platonic love-poetry relies upon the notion of human love as an imitation of divine. Yet, while the Courtly poets aspired to Platonic love, their yearning was undoubtedly fuelled by physical desire. Whether the divine love of the mystics, or the formalised conventions of Amour Courtois, love has been evoked over the centuries in terms of an insatiable and ever-increasing desire. Indeed, this is the paradox central to the Neo-Platonic tradition: the poet is acutely aware that love is inherently spiritual *and* physical, but Platonic philosophy tells him that while the soul survives eternally, the body must perish. Consequently, the lover-poet is faced with an agonising dilemma: love intensifies the desire for eternity, and in doing so, sharpens his awareness of his own mortality. The conventional response to this quandary for the Neo-Platonic poet is to adopt a posture of 'Vanitas', where the poet-lover resigns himself to the fact that love and its frustrations are salutary reminders of the transient nature of the flesh.[23]

However, it is probably true to say that as the Spanish love-lyric matures, and the formal conventions of the Courtly ethos loosen their grip, concessions to physical love increase considerably. The later poetry of Quevedo is less resigned to the frustration of physical love by mortality. In the sonnet "Amor impreso en el alma, que dura después de las cenizas", he argues that if love is life itself, and if life precludes death, then surely love will rob dread death of some of its sting.

> Si hija de mi amor mi muerte fuese,
> ¡qué parto tan dichoso que sería
> el de mi amor contra la vida mía!
> ¡Qué gloria, que el morir de amor naciese!   (ll. 1-4)[24]

With characteristic sleight of hand and concept, Quevedo demonstrates how love transforms death into a birth. As yet, this defiance of death remains purely intellectual and linguistic: as a conceit it is perfectly coherent, but it offers little consolation to the actual lover concerned with the perpetuation of love in the flesh. No matter how cleverly disguised with conceptual bravado, an element of martyrdom remains; the body, it appears, *will* be sacrificed to the soul; "Y el no ser, por amar, será mi gloria" (l.14). Quevedo comes closer to Salinas's aspiration to eternal incarnation in his famous, "Amor constante más allá de la muerte", where the flame of physical desire makes the forbidden passage across the river Styx, thus defying "la ley severa" that deems the flesh inalterably perishable: "nadar sabe mi llama la agua fría / y perder respeto a la ley severa" (ll.7-8).[25] Water will not quench love's fire, and although the lovers may be reduced to ashes, in accordance with natural laws - "serán ceniza, mas tendrán sentido, / polvo serán, mas polvo enamorado" (ll.13-14) - their ashes will be transfigured into a statement of love's survival. What emerges from this poem is the notion that love has altered the poet's perspective on death, which no longer seems absolute. This notion that love can somehow qualify mortality is taken up by Salinas, and developed by him to a degree that was impossible in the seventeenth century religious framework of *desengaño*.[26] Salinas's firm belief in the equal status of body and soul, and his striving after the 'entereza' of their total fusion, allows him to conceive of an eternity in the flesh as well as in the spirit. While the Baroque poet could intellectually conceive of a physical eternity, religious doctrine still specified that the body was unworthy of eternity. For the secular poet this mind-body dichotomy is less rigid. The limitations on the poet's conception of eternity are no longer doctrinal, but empirical and linguistic, and these, Salinas generally ignores. Defying mortality, he establishes the linguistic premise for a love that is "tan sepultado en su ser" (l.30) - so rooted in its flesh and blood physicality that like the dead, he has no fear of mortality:

> Tan cierto de no morir
> como está
> el gran amor de los muertos.
> (ll.37-9, Ahora te quiero, *Raz.*, p.385)

This twentieth-century poet-lover can freely aspire to eternal incarnation: through linguistic and poetic innovation he can orchestrate the glorification and assumption of the flesh.

Another interesting point about Quevedo's approximation to eternal incarnation is that he describes eternity in terms of a journey rather than an arrival; the crossing of the river that divides life from death is probably the poem's most enduring image. Similarly, in Salinas's love-poems, the "trasmundo" is expressed in terms of the aspiration to eternal love, rather than its fulfilment. Distance may separate the lovers, causing them loneliness; time's onslaught will inevitably bring changes; many obstacles will test their love. Their only chance for survival is their commitment to continue their love:

> ...viviendo una vida
> inocente entre errores,
> y que no quiere más
> que ser, querer, quererse. (ll.40-3, p.225)

Salinas, like so many poets before him, equates life with love, "ser" with "querer". Again, a primordial state of innocence is suggested, as the lovers act out "errores" in the eyes of those not in love, but these very errors make up part of the "razón de amor", love's logic, and allow the lovers to aspire to such seeming illogicalities as eternal incarnation, "la pura / gloria de su acertar", (ll.51-2, *La voz*, p.255).

The physical consummation of love does not satisfy desire in these poems, but only fuels its flames. Unlike the Courtly poet whose eternal desire was sustained by its own perpetual frustration, Salinas manages to consummate and instil further desire simultaneously. Sexuality therefore acts as a highly appropriate metaphor for the lover's quest for eternity: as long as the lovers continue to exercise the desire of one body for another, they guarantee an endless love that is "seguro de no acabar / cuando no terminan los besos" (ll.34-5, *Raz.*, p.385). Each caress invites another, at once anticipating and postponing ultimate consummation. Not only is love equated with life, but its place *in* this life is stressed in the line, "querer en vida" (l.32, p.384); the "trasmundo" will only be reached through the here and now.

The theory that physical desire is the most accurate metaphor for eternity available to the poet, because it regenerates itself ad infinitum, is put forward by

Salinas in relation to the works of Rubén Darío. His comments are equally applicable to his own love-poetry:

> El amor completo y profundo busca honduras donde anclar, repetida costumbre, asiento en una serena eternidad; el de los sentidos, como sólo se ejercita en apetecer, es un virtuoso de la traslación, porque lo que quiere es querer más.[27]

Eternal love cannot withstand prolonged abstraction, but requires the constant substantiation offered by the lovers' bodies. Accordingly, the traditional motif of the soul as a captive bird trapped within the cage of the body, is transformed to become that of a bird seeking a perch on which to rest. The soul is compelled to manifest itself in the flesh; otherwise it is condemned to perpetual, frenetic flight, without destination.

> Las almas, como alas
> sostiéndose solas
> a fuerza de aleteo
> desesperado, a fuerza
> de no pararse nunca...
> (ll.46-50, ¡Qué de pesos inmensos!, *La voz*, p.321)

The poet's love comes to rest in the 'other', the beloved, without whom there can be no realisation, no sense of completion or 'entereza'.[28] Ultimately, the lovers' quest for eternal love is dependent upon the intensity of their love, the strength of their desire to generate further love, and their capacity to fuse "alma y cuerpo", so overriding all considerations of mortality.

The perishable nature of human flesh presents physical, metaphysical, and considerable linguistic obstacles as the poet attempts to express the concept of an eternally incarnate love. Salinas's response to this problem is, again, to stress that human love is an irreducible composite of "alma y cuerpo". A poetic process of substantiation and unsubstantiation takes place in the love-cycle, where the immaterial is rendered material, and matter dematerialised to the point where they merge completely. The poet's aim is to blur all semantic distinctions between the physical and metaphysical as separately conceived realms of experience, and to demonstrate the degree of linguistic and conceptual 'entereza' arrived at in the love experience.[29]

Commenting on the poetic technique of Juan de la Cruz, Salinas observes that while the mystic poet replaces reality with a vision, the symbols he chooses are all drawn from material reality. And so, he concludes, the result is - "A sensation of unreal reality, or of real unreality", (*Reality*, Chapter Four, "The Escape from Reality, p.120). It is significant that he should discern this reciprocal process in another's work. Equally, his own love-poetry creates a sensation of immaterial matter, or of material immateriality. As the non-material life of the soul merges with that of the body, verbs of a particularly concrete character such as "fabricar", and "labrar", are applied to such unexpected and elusive entities as "nadas" and "sombras". Love-making is perceived as a materialising process that renders tenuous emotion palpable, and this is reflected in the degree of semantic substantiation exercised in the love-cycle.

> Y de estas nadas se ha ido
> fabricando, indestructible,
> nuestra dicha, nuestro amor,
> nuestra tarde.
> (ll.39-42, ¿Cómo me vas a explicar?, *Raz.*, p.399)

This "dicha", their love, extends beyond the realms of the senses, yet it is woven by their bodies, in a very concrete sense "fabricado".

There is great irony in Salinas's treatment of his feelings of physical attraction to the beloved. At times he wishes he could escape the influence of her physical charms, to somehow by-pass her body, and gain access to her essential self. By materialising her shadow in "Me estoy labrando tu sombra", he attempts to create a rival to her persuasive, physical reality. The underlying irony, of course, is that he claims to yearn for a non-material love, but can only evoke such a love with the decidedly material lexicon of "labrar" and "palpable". Salinas mocks his own conflicting desires with the consciously ambivalent lines -

> Y puedo vivir en ti
> sin temor
> a lo que yo más deseo,
> a tus besos, a tus abrazos. (ll.20-3)

The poet's true posture is finally revealed by the exclamation of l.30, "¡Yo, que los quería tanto!", (*La voz*, p.307), verifying our suspicion that he has not been entirely sincere or successful in his attempt to cast off physical desire. Like the Courtly love-poets, Salinas is here aspiring to a 'pure', Platonic love, of mind and soul alone; an immaterial love. Unlike his predecessors, he parodies his own aspirations, and his stated intentions are ultimately punctured by this tongue-in-cheek tone.

This apparent pursuit of purely Platonic love at the expense of the body runs counter to Salinas's true intention, which is to forge a love that is 'entero', a merging of flesh and spirit. A sequence of seven poems that explores the lovers' ambivalent status as material and/or immaterial entities, concludes the volume *La voz a ti debida*. Salinas speculates in the opening lines of the penultimate poem of the book:

> ¿Y si no fueron las sombras
> sombras? ¿Si las sombras fueron... (ll.1-2)
> cuerpos finos y delgados,
> todos miedosos de carne? (ll.6-7, p.328)

Reading the poems in sequence, it becomes evident that that these "sombras" are not just shadows, but the lovers' souls, psyches, minds, their non-material selves, here humanised and granted bodies. Salinas toys with the idea that, once substantiated, they would be modest creatures, even prudish, unused to the donning of flesh. After materialising the lovers' shadows, he sets about materialising shadows everywhere, postulating that they may in fact be bodies, simply posing as shadows: "cuerpos disfrazados / de sombras, sobre la tierra" (ll.20-1, *La voz*, p.328). The subject of the final poem in the sequence, and in the volume, "¿Las oyes cómo piden realidades?", is this same materialisation of the lovers' "sombras", which can only realise their "sueño de sombras" (ll.29-30) by becoming flesh and blood.

> Y su afanoso sueño
> de sombras, otra vez, será el retorno
> a esta corporeidad mortal y rosa
> donde el amor inventa su infinito.
> (ll.29-32, *La voz*, p.329)

Salinas implies that not only is the human soul fully realised in the flesh, but that this represents a 'retorno' - a restoration to a prelapsarian state of wholeness or 'entereza'. The reconciliation of these two facets of humanity: the body, "mortal y rosa", and the soul,"infinito", are married in love's new definition of eternity, which encompasses both.[30] Even dreams, ineffable by definition, are materialised in the beloved's body:

> ...un sueño sólo es sueño
> verdadero
> cuando en materia mortal
> se desensueña y se encarna...
> (ll.50-3, Torpemente el amor busca, *Raz.*, p.345)

The lover's awakening from a dream, in this instance, offers no sense of disappointment or *desengaño*. The lines invite comparison with that great manipulator of the dream/reality paradox, Calderón de la Barca, for whom the final awakening is a *desengaño* - an awakening to the 'true' life of the soul in death. For Salinas, however, the life of the body and the senses is as 'real' as that of the soul. Accordingly, Segismundo's assertion that "la vida es sueño", that mortal life is a dream - implying unreality and illusion - is subverted by Salinas's counter-assertion of the reality of dreams, as incarnate in the lovers' bodies.[31]

While "sombras" and "sueños" can be substantiated by love, they can also serve the purpose of dematerialising what previously seemed solid and palpable. These shadow and dream motifs typify Salinas's semantically flexible approach: in order to communicate the pristine, novel character of the "trasmundo", he must reach beyond inherited semantic categories, materialising that which previously had no physical form, and dematerialising matter. The latter process of dematerialisation can reduce an actual body to the condition of a shadow, as is the case in "Ha sido, ocurrió":

> Creeré que fue soñado.
> Que aquello tan de verdad,
> no tuvo cuerpo, ni nombre. (ll.33-5, *La voz*, p.226)

This poem is written from a perspective of separation, and the poet's dematerialisation of the beloved - his denial of her physical reality - serves the distinct purpose of relieving the anguish caused by her current absence.

Both conceptually and lexically, Salinas's attitude to matter is elastic: not only is it the case that feelings and dreams materialise, but that the physical world can turn out to be as ineffable as the spiritual or immaterial. Salinas can postulate the actual, corporeal nature of shadows in "¿Y si no fueron las sombras / sombras?" (p.328), while in the poem directly preceding it, he stresses the shadowy nature of the human form:

> ¡Qué cuerpos leves, sutiles
> hay, sin color,
> tan vagos como las sombras! (ll.1-3, *La voz*, p.327)

The same motif can both materialise and dematerialise, as this poet makes no real distinctions between physical and non-physical feelings. This becomes particularly clear when both processes - the substantiation of the immaterial and the dematerialisation of matter - converge. We find the materialisation of "sueño" in one line, "Por ti he cogido un sueño de las manos" (l.42), and the subsequent dematerialisation of the beloved, where the flesh and blood nature of her body seems to be denied in the next - "o de las que parecen manos, alas" (1.43, *Largo*, p.482); these are not hands, but celestial wings, extensions of her soul. This two-way process of semantic transformation has the effect of broadening our understanding of what comprises matter or spirit; and "alma y cuerpo" increasingly come to be perceived as a single, all-encompassing sphere of experience.

At times the tendency to dematerialise follows a pattern of progressive, or rather, regressive elimination, as in "Sí, por detrás de las gentes" (*La voz a ti debida*). Here, the poet attempts to define the beloved through a process of elimination: first he discards her name (1.3), then her physical image, then her non-physical self, or "alma" (1.8); and finally his own subjective definition of her, "lo que yo siento de ti" (1.12), reducing her to a state of non-being, "como si fuese morir" (1.24, p.223). It is clearly not the poet's intention to eradicate the beloved's existence, or deny her reality, whether in "alma" or "cuerpo" - this would constitute a denial of her 'entereza'. He aims rather to stress that her essential self is so elusive that she cannot be pigeon-holed within the confines of either material or immaterial existence. She is at once both, and beyond both: "detrás de todo" (1.21, Sí, por detrás de las gentes, p.223).

Where concrete verbs such as "fabricar" and "labrar" have been seen to materialise the lovers' aspirations, the antonymous "deshacer" strips away the the material world, revealing the more noumenal aspects of their love: "Se deshizo el abrazo..." (1.21, *Raz.*, p.349). Not only does love alter the perception of material reality, it would seem to alter matter quite radically. Salinas traces the effects of love's anarchy in "Amor, amor catástrofe", where, "se extinguen / las normas y los pesos" (11.9-10, *Raz.*, p.248). The materiality of matter is normally measured in terms of volume and weight, but here in Salinas's hands, it is repeatedly dematerialised to a state of weightlessness. The title-line of "La materia no pesa" (p.291), speaks for itself. In this poem the beloved's presence restores the poet to the "trasmundo" where he is unconfined by the physical laws of gravity that determine the motion of other material phenomena.

> ...tu dulce peso rosa,
> es lo que me volvía
> el mundo más ingrávido. (ll.35-7)

Paradoxically, it is her physical weight and mass that opens up to him a world that is weightless. This astounding effect is observed again in "¡Qué de pesos inmensos!" (*La voz a ti debida*, pp.320-1), where Salinas refines his definition of the beloved's "peso", or materiality to an "infinito, / gravitación, ahogo..." (l.19). She is made of an infinite weight, but not a dead weight, not an immovable mass. Her "peso" is infinite and immeasurable because it involves direction and motion. Gravitation pulls her irresistibly towards incarnation, and towards her lover, but this is not an end in itself - it is part of the process that leads to eternal incarnation. Salinas playfully challenges Newton's mechanistic view of the cosmos, in a motion that resembles drowning, "ahogo", a complete submergence in the flesh. The "trasmundo", he asserts, is held up by imponderable bodies: "en aires, en ausencias, / en papeles, en nada!" (ll.5-6), the epitome of which are the lovers' souls - "tan débiles / para sostén eterno / de los pesos más grandes!" (ll.43-5, *La voz*, p.321).

So rigorous is this tendency to dematerialise, that Salinas does not stop at stripping away substance and mass, rendering them weightless. Phenomena that are already non-material by nature, are treated as though they, too, need to be unsubstantiated, and are even further de-materialised. The cumulative effect this produces on the reader impedes any clear conception as to what constitutes empirical and/or non-empirical reality. For example, the beloved's voice has no palpable substance, though it is perceptible to the senses: at times it acts as a materialising mechanism, conjuring up an impression of the beloved's presence when she is in fact absent - "Porque tu voz crea su cuerpo" (l.17, "Si la voz sintiera con los ojos", *Raz.*, p.377); while on other occasions, its volatile quality is further emphasised:

> Un día, al fin, hablaste,
> pero tan desde el alma,
> tan desde lejos,
> que tu voz fue una pura
> sombra de voz, y yo
> nunca, nunca la oí.
> (ll.19-24, Cuántas veces he estado.., *La voz*, p.293)

"Pura" and "sombra" imply an ethereal quality: the beloved's voice is distant, so distant from the material world that she is inaudible to the ear. The lover will not make contact with her in this way; a form of communication that is both spiritual and physical, appropriate to the 'entereza' of love, has yet to be learned.

Many poems throw up examples of expression which is two stages removed from physicality, of the immaterial further dematerialised. These extreme states of immateriality sometimes convey a yearning for incarnation, as in "Antes vivías por el aire", where the beloved, having once experienced love in the flesh, is haunted by its memory. The ghost of her physical life, its "huella", stalks her disembodied existence, so that she is no more than a "huella de tu huella" (l.26, *Raz.*, p.348). Generally, where Salinas applies this device to the lovers' "almas", his intention is not so much to distance them further from their "cuerpos", as to reveal their very essence. Of love itself he writes:

> A su fugacidad,
> con el alma del alma,
> la llamamos lo eterno. (ll.36-8, p.374)

Far from distancing the lovers from their material selves, Salinas fuses "alma y cuerpo" to the extent that the soul's soul ceases to be a spiritual or non-material metonym, and can be read as an adjunct to the body, in much the same way as the dreamer's dream represented reality. Following the same logic, heaven and earth cease to be distinguishable, as "la tierra / es el cielo del cielo" (ll.15-16, *Raz.*, p.373).

Salinas's pursuit of 'entereza' is enacted in his love-poetry through an absolute confusion of body and soul. The result of his deliberate substantiation of "alma", and unsubstantiation of the "cuerpo" may be described as a kind of semantic "consubstantiality", and is exemplified by the poem "Salvación por el cuerpo": "Arribo a nuestra carne trascorpórea, / al cuerpo ya, del alma", (ll.146-7, *Raz.*, p.423).[32] The alternate dematerialisation of "cuerpos" (ll.1-7), and materialisation of "sombras" (ll.8-12) in "¡Qué de cuerpos leves, sutiles..!", culminates in the following example of this ideal state of 'entereza':

> Y qué trajín, ir, venir,   (l.13)
> sin parar, sin saber nunca
> si es alma de carne o sombra
> de cuerpo lo que besamos...   (ll.17-19, *La voz*, p.327)

The tone is more celebratory than perplexed, and it is significant that this consubstantiality is not portrayed as a fixed, static condition. It is itself a process, by necessity unceasing, so that love may be incarnated endlessly.

Not only does love heighten the poet's awareness of himself as consubstantially "alma y cuerpo", it also sharpens the feeling of consubstantiality between the lovers. It is not enough for the lovers' soul to possess its own body, it finds itself incomplete and lacking substance without that of the beloved:[33]

> Pero el alma, dime, el alma,
> que otro día de aquel
> se encuentra ya sin más ojos,
> sin más manos, sin más pies,
> que los tristemente suyos...
> (ll.19-23, ¡Qué contenta estará el agua!, *Largo*, p.544)

A semantic pattern emerges from many of these poems, which commence with a conventional Cartesian view of "alma" and "cuerpo" and conclude with an entirely transformed vision of "alma-y-cuerpo". One example is "¿Fue como beso o llanto?" (pp.350-1), where the initial 10 lines deal with the lovers' meeting as the collision of mass with mass, "choque de materia / y materia" (ll.7-8), which then expands to embrace "tu ser con mi ser / enteros" (ll.14-15), indicating that they are united utterly, both in body and in the non-physical dimension of the soul, and so achieve the desired state of 'entereza' as two fully realised individuals, and as a new joint entity.

Time is a crucial factor in the quest for eternal incarnation. While empirical evidence tells us that all matter must perish, Salinas seems to salvage the lovers' bodies from this mortal fate by transforming our understanding of materiality. As a poetic inversion of physical law is enacted, mortal love, previously subjected to time's tyranny, becomes time's master.[34] There are obvious inconsistencies in Salinas's approach to time at different periods of his literary development. In three finely-wrought sonnets which are structurally central to Salinas's first volume of published poetry, *Presagios*, he adopts the formalised sentiments of *desengaño* associated with this poetic form.

> Deja ya de mirar la arquitectura
> que va trazando el fuego de artificio
> en los cielos de agosto. Lleva el vicio
> en sí de toda humana criatura:
> vicio de no durar.   (ll.1-5, No.23, p.77)

The sonnet is clearly a formal exercise in both structure and theme, and merits contrast with later poems where Salinas argues that in order to attain eternity, the lovers need to break out of the limitations set by time. They want to control their own evolution, past and future, as indicated by the range of tenses in these lines from *Razón de amor* -

> Desesperadamente el mundo intenta
> todavía esta noche resistirnos,
> que vivamos, vivir, como ha vivido. (ll.64-6, pp.437-8)

The lovers resist any attempts to confine their existence: they look to an unspecified, endless future of the subjunctive "vivamos", and the infinity suggested by "vivir". Elsewhere, time acts as a co-conspirator, enabling them to arrive at eternal union and 'entereza'.

> El tiempo que circula
> por las venas del mundo
> y la sangre que corre
> aquí, por nuestras venas
> quieren lo mismo, ya:
> acercarnos, juntarnos. (ll.64-9, *Largo*, p.553)

Here the lovers are at one with time which now provides a friendly medium; it does not pass them by, rather they move with it, as their relationship evolves from enslavement to the possession of their own fate: "El tiempo es nuestro, nuestro / Nuestro dueño es esclavo" (ll.51-2, *Largo*, pp.552)[35].

Just as the physical laws that determine volume, weight and distance are transformed by love, so is time, the fourth dimension. For this reason, Salinas argues that memories are impossible for the lovers. Their experience cannot be defined in the conventional time-scales of past, present and future, and an interesting example of temporal oxymoron can be found in the poem "A ti sólo se llega / por tu voz", from *La voz a ti debida*:

> ¡Qué novedad tan inmensa
> eso, volver otra vez,
> repetir lo nunca igual
> de aquel asombroso infinito! (ll.28-31, p.312-3)

The apparent non-sensicality of l.30 drives home the fact that the lovers inhabit a unique time-sphere which does not proceed chronologically. Thus, they can 'repeat' events that are never the same in an infinitely varied, infinite world. This is the ideal state aspired to by the lovers, where notions of before and after, repetition or anticipation have no relevance; a time-scale where past, present and future co-exist simultaneously.

Lyrical poetry, especially the love-lyric, has traditionally been less concerned with historical time, or *chronos*, than with those intense moments which seem to halt, or crystallise time's passage - what Joyce described as "epiphanies". These moments are the product of a heightening of inner experience, when the individual's perception of time emanates from the inner consciousness, bearing little or no resemblance to the sequence of outer events that measure chronological time, or narrative. Salinas's love-cycle dwells very much in this inner time-sphere, and largely defies a linear, narrative interpretation. *La voz a ti debida* may, indeed, trace the early stages of a relationship; *Razón de amor* may deal with the emotional turmoil of the later stages of a relationship; but the degree of overlap in thematic content and tone, the consistency of contradiction in all three of Salinas's volumes of love poems, makes it difficult to establish with any certitude a clear-cut narrative development. The poems published posthumously under the title of *Largo lamento* were written in the late 1930s, and include many poems whose tone belies this title, as well as the many that strike a nostalgic chord. *Largo lamento* is more than the epitaph of a love-affair: it is also the continuation of a poetic exploration of the nature of the love experience. Salinas's love-poetry is certainly more exploratory than descriptive, concerning itself with inner, rather than outer temporal experience. The fact that love does not abide in the external, measured scales of 'chronos', is symbolised in *La voz a ti debida*, by the conflicting pulses of the beloved's wrist and the watch she wears on it: "¡Qué cruce en tu muñeca / del tiempo contra el tiempo!" (ll.1-2, p.267).

In order to arrive at a state of 'entereza', the poet-lover strives to fully integrate the realms of physical and metaphysical experience. His success in expressing their fusion in his verse, has the added effect of challenging the temporal limitations imposed upon the body by Cartesian and scholastic philosophy.

Nonetheless, while Salinas verbally defies the rigours of time's passage, there is no denying that reading his love-poetry requires some degree of suspension of disbelief on the part of the reader, who is gradually drawn into the lovers' experience, and begins to identify with their aspiration to eternal incarnation. Psychologically and emotionally, it can be argued that the cultivation of a truly satisfying bond with another person enhances a certain sense of timelessness and relieves some of the anguish that springs from the individual's consciousness of mortality. For this reason, Salinas is able to write to his fiancée -

> ...ve pues, en donde veo la inmortalidad, no en una voluntad divina
> que nos conserve, sino en nuestro impulso interior.[36]

What emerges from much love-poetry is the impression that the only feeling of permanence available to the individual in this world, is found in the "yo"-"tú" relationship. The coming together of two individuals to form a new entity of "nosotros" seems to create an inexorable dynamic of self-perpetuation. But these love-poems go a stage further, and the conception of eternal incarnation can be said to represent an ontological ideal of eternal relation in body and soul. In this way, the relationship forged between two people - essentially inner and subjective - begins to affect their relationship with the outer, empirical world which must now be re-conceived temporally in order to accommodate their 'eternity'.

The lovers' accession to the timeless realm of the "trasmundo" raises questions as to the nature of the relationship between poetry and experience. Through his communication of the consubstantial status of "alma y cuerpo" and love's 'entereza', it could be argued that Salinas's love-poetry in fact anticipates experience, more than describing it. Unlike his predecessor Gustavo Adolfo Bécquer, who laments the failure of language to capture the ineffable, Salinas seems to create a poetic vision of an unrealisable ideal.[37] Pre-conditioned by post-Romantic literary values, the modern reader is more familiar with the poetic expression of the inadequacies of language, than with demonstrations of its capacity to invent experience. The case, as Steven Gilman points out, is not so much that Bécquer's *Rimas* are the "habitación natural del poeta", as "nuestra habitación natural como lectores".[38] The question of whether language is here describing, or anticipating the love-experience, involves a fundamental temporal doubt. Does language create the "trasmundo" by anticipating it? Or does the poet simply describe an extraordinary experience already lived? In order to approach this question, it is necessary to examine the nature of the experience that this poetry either creates or re-creates.

Although Salinas writes in an intellectual framework that is secular, this is not to say that he does not acknowledge the existence of a 'spiritual life' - in fact this seems to have been a common topic in his correspondence with Jorge Guillén.[39] It is quite clear from Salinas's work that his conception of love involves metaphysical qualities as well as physical. This is why love-poetry is such an appropriate medium for the quest for 'entereza' as a personal and poetic goal. He draws extensively from the Neo-Platonic tradition that initiated the juxtaposition of divine and profane loves - but without adhering to any of the doctrinal limitations imposed by this tradition; to this extent, the modern poet has the best of both worlds, that of the flesh and the soul. The Courtly love poets may have woven a religion out of love, (C. S. Lewis describes the Courtly love cult as, "an extension of religion, an escape from religion, a rival religion" - all ritual, idolatry and humble subservience), but Salinas's presentation of human love also displays certain characteristics that are inherently religious.[40] It may be useful at this point to return to his commentary on the works of Garcilaso de la Vega, of whose Sonnet V, he writes the following:

> These words emit such spiritual heat that we cannot for a moment doubt the reality of the flame. The other was a game; here love bursts forth, implacably, in all its seriousness... And its two qualities that stir us deeply are two essentially religious qualities: seriousness and fervour. (*Reality*, p.84)

Two issues emerge from these comments, the first concerning the poem's origin and the second its tone. In relation to the origins of Garcilaso's celebrated sonnet, Salinas feels it necessary to stress the authenticity of the experience that has inspired the poet to write. He makes a value-distinction between this poem, which he claims can only have sprung from authentic experience, and the formulaic poetry so prevalent at this time. At another point in the same essay, Salinas asks:

> What was the reality behind his love? What was its poetry? Did he live spiritually in an amorous world? To what extent is his love real, to what extent poetic? (*Reality*, p.82).

These are questions which can be asked, very pertinently, of his own poetry, but they are questions not easily answered. It is not enough to say that Garcilaso's love for Doña Isabel Freire was "real" in the sense that Salinas applies the term, any more than it is sufficient to argue that an affaire conducted by Salinas in the early 1930s, is the sole "reality" behind these poems. While both relationships are historically verifiable and "real" in biographical terms, they are largely transformed by the poetic process into expressions of metaphysical wonder. In the case of Garcilaso, and to a lesser extent Salinas, idealisation of the love experience plays an important part in this transformation. Consequently, it would be limiting to confine the scope of Salinas's lengthy exploration of the love experience to the context of one relationship, however important it may have been as an initial source of inspiration.[41] The very questions posed by Salinas of his literary forbear, illustrate the opinion that the events of a poet's life frame only one aspect of his work. The precise wording of his questions is revealing: "What" and not "who", was the "reality" behind this love? In other words, the nature of the experience is given more emphasis than the actual object of the poet's affections. And perhaps more importantly, "did the poet live spiritually in an amorous world?" At this point spirituality and love are clearly inseparable in the poet's mind. Like religious feeling, human love is non-rational, ineffable, intuitive.[42] It is precisely because of these similarities that Juan de la Cruz chose to express divine love through the allegorical search, encounter and union of sexual love. The final union may be mystical or erotic, but the sensations it inspires are closely related. The sensation of elevation, flight, of weightlessness, is just one example:

> Apártalos, amado
> que voy de vuelo.   (Cántico espiritual, Verso 13)

> Por ti me arranco
> me voy volando...   (ll.62-3, Canción de la vida total, *Largo*, p.570)

Certain sensations felt by the poet-lover can be expressed as common to erotic and religious experience. Most characteristic of these sensations is that of transformation, or transfiguration. The following lines from Salinas and Juan de la Cruz reveal the same feelings of metamorphosis, effected by different kinds of love -

> ¡Oh noche que gustaste!
> ¡Oh noche amable más que alborada!
> ¡Oh noche que juntaste
> amado con amada,
> amada con amado transformada!
>   (La noche oscura del alma, Verso 5)[43]

> En la noche y el trasnoche
> y el amor y el trasamor,
> ya cambiados
> en horizontes finales
> tú y yo, de nosotros mismos.
>   (ll.27-31, Horizontal, sí te quiero, *La voz*, p.271)

Sexual love engenders new life, and in this way alleviates the individual's physical and metaphysical fear of extinction. Salinas's coining of the verb "transvivirse", articulates a concept of an eternity that is gained "tras" the life of the body, in the flesh and blood embrace of sexual love. The love of earthlings, flesh and blood, can thereby achieve the status of eternity -

...transvivirse
en beso o hueso,
en inmortalidad del incorpóreo
no querer morir nunca que es besarse...
(ll.15-18, Destino alegre, *Raz.*, p.430)

It is the very dramatic and exceptional nature of certain experiences, whether religious or amorous, that impels poets to take up their pens in direct response to their sheer elusiveness and incommunicability. Their resistance to the rational structures of language presents a challenge. It is therefore scarcely surprising that G. A. Bécquer should write that, "El amor es poesía; y la religión es amor."[44] By co-relating love, poetry and religion he underlines the great common factor of all three, their mystery. It was also Bécquer who most clearly enunciated that the only way to communicate such experiences is through poetry, the writing of which, like love and religion, is itself an ineffable experience. The love poet is particularly aware of his simultaneous dependence on words, and his struggle to transcend them. It is this problematic relationship with their medium that urges poets of the ineffable to forge new poetic idioms.

Having poetically realised the ideal of 'entereza', arriving at a point of complete union with the beloved - whether divine or human - Salinas seems to transcend the limited capacity of language. The simultaneous emotional intensity and nebulous atmosphere of Juan de la Cruz's work is comparable with the equal passion and ambivalence of Salinas's. If Bécquer can be described as a "visionario seglar", then perhaps the resonances of Salinas's love-poetry justify the use of the term, 'secular mysticism'.[45] However, it should be remembered that the lovers' accession to the "trasmundo" in this love-poetry is not a transcendental journey, in the accepted meaning of the word. Instead of rising above the material world, an upward motion implying a superiority of "trasmundo" over "mundo", the lovers immerse themselves in material reality, thereby forging a passage 'tras el mundo'. It is a motion which requires the conception of an extra-dimensional reality, at once material and immaterial, "más allá de" the measured confines of time and space. In this way the spirit's desire for eternal life can be realised in the body. Salinas takes Quevedo's conceit of "polvo enamorado" and love's passage across the river Styx, to its ultimate conclusion in the poem "Salvación por el cuerpo":

> para encontrar, al cabo, al otro lado,
> su cuerpo, el del amor, último y cierto.
> Ese
> que inútilmente esperarán las tumbas.   (ll.154-7,*Raz.*, p.423)

The most obvious similarity between human love and religion is the integrating impulse shared by both - the quest for 'entereza' in union with a godhead or with the beloved. The etymology of the word religion itself indicates a re-connecting: *re-ligare*, a re-unification and restoration to wholeness of what has been temporarily fragmented. This association has long been recognised by love-poets: Garcilaso, like all true artists of the Renaissance, painted human love as an imitation of divine; Bécquer deified both human love and poetry. Salinas steps outside the unspoken value-system that permeates love-poetry from the Troubadours to the Romantics, and which measures human love against the ideal of the divine. He acknowledges no distinctions between human and super-human love, and unlike Bécquer, has therefore no need to deify or idolise.

Salinas, while very much a man of his times in many respects, persists in his conception of human love as both a physical and metaphysical experience. His love-poetry seems to be inspired by a desire not only to describe, but to invoke feelings that are as intense as they are elusive. Always there is a desire to push back boundaries, not only those of language, but of human experience conveyed through language. This pioneering spirit recalls another era, and in "The Escape From Reality" Salinas comments on the motivation of seventeenth century Spanish poets.

> Our soldiers and conquistadores seemed to have as their motto:
> onward, plus ultra. And that desire to go further, that aspiration
> toward the spiritual beyond, vibrates like a flame in our literature
> and art. The great captains and conquistadores of the inner struggle
> are, to the end of the seventeenth century, the mystics.
> (*Reality*, pp.99-100)

Sentiments which clearly strike a chord in Salinas's own ideal of poetry, which he

elsewhere describes as "una aventura hacia el absoluto".[46] He too can be

described as a champion of the "inner struggle": the act of writing is for Salinas a

journey towards absolute, or complete experience; a quest for 'entereza' in both his

life and its expression. Like love, this aspiration is by nature self-perpetuating and

eternal. The poet's physical and metaphysical lust for knowledge is insatiable; it

comprises both "alma" and "cuerpo".

> ...Igual
> al gran amor en colmo
> buscando claridad
> a través del misterio
> nunca bastante claro,
> por desnudo que esté
> de la carne mortal.
> (ll.32-8, En ansias inflamada, *Raz*., p.662)[47]

This quest, this aspiration, is a constant in the Western tradition of the love-lyric,

and indeed affords much love-poetry a timeless quality which makes it readily

accessible to the reader of any period - so universally felt and stated are these

sentiments.

One aspect of love-poetry which facilitates its lasting appeal is its

preoccupation with the inner life, the life of the emotions, the soul. While it may

luxuriate in the realms of sensuality, it rarely dwells on description of the empirical

world inhabited by the lovers, being more inclined to create its own world, as

Salinas creates his own poetic "trasmundo", and Juan de la Cruz, a symbolic

topography of the soul, in his *Cántico espiritual*.[48] Certainly there is little reference in Salinas's love-poetry to the technological trappings of twentieth century urban life which figure so prominently in his earlier volumes. And what of the political turmoil that erupted in Spain in the 1930s, precisely when Salinas was composing the poems that make up *La voz a ti debida*, and *Razón de amor*? Salinas was not apolitical: not only was he deeply affected by the political events between 1930 and 1933, the year of publication of *La voz a ti debida*, but was an active supporter of the new Republic.[49] In his letters to Jorge Guillén at this time, Salinas laments the level of political factionalism and ambition of the worst kind that had contaminated his circle of acquaintances in Madrid at this time,

> Se acabó ya todo interés por las actividades espirituales que no desemboquen de un modo inmediato en lo que ellos llaman política... (2.4.31)[50]

By writing love-poetry, Salinas is able to express his personal quest for absolutes, his own 'spiritual' quest. If it seems bizarre that he should embark upon such a metaphysical quest when faced with the immediacy of great political upheaval, another letter to Guillén may help to clarify his reasons:

> ...estoy sintiendo que España llega a un punto en que todos los propósitos personales van a ser superados, lo mismo los del rey que los míos. Y eso es lo que me indigna por dentro. (20.2.31)[51]

These letters suggest that it was partly in response to the pressures of external, socio-political events at this time, that Salinas felt a great need to write poetry that was personal, intimate - the qualities that he would describe as 'spiritual'. Love is the ultimate of all personal experiences: whether erotic or religious, it is perhaps the only area that remains wholly private, entirely the property of the individual. Together, *La voz a ti debida*, *Razón de amor*, and *Largo lamento*, map out a quest for 'entereza' in the poet's inner life. During this period of his poetic career, the 'other' is embodied by the beloved, and union with 'otherness' is sought only in the private realms of the love relationship. This could be seen as a very human response to the turmoil so prevalent in the external, collective realm of politics in Salinas's world of the 1930s. Yet in his later works, Salinas's quest for 'entereza' will lead him to see the 'other' in the collective entity of society, a political, historical, and external reality. We witness how he will cease to flee from history, instead confronting it in the poems of *Todo más claro*, and the essays of *El defensor*, seeking involvement, interaction and ultimate union with that greater, collective 'other'.

Salinas continued to compose love-poetry throughout the 1930s, a period of great upheaval and change in his life, when he and his family left a Spain on the brink of war, and took up residence in the United States of America. In such troubled times, it is scarcely surprising that the poet should wish to remind himself that in a complex and divided world, the overwhelming simplicity of human love was still possible.

> Que el hecho más sencillo
> el primero y el último
> del mundo, fue querernos.
> (ll.81-3, ¡Pastora de milagros!, *Raz.*, p.343).

It is absolutely in keeping with his work, that this poet should feel it important to sustain a spiritual life during this period, to aspire to the ideal of 'entereza', whether as individual, poet or lover.

Notes

Chapter II

1. See C. J. Jung, "The Syzygy: Animus and Anima", in *Jung: Selected Writings*, Introduced by Anthony Storr, Fontana (London, 1986), pp.109-27.

2. As early as 1913, Salinas explores the interrelatedness self knowledge and knowledge of the beloved, in a letter to Margarita Bonmatí, where he cites the lines: "A mí has de buscarme en ti / A ti has de buscarte en mí". In her notes to this publication of Salinas' letters to his fiancée, Solita Salinas attributes these lines to St. Teresa, saying, "parecen ser una cita inexacta del poema de Santa Teresa que empieza así: 'Alma buscarte has en mí / Y a mí buscarme en ti...'" Carta XI, Madrid 1913, *Cartas de amor a Margarita, 1912-1915*, ed. Solita Salinas de Marichal, Alianza Tres (Madrid, 1984), p.59.

3. The fusion of two flames in these lines recalls Bécquer's metaphor in "Rima XXIV": "Dos rojas lenguas de fuego / que a un mismo tronco enlazadas / se aproximan, y al besarse / forman una sola llama" (ll.1-4), and Salinas' allusion to the unifying motion of the waves in ll.22-26 echoes the third stanza of the same poem.

Salinas:

Bécquer:

Vamos a probarnos olas
que corren una tras otra,
separados y jugando,
hasta que en la arena tibia
se les acaba el ser dos...
(ll.22-26, p.579)

Dos olas que vienen juntas
a morir sobre una playa
y que al romper se coronan
con un penacho de plata...
(ll.9-12)

G. A. Bécquer, *Rimas*, Clásicos Castellanos (Madrid, 1975), p.47.

4. Solita Salinas's reading of *Largo lamento*, is largely based on the assumption that an actual relationship took place in the 1930s, whose termination left the poet with a mixture of feelings such as abandonment and betrayal, as expressed in this collection. However she also concedes that Salinas's faith in love continues.

> Hemos asistido en *Largo lamento* a la desilusión de un hombre enamorado, a su tristeza, soledad, desánimo y casi muerte (poética al menos) y hemos visto con sorpresa que a lo largo del libro, fluye una corriente en sentido contrario: lo de la fe en el amor, el mismo que le ha traicionado.

Solita Salinas, Prólogo to, Pedro Salinas, *Poesías completas Vol. 4*, "Largo lamento", Alianza, Libro de Bolsillo (Madrid, 1990), pp.22-23.

5. This highly self-conscious coincidence of content and form is a very common feature of the Cancionero tradition, whose influence on Salinas's love-poetry has possibly been underestimated. J. G. Cummins outlines certain stylistic traits of the Cancionero in terms that can easily be applied to the love poetry of Pedro Salinas:

> ...preoccupation with repetition, insistence, echo; with phonetic, syntactical and conceptual parallelism. The results can vary from a largely unconscious use of sound repetition to a formal parallelism of idea and syntax in which the resources of poetic expression themselves become the primary elements of the poem. (J. G. Cummins, *The Spanish Traditional Lyric*, Pergamon, (Oxford, 1977), p.26).

Because Salinas's personal library did not survive the Civil War, it is difficult to establish with certainty that he purchased and read poetry of this kind in the period immediately prior to the composition of the love-cycle. However it is certain that throughout the 1920s there was considerable interest in the compilation of Cancioneros in Spain, and it is quite conceivable that some of these would have figured in Salinas's reading at this time. Likely examples are Alvarez Gato's *Obras completas*, ed. Jenaro Artiles (Madrid, 1928), or J. Cejador y Franca, *La verdadera poesía castellana*, Vols. l-V (Madrid, 1921-4). In the light of Salinas' probable interest in the Cancionero, Juan Marichal's judgement that this poet was utterly unaffected by traditional verse-forms is difficult to justify. See Juan Marichal, "La poesía de Pedro Salinas", *Letras*, No.70-74, XXXVII (Lima, 1965), pp.36-47.

6. These lines are reminiscent of Garcilaso de la Vega's Sonnet V, a late example of the Cancionero's thematic concern with the lover's indebtedness to the beloved, where Garcilaso makes a characteristic equation of love and life: "por vos nací, por vos tengo la vida, / por vos tengo que morir, y por vos muero" (ll.13-14). Salinas takes the title of *La voz a ti debida* from Garcilaso, and comments at considerable length on Sonnet V in his critical essay, "The Idealisation of Reality", in *Reality and the Poet in Spanish Poetry*, John Hopkins Press (Baltimore, 1966). See See

Garcilaso de la Vega, *Poesías castellanas completas*, ed. Elias L. Rivers, Clásicos Castalia (Madrid, 1972), p.41.

7. Juan del Encina, *Poesía lírica y cancionero musical*, ed. R. O. Jones and Carolyn R. Lee, Clásicos Castalia (Madrid, 1975), pp.131 and 82 respectively.

8. Stixrude summarises this most eloquently when he comments: "Love is, after all, neither more nor less than its longing to take on life anew; awakened by the force of its own invention". See David Stixrude, *The Early Poetry of Pedro Salinas*, Princeton University/Editorial Castalia (Madrid, 1975), p.131.

9. Pedro Salinas, *Reality and the Poet in Spanish Poetry*, John Hopkins Press (Baltimore, 1966), Chapter Three, "The Idealistion of Reality", p.81.

10. As Robert Havard has commented: "Intrinsically, Salinas' poetry is more concerned with tradition than with novelty... In one very real sense, Salinas' muse is tradition". See Robert Havard, "Pedro Salinas and Courtly Love", *Bulletin of Hispanic Studies* LVI (1979), pp.135-6.

11. As in Note 2, p.16.

12. As in Note 2, Carta XXV, p.95.

13. In another of his letters to Margarita in 1913, Salinas elevates his fiancée to the point of painting their relationship as that of supplicant worshipper to divine intercessor, evoking her as a latter-day Madonna.

> Cada vez que me dices 'te quiero' siento algo inefable en el alma; quisiera ir hacia ti como van hacia la Virgen María esos ángeles de las Anunciaciones, todos vestidos de candor, con un lirio en la mano. Tú eres para mí lo más alto, lo más puro, lo más bello de la vida, y te adoro místicamente.

Cartas de amor a Margarita, 1912-1915, Carta XI, Madrid 1913, p.5. As in Note 2.

14. See lines 6, 11, 12, 17, 31, 38, 40, 47, 58, 60, 62, 70, 81, 83, and 87 of "Canción de la vida total", *Largo lamento*, pp.568-71.

15. As early as 1914, it would appear that Salinas was aware of the rich resources offered by religious expression as a means of communicating feelings of love. In a letter to Margarita he outlines his aspiration to a love that is total, complete,

140

whole - and does so in precisely the terms that will appear many years later in the poem "¡Pastora de milagros!".

> Por eso, Margarita, miro a todo el futuro lleno de fe y de esperanza porque sé que mi vida a tu lado será mi máxima vida, que amándote mi vivir será total. (Carta LIII, p.152, as in Note 2)

16. In his *Dictionary of Symbols*, J. E. Cirlot has the following to say about tree symbolism:

> The tree is one of the most essential of traditional symbols... It stands for inexhaustible life, and is therefore equivalent to a symbol of immortality. According to Eliade, the concept of 'life without death' stands, ontologically speaking, for 'absolute reality', and consequently, the tree becomes a symbol for this absolute reality, that is, at the centre of the world. Because the tree has a long, vertical shape, the centre-of-the-world symbolism is expressed in terms of a world axis. The tree, with its roots underground and its branches rising to the sky, symbolises an upward trend related to other symbols, such as the ladder and the mountain, which stand for the general relationship between the 'three worlds', (the lower world: the underworld, hell; the middle world: earth; the upper world: heaven).

Translated from the Spanish by Jack Sage, Routledge and Kegan Paul (London, 1971), pp.346-7.

17. Juan de la Cruz, "Introducción" to the "Noche oscura del alma", in *The Poems of St. John of the Cross*, ed. Roy Campbell, Pantheon Books (London, 1951), p.10

18. "De el alma que se goza de haber llegado al alto estado de la perfección, que es la unión con Dios, por el camino de la negación espiritual", as in Note 17.

19. Juan de la Cruz, "Cántico espiritual", *The Poems of St. John of the Cross*, ed. Roy Campbell, Pantheon Books (London, 1951), pp.18 and 26.

20. Pedro Salinas, *Reality and the Poet in Spanish Poetry*, Chapter Four, "The Escape from Reality". As in Note 9.

21. Antonio Machado, *Poesías completas*, ed. Manual Alvar, Austral (Madrid, 1982), pp.118-9.

22. Machado reflects on this mysterious link between ascent and descent in the context of subconscious dream experience: in another poem from *Del camino* "el sueño" leads the poet to "criptas hondas" and "escalas sobre estrellas", (*Del camino*, XXII, ll.5, *Poesías completas*, as in Note 21). By delving into the subconscious, perhaps the poet can emerge illuminated, and so embark upon a pathway to the stars. This would be one psychological reading of the process of ascent via descent.

23. Juan del Encina's response to this Platonic paradox is typically resigned:

Partir, coracon, partir,
alegre para morir.

¿Qué me aprovecha el querer
sin esperanca tener?
No hay plazer que dé plazer
saviendo que ha de morir.   (Canción No.110)

Juan del Encina, *Poesía lírica y cancionero musical*, ed. R. O. Jones and Carolyn R. Lee, Clásicos Castalia (Madrid, 1975), p.222.

24. Francisco de Quevedo, *Poemas escogidos* LXXXXVIII, ed. José Manuel Blecua, Clásicos Castalia (Madrid, 1981), p.174.

25. Quevedo, *Poemas escogidos* CIII, p.178. As in Note 24.

26. Arthur Terry writes most succinctly on the conflict between body and mind in Quevedo's poetry:

...for Quevedo there is an agonising conflict between body and mind. The latter 'wooes' and 'is wooed by' God; but this is a source of torment to man while he is imprisoned, 'encarcelado' in the body, 'el claustro mortal'.

Arthur Terry, Introduction to, *An Anthology of Spanish Poetry, Part II, 1580-1700*, Pergamon Press (Oxford, London, 1968), pp.xxv-xxvi.

27. Pedro Salinas, *La poesía de Rubén Darío*, Seix Barral (Barcelona, 1975), Chapter VI, p.106.

28. Salinas resorts to this bird-soul metaphor in more than one poem: another example can be found in *Largo lamento*: "y toda ala de querer o pájaro / necesita posarse..." (ll.124-5, "Volverse sombra", p.476).

29. In the light of this semantic destabilization, the body-soul dichotomy presented by Feal Deibe seems altogether too simplistic, when he states that, "El alma es siempre igual, una, pero el cuerpo varía: hoy presenta una forma y mañana otra". In fact both body and soul constantly change throughout this poetry, and by changing, draw ever closer to the nature of the other: matter becomes increasingly ethereal, the spirit seems almost palpable. Rather than change preventing ultimate union, as Feal Deibe suggests, it facilitates it: "El deseo es reconciliar el cuerpo con el alma que no varía... El cambio constante... impide el encuentro". See Carlos Feal Deibe, *La poesía de Pedro Salinas*, Gredos (Madrid, 1971), pp.65-6.

30. In relation to this poem and the final poem of *Razón de amor*, David Stixrude comments that "Both *La voz a ti debida* and *Razón de amor* end by stressing the urgency of love's incarnation" (p.137). The reasoning behind this urgency is glossed as follows:

> The poet's sojourn in the physical world creates in the soul an intense, but formless, usually unspoken desire for incarnation, and yet the soul incarnate would cease to survive. Therefore it must content itself with what it was and is (the evidence of the outer world) and go on yearning for what may or may not be (substantiality of the inner world), forever discontented.
> (Stixrude, p.131. As in Note 8)

It seems that the quest for eternal incarnation (which resembles Stixrude's "substantiality of the inner world"), is a necessary prerequisite to love's perpetuation. Moreover, the poetic process executed by Salinas in these poems undermines such strict Cartesian certainties as the impossibility of the soul incarnate's survival.

31. This conceptual play on the dream-reality motif cannot fail to bring to mind Segismundo's famous words in *La vida es sueño*.

Segismundo: ¿Qué es la vida? Una ilusión,
        una sombra, una ficción.
        Y el mayor bien es pequeño,
        que toda la vida es sueño
        y los sueños, sueños son.

Calderón de la Barca, *Obras completas, Vol. I*, Aguilar (Madrid, 1959), p.387.

32. In his commentary on Garcilaso's Sonnet V, "mi alma os ha cortado a su medida" (l.10), Salinas states that the poet regards the beloved as "consubstantial with his soul". See Pedro Salinas, *Reality and the Poet in Spanish Poetry*, p.83. As in Note 9.

33. One is reminded of the lines from J. R. Jiménez -

¡Qué dulce esta inmensa trama!
Tu cuerpo con mi alma, amor
y mi cuerpo con tu alma.

J. R. Jiménez, *Segunda Antolojía*, "Diario de un poeta recién casado", No.17, ed. Leopoldo de Luis, Austral (Madrid, 1983), p.226.

The analogy of a 'trama' is extremely apt, as Salinas interweaves body and soul in a gradual, poetic process that leads to complete integration, the fabric of love. Not only do "alma y cuerpo" fuse within the boundaries of individual experience, but the lovers can no longer distinguish their own bodies and souls from each other's.

34. In a letter to Guillén, concerning the poem "Cero", Salinas says: "...el tema, en general, es la imposibilidad de realizar un destino en lo temporal". Quoting this letter in his book *La casa de Anteo*, Taurus (Madrid, 1985), Philip Silver reaches a blanket conclusion that -

...toda la poesía de Salinas, la amorosa inclusive, es una continua meditación acerca de 'la imposibilidad de realizar un destino en el tiempo'; sentencia pesimista que abarca la poesía, el amor, la cultura y la tecnología contemporánea (p.131).

This time-bound, pessimistic interpretation is not satisfactorily borne out by Salinas's love-poetry which, rather than admitting the limitations of mortality, sets out to transform received temporal and spatial definitions.

35. This evolving relationship between the lovers and time, is already hinted at in a letter from Salinas to Margarita Bonmatí in July 1915, with the words: "He aquí lo que es el tiempo, Margarita, algo que nos vence y algo que podemos vencer". *Cartas de amor a Margarita, 1912-1915*, Carta XXVI, p.97. As in Note 2.

36. *Cartas de amor a Margarita, 1912-1915*, Carta LIII, p.152. As in Note 2.

37.   Yo sé un himno gigante y extraño...   (l.1)
      Yo quisiera escibirle, del hombre
      domando el rebelde mezquino idioma,
      con palabras que fuesen a un tiempo
      suspiros y risas, colores y notas.   (ll.5-8, Rima No.1)

G. A. Bécquer, *Rimas*, Clásicos Castellanos (Madrid, 1975), p.11.

38. Steven Gilman, "El proemio a la voz a ti debida", in *Pedro Salinas*, ed. A. P. Debicki, El escritor y la crítica, Taurus (Madrid, 1976), pp.126-7.

39. Salinas's use of the term 'spiritual' in his letters to Guillén, as in much of his literary criticism, is characteristically loose: "la vida espiritual" seems to denote, for this poet, his innermost feelings, his sense of identity, his most intimate "yo".

> En fin, chico, esto de la política es uno de los elementos de perturbación y de incoherencia que es menester rechazar para que la vida espiritual no sea un caos completo. (6.6.30)

Christopher Maurer, "Sobre 'joven literatura' y política: cartas de Pedro Salinas y de Federico García Lorca, la Guerra Civil", in *Estelas, laberintos, nuevas sendas. Umamuno, Valle-Inclán, García Lorca, la Guerra Civil*, Co-Ord. Angel de Loureiro, Anthropos (Barcelona, 1988), p.300.

40. C. S. Lewis, *The Allegory of Love: A Study in Medieval Tradition*, Oxford University Press (Oxford, 1973), p.21.

41. By limiting his reading of the love cycle in this way, Robert Havard effectively excludes all prior evidence in Salinas's poetry and letters of an evolving conception of love as a metaphysical experience. See Robert Havard, *"Pedro Salinas and Courtly Love"*, *Bulletin of Hispanic Studies* LVI (1979), and "Pedro Salinas: the poetics of motion", *From Romanticism to Surrealism. Seven Spanish Poets*, University of Wales Press (Cardiff, 1988).

42. On reading Juan de la Cruz in August 1913, and thinking of his absent fiancée, Salinas is very aware of the similarities between the experiences recorded by the mystic, and his own feelings. In a letter date 20 July 1913 he writes:

> Y té juro, Margarita, que jamás he sentido, estando lejos de ti, una emoción, un amor tan inefable, tan infinito, como sentí ayer en este místico momento en que dejé de leer, y me puse a escuchar a mi corazón. Jamás te he querido tan apasionadamente, jamás he tenido

tan clara conciencia de un amor, era algo casi religioso, místico propiamente. (Carta XXV, p.96)

And in various other letters, Salinas draws explicit connections between his experience of love, and the nature of religious or mystical experience. For example:

> Los poetas que han amado mucho no han escrito de amor; lo han guardado dentro. Es decir, el amor les ha sugerido muchos cantos, es verdad, pero cantos trascendentales. (Carta XL, Madrid 1914, p.125). As in Note 2.

43. *Cántico espiritual*, pp.11-12. As in Note 19.

44. G. A. Bécquer, "Cartas literarias a una mujer", Carta IV, *Rimas y prosas*, Ediciones Rialp (Madrid, 1968), p.260.

45. Jorge Guillén coins the title of, "visionario seglar" in his essay on G. A. Bécquer: "Bécquer o lo inefable soñado", *Lenguaje y poesía*, Alianza (Madrid, 1983), p.113.

46. The quotation is taken from Salinas' preface to a selection of his poems, as published in Gerardo Diego's anthology, *Poesía española contemporánea 1931-34*, Taurus (Madrid, 1959).

47. Both the title and content of this poem are derived from Juan de la Cruz's *Noche oscura del alma*: "En una noche oscura / con ansias en amores, inflamadas / Oh, dichosa ventura! (ll.1-3, as in Note 19).

48. Commenting on the works of Garcilaso, el Conde de Salinas and Villamedina, Arthur Terry suggests that -

> ...poetry was not so much an art as an expression of an ideal of life, a possibility which would explain both the lack of contemporary influence in their love poems and the depth of feeling which they express.

Arthur Terry, Introduction to *An Anthology of Spanish Poetry 1500-1700, Part II, 1580-1700*, Pergamon Press (Oxford, London, 1968), p.xxviii.

49. Christopher Maurer stresses that Salinas's political involvement in the Second Republic was of a very private nature, characterised as much by modesty and discretion as by a distrust of ideological alignments.

Actividad privada. Firme rechazo de la coerción ideológica, de doctrinas impuestas. La política sería, para Salinas, una labor casi silenciosa, callada... Si no fuera por las cartas a Guillén, apenas quedaría testimonio escrito de su trabajo como fundador de la Universidad Internacional de Santander. El mismo silencio rodea su proyecto de editar, en edición triple, a los autores clásicos. (pp.308-9) As in Note 39.

50. See Christopher Maurer, p.304. As in Note 39.

51. See Christopher Maurer, p.303. As in Note 39.

Chapter III

Ausencia y presencia

Separation and Synthesis.

Separation is a complex issue for Salinas, paradoxically involving both synthesis and scission. This is especially true of his love poetry, where absence emerges as a predominant thematic concern. Because Salinas's definition of love necessitates the equal participation of body and soul, the beloved's physical absence represents a threat to love's fruition and fulfilment. Physical separation prevents the lovers from achieving their ideal of 'entereza', that sense of wholeness arrived at by the individual in union with the 'other'. However this is just one aspect of a complex theme which is riddled with paradox and contradiction. The condition of absence in itself presupposes and pre-contains a condition of presence; thus, every absence becomes a problematic absent presence.[1] Indeed, separation is presented in many of Salinas's poems as a rather circuitous route to ultimate union. Without disjunction there can be no sensation of re-unification, and the experience of absence at times serves to intensify the lovers' appreciation of each others' presence, of their togetherness.

"La Ausencia" figures in Salinas's poetry as early as *Seguro azar*, emerging as a significant thematic strain in *Fábula y signo*, and is rigorously explored in the love cycle, reaching a thematic climax that can truly be described as obsessive in

Largo lamento. This sharp crescendo of interest between the composition of *Fábula y signo* in the late 1920s, and that of *Largo lamento* in the mid-to-late 1930s, has provoked speculation as to the possible source of this melancholy condition of absence in the poet's life during this period. The problems underlying such speculation are manifold. Firstly, it rests on an assumption that all absence is negative *per se*; in addition to this, it confines consideration of possible influences on the poet's work to a short temporal period of less than ten years; and perhaps most importantly, it reads the condition of absence as solely referential to the beloved, thus limiting any reflection on what is a broad thematic area in Salinas's poetic development to the relatively narrow arena of the poet's sentimental life.

Certainly the whole question of absence is most thoroughly developed by Salinas in the context of the love relationship, but this need not preclude the influence of extra-amorous considerations. Is it not probable, for example, that the emotional and cultural shock induced by the urgent (and ultimately not so voluntary) exile from Spain in 1936, may have influenced Salinas's thoughts on the whole question of absence? For this poet, banishment from Spain to an alien culture and linguistic environment represented a temporary banishment from creative writing. At a profound level, the poet's inner dialogue with the creative self was silenced. Writing to Guillermo de Torre, Salinas describes this state of linguistic estrangement: "Vd., amigo mío..., no se da cuenta de que los que residimos en un país de lengua extraña somos dos veces desterrados".[2] Between 1937 and 1942, Salinas gives himself over to the production of literary criticism.[3] A reconciliation of his creative and critical voices is only fully realised in the presence of a living, breathing, Hispanic culture in Puerto Rico where he lived from 1943 to 1946. Exile, like separation fom the beloved, encourages the poet to re-define himself. Patria, like amada, becomes a symbol of a Paradise Lost, of an ideal state of integration with, and presence in, the other - in the broadest sense of

Salinas's phrase, "all that lives outside of the poet".[4] Birute Ciplijauskaite sums up the process whereby Salinas finds 'entereza' in exile with the phrase, "Salinas se completa en el destierro".[5]

While acknowledging the importance of these biographical factors and recognising that the emotional and cultural circumstances in which Salinas wrote undoubtedly influenced his work, it is not the intention of this study to present an unduly simplistic picture of his profoundly ambivalent treatment of the absence theme. There is an obvious temptation to somehow explain away Salinas's persistent examination of the inseparable conditions of absence and presence in biographical terms. While endeavouring not to fall into the trap of looking for direct correspondence of cause and effect between biographical data and the poetry itself, we can ascertain certain circumstances in Salinas's life which may have influenced the development of his ideas in this area, and the evolving patterns of emotional association that emerge in his complex psychological treatment of the "ausencia" theme. One such circumstance was the prolonged 'noviazgo' with his future wife Margarita Bonmatí, between 1912 and 1915, formative years for the young poet who was then in his early twenties. The relationship was conducted in a state of "ausencia", Margarita residing with her parents in Algeria while Salinas pursued his studies in Madrid and Paris. Another significant experience of separation in this poet's life was that of exile. In a letter to Dámaso Alonso dated 11 April 1951, Salinas alludes to his condition as exile in terms of painful separation:

> Sí señor; es absurdo todo esto. Y yo tampoco me echo a gemir (no soy ningún Cid que pueda permitirse esos lujos), pero casi, casi, cuando me veo metido en este mundo ajeno, y, por ahora, sin salida. Mucho me alegrará siempre saber que Vd. del otro lado de la puerta, sintió conmigo, una vez, todo lo absurdo de mi gran y aceptada enfermedad: la separación.[6]

His distress, even after twenty-five years in his adopted home, is still patent; it appears that Salinas suffered from an on-going sensation of "ausencia" until his death.

The quest for presence that colours much of Salinas's work, whether it be presence in the patria, the presence of the beloved, a divine presence, or that of the poetic impulse, is closely related to the quest for 'entereza'. Absence represents incompleteness, the absence of 'otherness', and is an impediment to self-realisation. "Distancia", "separación" and "ausencia" form a single semantic unit in much of Salinas's poetry: the absence of a beloved person, absence from a beloved place, are synonymous with the concept of distance, the physical space that separates two entities, be they lover and beloved, or poet and patria - "Distancia vista es / lejanía medida", (ll.6-7, "Los equívocos", Seg., p.119). Distance has no objective measure: it can only be quantified in terms of "lejanía", a state which implies relationship - the distance from another person or place. To experience distance is to know separation and absence.

This semantic fusion of absence, distance and separation is clearly delineated in the poet's mind as early as the composition of Seguro azar, (1924-28), and is expanded in the later love cycle, where distance can only be measured in terms of the vacuum left by beloved's physical absence.

> Pero lo insoportable   (l.38)
> es la distancia, es
> el hueco de tu cuerpo...
>   (ll.42-3, La materia no pesa, La voz, p.292)

The beloved's absence is expressed quite explicitly as a feeling of exile - not just from the beloved "tú" but also from the "yo" that is part of this relationship. The poet experiences feelings of displacement, despite the fact that he occupies the same physical space as he did with the beloved.

> Pero ahora,

¡qué desterrado, qué ausente
es estar donde uno está!   (ll.18-20, p.312)

Even prior to Salinas's direct experience of exile after 1936, the beloved's presence
is perceived as a passport to an emotional and spiritual homeland:

Porque sé que adonde estuve
sólo
se va contigo, por ti.
(ll.40-2, A ti sólo se llega / por ti, *La voz*, p.313)

Her absence is keenly felt in spatial terms as a "hueco" (l.43, p.292), but time is
also measured in relation to absence or presence: a set of temporal equations
underlies many of Salinas's love poems. Thus, "ayer" can be read as the memory
of past presence; "mañana" the anticipation of future presence; "hoy", the
experience of absence in the present:

En un siempre se hinca:
el tiempo, que era un siempre,
partido: ayer, mañana.
Y aquella sombra sola,
única, por la arena,
truncada en dos: tú y yo.
(ll.4-9, Los despedidos, *Seg.*, p.157)

Time is cleft, just like the single shadow cast by entwined lovers when they part,
there can be no continuity in its passage without the constant presence of the
beloved. Indeed it may be said that the time-scale of the love cycle is wholly
dependent on the condition of togetherness or separateness. This is evident in
Salinas's manipulation of temporal expression. Each tense implies either absence
or presence, as in the title "Fue es duro como piedra", (*Largo lamento*, p.587),
where the past tense recalls the past presence of the beloved, thereby heightening
the poet's awareness of her absence in the here and now. However, Salinas departs
from the purely temporal function of the past tense, expanding its meaning to
encompass the beloved's absence, and evoke the consoling powers of memory.

Fue es duro como piedra.
Pero a veces las almas
cuando no tienen más
descansan en un "fue".   (ll.1-4)

In the same way the future tense looks forward both emotionally and temporally, becoming an expression of hope in the possibility of future presence:

Otras veces las almas
esperan, esperanzas
que se llaman "va a ser"
o "sí, será", o "ya viene".   (ll.8-11, *Largo*, p.587)

Faced with the dilemma of absence, and the consequent loss of 'entereza', the poet strives to recover presence from the past through the power of memory, defined elsewhere by Salinas as "el recuerdo, forma psicológica del tiempo".[7] Memory salvages the past from oblivion; it renders past, present. By committing past event to memory, he seems to outwit Time's inexorable motion. To quote Salinas's own comments again - "Pero he aquí la memoria, que lleva mucho poder, que detiene a las cosas, las para".[8] Memory, in other words, gives us the illusion of stopping time in its tracks. In an early poem "Tú, mía", Salinas fixes the beloved's memory at one particular moment, one date: "Tú eres ya una fecha sola" (l.23, *Fáb.*, p.194). The effect resembles that of a freeze-frame in a motion picture; memory has resisted the actual passage of time. Unfortunately, this applies to unpleasant and pleasant experiences alike: "Hay que vivirse en la memoria, aunque sea pena, porque la pena es cuando ya lo demás cesó de ser, ha sido".[9]

When the beloved is absent, leaving no material evidence of her presence, the image imprinted in the lover's mind is the only living proof of the reality of the past. His acute pain at losing the beloved and the vividness of her memory fuse, so that the very sensation of pain triggers a response of recall. The pain of absence at least, is present, living proof of previous joy -

La gran prueba, a lo lejos,

de que existió, que existe,
de que me quiso, sí,
de que aún la estoy queriendo.
(ll.26-9, No quiero que te vayas.., *La voz*, p.319)

Even Salinas's reflections on the pain of separation, of lost love, are characterised by a relentless play on tenses. The change in the poet's circumstances from past to present is traced by the temporal sequences of "existió - existe" (1.27), and "quiso - estoy queriendo" (1.29). The transference of the subject of 'querer' from the third person to the first, reflects how past mutual love has given way to the unrequited love of the lover for the absent beloved. Remembrance of better times provides some consolation for the bereft lover. Yet the stark contrast of past definite with future indefinite tenses lends this poetry an agonising edge. Memories can console, they can sustain contact with the past, but they cannot provide hope for the future.[10] The lover tries to convince himself, in a series of rhythmic temporal contrasts, that -

No importa que no te tenga,
no importa que no te vea.
Antes te abrazaba,
antes te miraba.   (ll.1-4, Eterna presencia, *Largo*, p.460)

And there are moments of affirmation, when it seems that memory allows the poet to possess the past utterly, permanently, in such a way that - unlike the beloved - it can never be taken from him. He looks back on the relationship as "un nudo" (l.1) which has now been untied. However -

el recuerdo de ese nudo
en que los dos fuimos uno,
porque queríamos serlo,
ha de durar, sin atarnos,
no ya como nudo, no,
sino como lazo eterno.
(ll.45-50, ¿Por qué querer deshacer?, *Largo*, p.594)

Unlike life in the present, memory is no longer subject to change: immutable, it captures the now past unity of the lovers for posterity.

Memory empowers the poet to re-create the past, to conjure up what is absent so vividly that at times it feels almost physically palpable. The materialisation of memory in the title of "La memoria en las manos" (*Largo lamento*, pp.469-71), brings home to the reader the sheer physical immediacy of the poet's recollections. The beloved's remembered presence may be invisible, but it is no less palpable for all that. This "mano / memoria" association is sustained, and taken a stage further in another poem from the same collection, "No me sueltes":

> el cálido recuerdo de una mano
> está siempre estrechándote a lo lejos,
> y soltarlo porque es pura memoria,
> es más traición que abandonar un tacto.   (ll.91-4, *Largo*, pp.541-2)

This time it is the beloved's turn to remember her past lover, whose touch is all the more compelling for being the subtle remembrance of an embrace, rather than its physical reality. At times it seems well nigh impossible to forget the past: the beloved's presence persists in her lover's consciousness, and the inescapable nature of memory is the subject of some of Salinas's more playful poems, such as "Hallazgo" from *Fábula y signo*:

> Te dejaré
> como olvidada
> y pensando en otros cosas
> para no pensar en ti,
>
> pero pensándote a ti
> en ellas, disimulada.   (ll.4-9, p.171)

The beloved permeates every area of thought, she cannot be banished to the realms of oblivion. Secure in the knowledge that she is safely housed in his memory, the lover feels free to toy with the dangerous notion of absence, even feigning forgetfulness.

However in another poem, again from *Fábula y signo*, Salinas seems to suggest quite seriously that in order to remember the beloved, he must first forget her. The thematic structure of "Vida segunda" is based on an unspoken distinction between memory as the ability to re-create through recall and imagination, and the poet's potential for invention and original creation.

> Sí, tú naciste al borrárseme
> tu forma.
> Mientras yo te recordé ¡qué muerta estabas! (ll.1-3, p.188)

The poet sets himself the hypothetical task of creating the beloved as his own conception, giving her a 'second life'. In order to execute this task he must of course forget her 'first life', or actual self:

> perdida en la desmemoria
> y te tuve que inventar...   (ll.20-1)
> a mis medidas de dentro.   (l.29, p.188)

Memory acts upon past experience in two starkly contrasting ways: primarily, it renders the past more immediately accessible - even creating the sensation of tangible presence. But it can also, as the above poem exemplifies, extract the past from the realms of empiricism, internalising it, rendering it irrevocably subjective. Salinas repeatedly expresses dissatisfaction with an empirically replete world.[11] For this very reason, he defines the poet's objective as "the creation of a new reality within the old reality".[12] At times the sensory experience of his coming together with the beloved is insufficient: he must internalise the experience in order to possess it completely, commit it to memory and eventually re-create it in his own image -

> Ha sido, ocurrió, es verdad, (l.1)
> No.
> Tengo que vivirlo dentro

me lo tengo que soñar.   (ll.19-21, *La voz*, p.225)

In a playful inversion of this process of internalisation, the beloved, in turn, absorbs the poet, so that he becomes part of her memory and has access to a past he has not lived:

> recordaré
> estrellas que no vi, que ella miraba,
> y nieve que nevaba allí en su cielo...
>   (ll.27-9, Qué alegría, vivir.., *La voz*, p.256)

The tone is entirely illogical, a playful evocation of how intimacy can create the impression of first-hand knowledge of another's past. And yet, it is interesting to note that while the beloved can be utterly possessed by the poet's memory, he remains wholly autonomous and active, even when he is technically a mere fragment of her memory, and the object of her reflections. The poet-lover does not want to be possessed by her memory, so much as to raid her thoughts, and penetrate her innermost feelings. By achieving the status of memory in her mind, he is also shielded from the changes of fortune endured by all matter. He would be the very rose that he presents to her as a token, which outlasts its organic form in the beloved's memory:

> vivida en ti, por ti,
> en su olor, en su tacto.
> Hasta que tú la asciendas
> sobre su deshojarse
> a un recuerdo de rosa.
> (ll.30-4, Regalo, don, entrega.., *La voz*, pp.263-4)

The materialising and internalising tendencies of memory are manifest in physical symptoms such as fatigue after love-making, reminding the poet-lover of the beloved's continued presence or "traspresencia" (l.5), despite separation:

> ...la fervorosa
> negación de tu ausencia, tu recuerdo,

va por mi ser entero, por mis venas,
fluye dentro de mí, y es el cansancio.
(ll.23-26, ¿No sientes el cansancio..?, *Raz.*, p.382)

This fatigue is a form of evidence of past experience, now internalised so that it is physically present, permeating his entire body, intravenously.

The process of internalisation through memory is not exclusively applicable to the beloved, but to other empirical realities. In the same way, the sea of San Juan, in *El Contemplado* is captured by the eye of perception and stored in the mind's eye: a process of enamourment between 'contemplado' and 'contemplador', similar to that between 'amada' and 'amante' is enacted.

Lo que se ha mirado así,
día a día, enamorándolo,
nunca se pierde
porque ya está enamorado.
Míralo aunque se haya ido. (ll.69-73, Var. V, p.621)

The exercise of memory is just one method of avoiding the void produced by absence. Another antidote to this problem, as already indicated in "Vida segunda", is by exercising the poetic imagination.[13] "Luz de la noche", also from *Fábula y signo*, is a rather complex poem built around a paradoxical system of conceits equating sleep with light and wakefulness with darkness. In this instance the beloved is not physically absent, yet her peaceful slumber is felt by the wakeful lover to put distance between them; they no longer seem to inhabit the same space or time. His response to this situation is -

que pienso en el otro lado
de tu sueño, donde hay luz
que yo no veo.   (ll.24-6, p.210)

He tries, through sheer dint of imagination, to penetrate her sleep, to share the daylight of her dreamworld, and so cross the boundaries of experience that separate them. At moments such as this, absence can be seen as a poetically fruitful frame

of mind, fuelling the poetic imagination. Distance can even inspire: this positive
nuance is afforded to the condition of absence by Salinas's use of the term
"ensueño", a term closely associated with the poetically fertile frame of mind
aspired to by Romantic poets -

> los cristales sutiles
> de distancia y ensueño
> de que está hecha la ausencia.
>> (ll.59-61, El dolor, *Raz*., p.428)

Unfortunately, these instances of inspirational absence are few and far
between: the overriding feeling is one of loss, which the poet strives to overcome
through the mental processes of memory and anticipation. From the starting-point
of present absence, the poet can derive consolation from either of two temporal
perspectives: looking backward to the memory of past presence; or looking
forward, in anticipation of renewed presence and the ultimate 'entereza' brought
by the lovers' reunification in the future - "de una ausencia que pronto /
acabará
en presencia" (ll.74-5, *Largo*, p.553). Any realisation of these joint aspirations is
utterly dependent upon the beloved's continued presence in the future: even
linguistic expressions of tomorrow only acquire semantic value in this context. The
word "mañana" is therefore "ingrávida" (l.3), "sin alma y sin cuerpo" (l.4), until
spoken by the beloved, giving credence to her future presence:

> dijiste: "Yo, mañana..."
> Y todo se pobló
> de carne y de banderas. (ll.9-11, Mañana, *La voz*, p.229)

It seems, on occasion, that the promise of the beloved's future presence eclipses
her presence in the here and now. Such insecurity contrasts sharply with the
confidence of the poet's later relationship with 'the other' as embodied in the sea
of San Juan and expressed in the poems of *El Contemplado*: physical absence is

no longer feared, nor is the continuation of the relationship entirely dependent on physical presence.

> ¿Conservar
> un amor entre los brazos?
> No. En el aire de los ojos,
> entre el vivir y el recuerdo...
> (ll.59-62, Var V, *El Cont.*, p.620)

The expression of future action can be intrinsically indefinite in the Spanish use of the subjunctive, which, in the following example from *Razón de amor*, creates an ambience of suspended emotion, as the lover awaits a definite presence. He eagerly anticipates the completion and 'entereza' which only the beloved can give him: "todo / esto que nada es.." (ll.10-11), "espera su cumplirse, cuando llegues" (l.13, p.386). The anticipation of her presence has the effect of intensifying experience, compressing the poet's vision to focus on details in an almost obsessive manner. Here, he can think only of her lips:

> Todo es labios, los míos y los tuyos,
> hoy separados...   (ll.14-15)
> beso será, se encontrarán en beso,
> dado por esos labios ardorosos
> que se llaman la ausencia, cuando acaba.(ll.23-25, *Raz.*, p.386)

With the syntactic manipulation necessary to produce an effect of hyperbaton, the separation of l.15 is not fully resolved until l.24. The kiss of l.22 is still only a future reality, "beso será", and certainty that absence will give way to presence is only finally established when the indicative of "cuando acaba" resolves the earlier subjunctive of l.13, "cuando llegues". The poem also raises an intriguing linguistic point: can experience be named before it has been lived? How can the poet describe a still unknown future? Salinas only names "ausencia" with the wisdom of hindsight from the secure standpoint of reunification in the present, thereby banishing it squarely and safely to the past.

Conventional temporal sequences break down, as is so often the case in Salinas's poetry, so that the two principal techniques for evading absence, memory and anticipation, begin to merge. In a curious chronological inversion, Salinas presents us with memory as an indicator of the future rather than a record of the past. He cannot think of his time with the beloved as a past event; cannot furnish it with linguistic signifiers of the past such as past participles; "nuestra vida / no parece vivida" (ll.35-6, *La voz*, p.323). The poet is reluctant to define their life together in terms of memory, committing it to the past. He prefers to think of it as ever latent, not recalled but predicted.

Not only does memory act as a pointer to the future, there are also cases in Salinas's love-cycle where anticipation poses as memory: one example is "Salvación por el cuerpo", from *Razón de amor*, where the future comprises unrecorded memories and presages of a future past -

> se puebla de recuerdos no tenidos,
> le recorren presagios sonrosados
> de aquel rosado bulto que tú eras.   (ll.110-12, p.421)

Again the chronological to-ing and fro-ing is significant. We begin with a reference to the beloved's anticipated presence in the future, "estarás" (l.108); which is then defined as a yet unlived past - unremembered memories - (l.110); and the final temporal oxymoron of "presagios" "que tú eras" (ll.111-12). This deliberate confusion of past and future tenses is reiterated in another poem from *Razón de amor*, again dealing with the comparable natures of memory and anticipation, and their mutual instrumentality in the evasion of absence. This time the beloved's presence is defined as - "el recuerdo de tu planta un día / sobre la arena que llamamos tiempo" (ll.23-4, p.348). Where Longfellow's notorious mixed metaphor of "footsteps in the sands of time" was intended to express permanence, Salinas's intention is to highlight times's unerring forward motion: all that will remain of today's physical presence tomorrow is a footprint;

a metaphor for memory. However it also serves the poet as a metaphor for the future: "Su anhelado futuro / tiene la forma exacta de una huella" (ll.33-4, Antes, vivías por el aire, p.348). In the first instance the footprint is evidence of a path already walked; in the latter, it points to a possible route to the future; one metaphor serves two functions and resists the chronological distinctions of past and future.

Salinas's yearning for presence is at times expressed in terms which transcend the limits of conventional sentimental experience. Both ontological and emotional aspirations underpin the anticipation of presence. In the love-cycle, the beloved not only represents the path to emotional fulfilment but symbolises all 'otherness', all that the poet lacks in order to achieve self-realisation and experience 'entereza'. There is a distinct implication that the poet looks to the beloved to fill a space in his 'soul' or inner being that is vacant, awaiting occupation; an implication that is borne out by the lines -

> un gran espacio blanco
> azul, en mí, no acepta
> más que los vuelos tuyos,
> los pasos de tus pies...
> (ll.16-19, No te detengas nunca, *Raz.*, p.369)

Allusions to blue and white airy spaces, to the beloved's flights, lend an other-worldly quality to the scene. The beloved walks with human tread, but nonetheless represents all that is other-worldly and 'other' than himself.

The apparent perversity of the following lines stems from the same hypothesis: that the beloved brings to the poet all that is not readily accessible to him in his own consciousness.

> Tú ya sabes que yo,
> como siempre te espero
> nunca atiendo a las cartas
> ni al teléfono.
> (ll.1-4, Ruptura de las cosas, *Largo*, p.509)

Mundane methods of communication will not establish contact with these mysterious qualities which she represents. And if the poet lives in a state of perpetual expectation, he asks himself: "¿Por qué eres sorpresa?" (1.2, Si te espero siempre, *Largo*, p.590). The answer is that it is precisely because she comes from beyond the poet's ken; because her presence will always be 'other' than his.

In his exploration of the 'ausencia' theme, Salinas does not stop at the levels of evading or coping with absence, but strives to penetrate the essential nature of the experience itself, which emerges as a deeply baffling sensation of perceiving what is not. This striving after essence leads, in turn, to a radical redefining of absence and separation. Implicit in every separation is the presage of a reunion: whether we read separation as synthesis or schism is therefore a question of perspective and emphasis. One rather surprising result of this poetic re-evaluation is that the 'entereza' of the individual and/or the couple can survive separation and absence. In the love relationship presented by Salinas's poetry, temporary absence becomes a means of continuous renewal.[14] The young poet can therefore address his absent novia as an "Ensueño constante y renovada", and repeatedly asserts the interrelatedness of separation and union in his subseqent love poetry.[15] Every departure predicts a return, and absence is simply a rather circuitous route to eventual presence.

> la ausencia, ese largo
> rodeo
> que das para volver.
> (ll.41-3, Apenas te has marchado.., *Raz.*, p.393)

The delaying tactic of hyperbaton, together with the circumlocutory insertion of an extra line purely to house "rodeo", all enhance the discovery of a new, positive definition of separation as return.

In order to preserve that vital sense of 'otherness', temporary absence is necessary. Just as familiarity robs "las cosas" of their 'otherness', it also erodes the quality of strangeness that is so vital to the poetic imagination, and to the constant renewal of love. Periodic partings, therefore, allow the lovers to recover the sense of novelty they experienced on their first encounter:

Por eso nos marchamos.
Se deshizo el abrazo,
se apartaron los ojos,
dejaron de mirarse
para buscar el mundo
donde nos encontráramos.
(ll.20-5, ¡Sensación de retorno!, *Raz.*, p.349)

By renewing the intensity of their awareness of 'otherness', temporary separation provides an emotional insurance policy for the lovers. Salinas goes as far as to suggest that by allowing space to exist between them, they will draw closer, finding deeper connections than the physical, until a new concept of togetherness is arrived at:

...sólo
puedes estar junto a mí
cuando sientes muy abiertos
para irte, para quedarte,
los rumbos y los caminos.
(ll.29-33, ¿Te acuerdas del laberinto?, *Largo*, pp.565-6)

True union and 'entereza' can only grow from discrete entities, who through mutual cognition, overcome the boundaries of individual personality, arriving at a state of integration so complete that it represents a new joint entity, the sum of two distinct parts. This requires total submersion in their differences - the qualities that distinguish each individual from the other. The love relationship forces lovers to acknowledge these differences (a form of separation), in order to then embrace them (re-unification, integration):

Y al final, el hallazgo,
el contacto, la nueva
separación vencida,
la unión pura brotando

de lo que desunía.
(ll.36-40, ¡Gloria a las diferencias!, *Raz.*, p.379)

Having discovered the potentially positive nature of separation, the poet takes the next logical step of seeking out this condition, of creating absence in order to regenerate a frame of mind that is poetically fruitful.[16] The sensation of absence can be so bitter-sweet that on occasion the poet chooses to overlook the beloved's physical presence and conjure up instead the condition of absence -

Y tengo que creer
aunque palpitas en lo más cercano
- sólo porque tu cuerpo no se ve -
en la vaga ficción de estar yo solo.
(ll.24-7, Tan convencido estoy.., *Raz.*, p.403)

Salinas exploits the fact that darkness conceals the beloved's physical form, in order to sense an internalised, immaterial presence.

Any redefinition of separation will by extension affect the nature of farewells and partings. "Los adioses" form a motif running through almost all Salinas's poetry, from *Seguro azar* to *Todo más claro*. Here again, Salinas upsets an inherited semantic order. Generally "los adioses" are understood as the verbal expression of the particular point in time and space where people part: here, they are more likely to indicate a point of encounter than one of separation. The experience of parting generally cuts like a knife, wounds, inducing feelings of loss and diminishment. In this early treatment of the parting theme, there is knife-edged separation, as the sharpness of the autumnal air signals the end of a shared season -

...El acero
del otoño, la vida
nos parte en dos mitades.   (ll.15-17, p.157)

The difference here is that the slicing of one whole entity into two halves does not necessarily signify a fatal loss of unity and presence. There is probably an implicit play on the popular expression for lovers as each other's 'media naranja', and their togetherness is stressed by the final, redeeming image of life as ripened fruit -

> La vida
> toda entera, dorada,
> redonda, allí colgando
> en la rama de agosto
> donde tú lo cogiste.
> (ll.18-22, Los despedidos, *Seg.*, p.157)

It is difficult to read this poem without thinking of Salinas's partings from Margarita Bonmatí at the close of the season in the summer resort of Santa Pola, Alicante. Autumn brings separation, but it is also a time of harvest, when lovers reap the fruit of a "vida entera", the wholeness they create in their togetherness, despite seasonal separation.

The wonderful irony of every farewell is that, while it announces the commencement of a separation, it can only be enacted in a state of presence. And so every 'adiós' prolongs presence, postponing the eventual absence it postulates. Salinas maximises this paradox to such an extreme that farewells can actually rescue the lovers from possible separation and absence:

> Juntos ya siempre por la despedida
> inseparables
> al borde mismo - adiós - del separarse.
> (ll.20-2, Los adioses, *Fáb.*, p.205)

The very act of saying goodbye is a form of procrastination, interrupting the inevitable sequence of events that forces the lovers apart - just like the syntactic interjection of "adiós" in l.22.[17] There is no denying the intensity of the experience of parting, as captured by these poems. Perhaps it is because such moments are experienced with great emotional intensity that Salinas concludes the above poem with a metaphoric equation of life as a confrontation with farewells: "vivir: / mirarnos en el adiós" (ll.58-9, p.207). In order to live fully, embracing all experience in its entirety, absence must be reckoned with as well as presence, separation as well as union.

If every separation sets the scene for a future coming together, then the definition of love as "un largo adiós que no se acaba" (1.2), is not as absurd as it might first appear. If the theory that every parting constitutes a prolonged coming together is taken to its logical conclusion, then "lo más seguro es el adiós" (*Raz.*, pp.337-8). In this poem, Salinas also highlights the fundamental truism that "vivir, desde el principio, es separarse" (1.3), a point borne out by both biology and psychology. The division of cells or fission as a means of reproduction; the separation of new life from the mother's at birth; and with the birth of human consciousness, an awareness of separate identity, the distinction between self and 'other'. Love's greatest achievement is that it resists this universal law - "la primera condena de la vida"(1.12). The great irony here, is that only by acting out the process of a neverending goodbye are the lovers shielded from the ultimate destiny of finding themselves alone. Each "adiós" verbally and socially ritualises separation, thereby diminishing its sting:

> Si se estrechan las manos, si se abraza,
> nunca es para apartarse,
> es porque el alma ciegamente siente
> que la forma posible de estar juntos
> es una despedida larga, clara.
> (ll.32-6, Serás, amor.., *Raz.*, p.337)

The whole purpose of separation here, seems to be re-unification: one is not possible without the other, just as absence cannot be conceived without knowledge of presence, its binary opposite. The mere articulation of the word "adiós", inspires the anticipation of return -

> Se te vio en tu marchar
> el revés: tu venida,
> vibrante en el adiós.
> (ll.44-6, Apenas te has marchado, *Raz.*, p.393)

The beloved's presence is already "vibrante", vividly emanating from her departure - so much so, that she is visualised re-tracing her steps like a film running backwards.

Love's capacity to effect transformation is one of Salinas's most constant preoccupations in the love cycle. Through a process of transmutation, farewells are changed quite mysteriously into welcomes: "nuestro tacto / de adiós se nos trasmuta en bienvenida" (ll.49-50, *Largo*, p.482). Separation and togetherness cannot be defined without mutual reference, and eventually lovers find that they can -

> transformar las despedidas tanto
> diciendo adiós, que nadie se separe.
> (ll.95-6, Dueña de ti misma, *Largo*, p.488)

This degree of transformation results from Salinas's persistent confusion of parting and re-unification; there can be no absolute separation. The process of semantic fusion already seen to apply to the terms "alma" and "cuerpo", is here applied to "ausencia" and "presencia". By breaking down semantic boundaries, Salinas opens up areas of experience and sensation that do not lend themselves to antithetical definition; they are mutually inclusive rather than exclusive. The love experience in particular inspires a quest for entirety of vision, where experience of one condition does not preclude the simultaneous experiencing of its binary opposite.

An added advantage of this all-embracing vision is that it allows Salinas to draw on diverging aspects of any given literary theme or motif. Daybreak forms part of a rich repertoire of literary settings in the European love lyric, and is conventionally associated with the parting of lovers.[18] However it is also, as J. G. Cummins points out, the setting for many lyrics that celebrate togetherness, and Salinas draws on both threads of the tradition. In some of his poems, dawn represents the intrusion of the outside world upon the lovers' intimate world of their own invention: daylight, in these cases, represents the demands and obligations to be met separately, and the subsequent necessity to part. One

168

example from *Razón de amor*, commences with the ominous statement that
"Sabemos, sí, que hay luz..." -

> La resistimos, obstinadamente
> en la prolongación, cuarto cerrado,
> de la felicidad oscura
> caliente, aún, en los cuerpos de la noche. (ll.7-10, p.424)

The warmth of their bodies retains the darkness of night, (an original example of
synaesthesia), which they strive to prolong. Daylight proffers a world that existed
prior to their love, a 'reality' the lovers prefer to discard in favour of the highly
personal 'reality' that commenced with that love -

> esta noche, gran madre de nosotros:
> vamos hacia el hacer.
> Nuestro existir de antes
> presagio era...   (ll.75-8, *Raz.*, p.426)

Their baptism to the new life of love is celebrated through total submersion in
darkness.

In other instances, although dawn may reveal the beloved's absence, it is
not the direct cause of her departure: darkness has concealed her absence, allowing
the poet to imagine that she is present, until daybreak forces the truth of absence
onto his consciousness. This is yet another case of Salinas's enthusiasm for
creative contradiction in the love cycle. The cover of darkness obliterates absence
and presence alike, but here Salinas executes a perfect inversion of the kind of
contrived absence we previously encountered in lines such as -

> Y tengo que creer
> aunque palpitas en lo más cercano
> - sólo porque tu cuerpo no se ve -
> en la vaga ficción de estar yo solo.
>   (ll.24-7, Tan convencido estoy.., *Raz.*, p.403)

Darkness now sustains the illusion of presence by disguising the true nature of distance:

> De noche la distancia
> parece sólo oscuridad, tiniebla
> que no separa sino por los ojos. (ll.1-3, p.390)

However when dawn breaks, the physical reality of absence is undeniable: "es la luz, la distancia" (l.26), drawing an equation between light and separation that is in keeping with the strictly conventional Courtly "aubade". An additional equation is introduced, of "luz" and "amor", which seems to undermine the original conceit of light as a source of separation:

> los anhelosos huecos
> que amor y luz abrieron en las almas.
> (ll.36-7, De noche la distancia, *Raz.*, p.391)

Love exposes great hollow spaces in the soul in the same way that light reveals the vacuums concealed by darkness; these are spaces which can only be filled by the beloved "tú". The beloved, yet again, emerges as a source of fulfilment: without her, the lover cannot achieve love's desired end of self-realisation and 'entereza' in the 'other'.

Salinas's "aubades", like his "adioses", tend to deviate from conventional expectations. Like the farewells in his lyrics, dawn is more often a source of joy than of sorrow. The tone of the circuitous "El sueño es una larga / despedida de ti" (*La voz a ti debida*, pp.265-6), is characteristically ironic. The presence of two beloveds in this poem allows for mischievous ambiguity. Initially, there is the beloved of his dreams, to whom he must bid farewell as dawn breaks - "Te abrazo por vez última: / eso es abrir los ojos" (ll.23-4, p.265). But he loses this "tú" only to recover another, his daylit, material companion of the waking world. The lover is saved any anguish by the more than compensatory presence of -

> tu cuerpo limpio, exacto,

> ofreciéndome en labios
> el gran error del día. (ll.48-50, *La voz*, p.266)

The irony of daylight's "error" is twofold: firstly it subverts the traditional associations of dawn with separation; secondly, it toys with the ambiguous status of each beloved - which is 'real' which 'unreal', which authentic and which 'erroneous'? (Error is best interpreted here as implying the absence of authenticity, as something counterfeit). Above all, the poem effectively demonstrates Salinas's ability to exploit more than one facet of any given theme or motif, in one poem. This plurality of perspective, sometimes dizzying, indicates a reluctance to settle for semantic singularity. The same reluctance resists fixed poetic form, opting instead for free verse, and illustrates how the quest for 'entereza' extends beyond the thematic content of Salinas's poetry, and is also present in his poetic expression.

Presence and absence are both familiar territory to the lovers, but somewhere in between these two conditions there is a grey area which is disorientating, because it is recognisable neither as separation nor union - "Amor: distancias, vaivén / sin parar. / En medio del camino, nada" (ll.7-9, "La difícil", *Seg.*, p.127). The poet-lover experiences distress when the beloved is in transit - neither in the space that he associates with her absence from him, (a presence elsewhere), nor in the same space that he occupies; she cannot be physically or psychologically located - "Saliste de tu ausencia / y aún no te veo y no sé dónde estás" (ll.5-6, p.274). He cannot define himself as either in or out of her presence, and finds himself paralysed in a state of "absoluta espera inmóvil", (l.30, *La voz*, p.274).[19]

The lover's concern with absence or presence in Salinas's love poetry, ultimately has less to do with the beloved's physical manifestation, and more to do with the relative absence or presence of her love for him:

> Porque te veo ahora
> mientras no te me quites el amor
> porque no te veré ya nunca más
> el día que te vayas,
> tú   (11.19-23, Cuando te digo "alta".., *Raz.*, p.380)

Once this love is withdrawn, despair makes anticipation impossible, and subsequently it ceases to function as a technique for alleviating the pain of absence. Memory also fails to compensate: as an early poem "Amada exacta" suggests, the beloved was designed "para la presencia pura" (1.6), and she cannot be accurately re-constructed by memory, whose obvious shortcomings are enumerated in a tragi-comic complaint:

> Todo yo a recomponerte
> con sólo recuerdos vagos:
> te equivocaré la voz,
> el cabello, ¿cómo era?
> te pondré los ojos falsos.
>   (ll.7-11, Amada exacta, *Seg.*, p.142)

The only possible rendering of this "amada exacta" is her actual presence; anything else is a travesty. This constitutes an obvious contradiction of Salinas's evocation in other poems of memory's ability to conjure up past experience, and typifies his semantic attitude, which is flexible to the point of being improvisatory.[20]

In the light of so many conflicting views on the capacity of human memory to compensate for absence, we can quickly surmise that for Salinas, memory's power to recover the past is by no means constant, and sometimes only increases the awareness of what is lacking -

> porque el recuerdo es
> la pena de sí mismo,
>
> el dolor del tamaño,
> del tiempo...
> (ll.37-40, ¿Fue como beso o llanto?, *Raz.*, p.351)

Occasionally, the beloved seems to elude memory utterly, as though she had never been materially present, as though she were not composed of matter, but pure essence:

> Tan pura ya, tan sin pruebas
> que cuando no vivas más
> yo no sé en qué voy a ver
> que vivías...   (ll.32-5, La sin pruebas, *Fáb.*, p.208)

When his memories fail to provide consolation, the poet faces the prospect of unrecoverable loss, of "olvido" and oblivion. The above lines from *Fábula y signo* demonstrate a consciousness of this void as a distinct possibility even in Salinas's early works. The threat of irretrievable absence increases as the love poetry develops chronologically, and is most prevalent in *Largo lamento*, as memory fails to call the beloved to mind. Likewise, forgetfulness obliterates her memories of their love:

> Y las has olvidado, porque nadie,
> con una ingratitud común a todos,
> se acuerda a la mañana
> de las telas que el cuerpo nos guardaron...
>   (ll.130-3, Como ya no me quieres.., *Largo*, p.519)

The tone of this poem is singularly resigned: there is no personal rancour, no bitterness, but the poet has clearly given up any hope for the survival of feeling. The beloved's forgetfulness, he stoically reflects, is only human nature. In an almost pathetic example of grasping after straws, the solitary lover tries to convince himself that the remembrance of anything - even of forgetfulness - is better than no remembrance at all:

> Recordar el olvido,
> aunque no tenga rostro, nombre, cuerpo,
> es casi no olvidar lo que se olvida.
> (ll.20-22, ¡Qué olvidadas están las sortijas!, *Largo*, p.498)

The interjection of "casi" and the air of inevitability inherent in the impersonal "se olvida", gives the lie to any self-deception by metaphysics.

Because of love's constant need for regeneration, we find that presence in the present tends to project forward, semantically and temporally anxious to secure future presence. Salinas's poetic ear is highly sensitised to temporal nuance. Like Antonio Machado, he writes from the standpoint that language and thought are inextricably connected with our perception of time. Every concept implicitly occupies its own position in time; absence requires a prior knowledge of presence; presence is always faced with a possible future of absence, the antonym it precontains. Remembering the past, predicting the future: all the language we deploy in association with absence and presence is heavily laden with temporal values. The very inception of presence already looks ahead to a time of absence -

> En el primer encuentro
> con la luz, con los labios,
> el corazón percibe la congoja
> de tener que estar ciego y sólo un día.
> (ll.4-7, Serás, amor.., *Raz.*, p.337)

Even when the desired presence has arrived the poet is incredulous, and cannot accept that such good fortune can last. There is always a nagging awareness that absence inheres in every presence.

Another uncharacteristically melancholy poem from *La voz a ti debida*, "No preguntarme nada", postulates the rather perverse thesis that the beloved's physical presence in the here and now is no more and no less than proof of her absence in the future. Indeed, the only beloved he can be sure of is the one who is absent now, and who therefore abides permanently as a possible presence in the future:

> Mi única amante ya siempre,
> y yo a tu lado, sin ti,
> Yo solo con la verdad. (ll.24-6, *La voz*, p.306)

This conception of a presence that predicts absence, and of an absence implying presence, leads to considerable semantic confusion.[21] The prophetic lines from an early poem -

> Tu presencia y tu ausencia
> sombra son una de otra
> sombras me dan y quitan, (ll.9-11, *Pres*. No.5, p.57)

- are developed both thematically and linguistically in the collections of poetry to follow, until absence and presence become virtually interchangeable.[22] This is the case in the lines "¡Qué paseo de noche / con tu ausencia a mi lado!" (ll.1-2, *La voz*, p.289) where the physicality of the beloved's absence makes it a valid substitute for her presence. This device of materialisation as a source of consolation for the beloved's absence, pervades Salinas's love poetry. The fact that absence acquires a physically perceptible presence is an indication of how intensely it is lived by the poet. In his probing examination of the terms "ausencia" and "presencia", Salinas reveals how they encroach shamelessly upon each other's territory, until seeming to occupy one single semantic space.

If absence and presence are no longer semantically distinct in Salinas's poetic scheme, can either be an absolute condition? As early as *Presagios*, the notion of absolute absence is mooted in "la divina mentira de estar solo" (l.15, "Soledad, soledad, tú me acompañas", p.65); presence is always implied. By the same token, absolute presence eludes the poet again and again, as absence hovers, never far away. In the search for absolute presence, we encounter references to the all-pervasiveness of the beloved, whose presence extends "más allá de" the boundaries of her own physicality, to inhabit the natural environment:

> un amor vuelto estrellas, calma, mundo,
> salvado ya del miedo
> al cadáver que queda si se olvida.
> (ll.34-6, Pensar en ti esta noche, *Raz*., p.368)

Their love is recorded by the elements, its evidence no longer confined to the lovers' materiality; they are 'saved' from the fate of one day inhabiting bodies that will be forgotten, bereft of love and thereby devoid of life, as implied by the use of "cadáver". This vision of the body as empty vessel is directly antithetical to love's cherished goal of 'entereza' in body and soul, as described in Chapter Two.

Significantly, this "traspresencia" or all-pervasiveness tends to be located in the beloved's physical absence, and therefore constitutes more a compensatory than an absolute presence. Emotional transference effectively transposes the poet's internalised memory of her onto his physical surroundings. As though to bear out this distinction between 'real' and compensatory presence, the beloved's arrival in another poem effectively blots out the perception of anything outside her immediate presence. The poet only resumes interest in the rest of the world when she is once again absent: "El mundo material / nace cuando te marchas" (ll.24-5, *La voz*, p.291). By observing the beloved, he records and internalises her image, then re-invents her in the void of her physical absence. We can thereby conclude that the only evocation of permanent presence in this love poetry is firmly set in the context of absence. Ironically, the beloved's physical 'reality' cannot offer the same degree of security as the poet's invention of her:

> Lo que yo te pido
> es que la corpórea
> pasajera ausencia
> no nos sea olvido,
> ni fuga, ni falta:
> sino que me sea
> posesión total
> del alma lejana,
> eterna presencia.   (ll.63-71, Eterna presencia, *Largo*, pp.461-2)

The term "posesión" is significant here, as is the shift (conscious or unconscious?) from the "nos" of l.66 to "me" in l.68. We begin with a collective wish that physical separation will not banish the lovers to the oblivion of each others' forgetfulness. But another criterion creeps in at this point - the poet's personal aspiration to possess the beloved in his own internalised image, an image that must, by necessity, exclude the body. In perverse opposition to the dominant tendency to materialise the beloved's absence in these poems, there occasionally arises a figurative preference for "alma" (as an internalised vision of essence), over "cuerpo" (physical presence). Another example of this ploy can be found as early as *Presagios*:

> Pero tu cuerpo nunca,
> pero tus labios nunca,
> felicidad, alma sin cuerpo, sombra pura. (ll.13-15, p.57)

The overall theme of this poem is the power of language to invoke presence. It emerges that any verbally created presence is by definition immaterial: it is in fact the poet's internalised image of the phenomenon, not the thing itself. In the same poem, the beloved's physical presence poses an obstacle to the poet's insatiable desire to articulate her: "Dentro de mí te llevo / porque digo tu nombre" (ll.4-5, *Pres.*, No.5, p.57). Salinas's desire for permanent presence leads him inexorably back to poetic re-creation, which transcends the intermittent absences of physical reality.[23] His idea of her is more 'real' in Cartesian terms than her actual materiality, because ideas are permanent and the flesh is not.

But surely this Cartesian resolution undermines the poet's fundamental aim of 'entereza'? How can this view of the beloved be acceptable to the poet-lover who, as already demonstrated in Chapter Two, aspires to an eternal love of both body and soul, and for whom the beloved's presence as a psychological and/or spiritual reality alone is insufficient? For the most part, we perceive in Salinas's poetry an inexorable drive to break free of Cartesian modes of thought and expression, in order to achieve fusion with the 'other' and a fully integrated self. From whence do these 'lapses' into Cartesian subjectivity stem? Is there some inherent conflict between the need of the lover for equal presence of body and soul, and the need of the poet, whose poetic project requires only the presence of the beloved's 'alma' or essence? The poet's aim in this early poem is to re-create her in his own image, and in the act of creation to achieve eternity - not the eternal incarnation of a love comprising 'alma y cuerpo' - but the immortality of the individual ego gained in self-expression. This desire for eternity is really another means of expressing the desire to experience absolute presence. For the lover, this embraces the beloved's physical, as well as idealised self - but absolute physical presence proves impossible, constantly eluding him; he cannot permanently possess the beloved in the flesh. For the poet, however, the goal of absolute presence is more readily attainable, as the poetic process does not require the beloved's physical presence. The persistence of the quest for absolute presence becomes more comprehensible if we acknowledge that to the poet, the beloved represents quite different qualities than she does to the lover. More than a physical presence, a personality, more even than his partner in body and soul, the poet's beloved serves as a potent symbol of all 'otherness', that precise but unknown quality that the individual requires to feel whole, or 'entero'.[24] This deployment of the beloved as symbol is not only familiar to the reader, but readily accepted, as it stems from a long tradition of the invocation of the beloved as muse, as a source of inspiration. The creative force that impels the poet to write is externalised in the form of the woman he loves, only to be internalised again through his poetic re-invention of her.[25]

But what are the implications of this conversion from woman to muse for the beloved? Is it a case of pure abstraction, as Spitzer claimed in 1941?[26] Certain poems suggest that this is indeed the case. The title of "Tú mía" (*Fábula y signo*), indicates that the poet desires only to re-invent the beloved in his own image, and seems to usurp her autonomy; she merely serves a literary purpose -

Aunque hables días y noches,
nada dices ya,

tu palabra última fue
aquella que yo te oí.   (ll.4-7, p.194)

It would be erroneous to read these intentions at face value: there is a sizeable measure of irony and self-parody at work in Salinas's evocation of the creative process. But it can justifiably be said that for poetic purposes, the beloved's existence is entirely dependent on the poet's perception of her, a tendency which finds its most extreme expression in *Razón de amor*, in the lines, "Apenas te has marchado / - o te has muerto" (ll.1-2, p.392), where she may as well be dead once she has absented herself from the range of the poet's sense perception.

Spitzer's thesis that the beloved "tú" of these poems is "un concepto puro" and not a 'real' person was met by a plethora of indignant opposition at the time of its publication. Yet it contains some portion of truth: it is disingenuous to suggest that the beloved as an actual personality is portrayed in these love poems. In this respect, Salinas only departs from the very traditional poet-centred love-lyric, insofar as he presents a Jungian picture of the yo-tú relationship: poet and beloved depend upon reciprocal 'otherness' to fulfil themselves both individually and as a couple.[27] A feminist critique of the poems would stress the consistent objectivisation of the beloved, perhaps even pointing up Freudian echoes where the feminine is strongly identified with absence, or a lack.[28]

Apart from the tendency to objectivise the beloved, another inevitable result of her 'poetización' is sublimation - from a single, real woman to an idealised, generic archetype. Salinas was fully aware of this process at work in the poetry of others. Writing on the works of Rubén Darío, he quotes Darío's own view that while love of a particular woman leads inevitably to love of 'woman' - "En la mujer, aún en lo mujer" - this does not diminish in any way the poet's ability to relate to that actual person: "La mejor musa es la de carne y hueso"[29] Nonetheless, the question remains. Sublimation of the beloved in poetic form may have no effect whatsoever on the poet's feelings for a particular woman, but it will profoundly influence how that woman is portrayed in his writing. Can the poet's subject be presented as both ideal and real, generic and particular? Or is the real woman invariably supplanted by the archetypal figure of the muse? Salinas poses this very question in relation to Darío's work: glossing the Nicaraguan poet's theory of "la diversificación de la mujer", he asks - "¿no se perderá la realidad de la mujer verdadera?" (p.133). The problem is never satisfactorily addressed. Salinas attempts to resolve the inherent conflict between woman and muse with a rather woolly statement that - "esa pluralidad de féminas ha de ser susceptible de reducirse a una, compendio de todas las otras" (p.134).[30] The unspoken reality, of course, is less a "compendio" and more an archetypal, literary conception of woman.[31] None of Salinas's reflections on the nature of the muse seem to support the theory put forward by Robert Havard that this love poetry is the direct product of just one relationship, inspired by one woman. There is a stronger case for arguing that the love-cycle maps out one man's experience of love, rather than the experience of one affair.

Salinas himself refutes the notion that literary archetype can convey the essence or identity of a single person. In an essay on the literary figure of Don Juan, he states - "Don Juan es una figura plural.. hemos llegado a una forme deforme... de Don Juan" - that the plurality of associations imposed upon the literary persona distort the real identity of the actual person: "Don Juan es una idea, Don Juan es una invención; Don Juan es un mito".[32] Can the same be said of the beloved in Salinas's love poetry? There is ample evidence of a quite self-conscious mythologising of the beloved. In "Atalanta", (*Seguro azar*), the poet claims not to be deceived by her everyday appearance, her apparent ordinariness. He suspects that her true nature is nothing less than mythical:

> y luego
> el mito, ascensor antiguo
> que te sube, allá, a la fábula. (ll.27-9, pp.154-5)

For this poet at least, this is the rightful status of his muse. Again, in *Fábula y signo*, the poetic process transports the beloved from her earthly habitat to Olympian heights; in this example she is not only sublimated and mythologised, but even deified by the poet's creative powers: "A mis medidas de dentro / te fui inventando, Afrodita" (ll.29-30, Vida segunda, pp.188-9). At times she is elevated to heights where the lover (here distinct from the omnipotent poet), cannot follow: he fears that she will completely abandon her human-ness in favour of her mythical-ness, leaving him bereft.

> ...volver puedes
> a tu mito y dejarme a mí llorando
> al pie de un árbol.
> (ll.69-71, No me sueltes, *Largo*, p.541)

The concomitant existence of two relationships should be acknowledged in any meaningful assessment of Salinas's love poetry: the love relationship of lover and beloved, and the literary relationship of poet and muse. Confusion of the two lends itself too easily to a cause and effect explanation of the text on biographical grounds. In the literary relationship, the beloved's role is functional: she fulfills the necessary role of muse. This in no way denies authenticity of feeling or questions the 'reality' of a specific love relationship; it is simply the inevitable result of the 'poetización' of that relationship.[33]

The *intimismo* of Salinas's love-cycle, where the voice of "yo", the lover, addresses the beloved "tu", has led to many critical assertions that the love experience strongly resembles a dialogue.[34] And indeed, love is regularly depicted as a dialogue in Salinas's poetry:

> ¿Hablamos, desde cuando?
> ¿Quién empezó? No sé.
> Los días, mis preguntas;
> oscuras, anchas, vagas
> las respuestas: las noches.
> (ll.1-5, *La voz*, p.286)

Their relationship is described as a mysterious discourse, where days formulate questions that only the lovers' nights together can answer.

In the inherited scheme of "muse poetry", the beloved functions as the inspiration of dialogue, initially between poet and beloved. This dialogue leads the poet to the knowledge of 'otherness' both externally in the beloved, and internally in himself. In direct response to the love experience, the poet embarks upon a voyage of self-discovery, a dialogue with his "alma" or "ánima", that will hopefully end in self-realisation.[35] This is precisely the kind of internal dialogue conceived by Hinks, with whose writings Salinas was clearly familiar:

> Según Hinks esta concepción de la vida mental como diálogo sirvió de fundamento a la representación de la musa. Poeta y musa no serían, conforme a eso, sino el hombre que habla con su alma, el diálogo interior.
> (*El defensor*, p.286).

In this sense, the love-cycle can justifiably be said to bear a closer resemblance to soliloquy than to dialogue.[36] Through the beloved, the poet discovers the muse in himself, and in doing so, finds his poetic voice.[37]

The voice alluded to most often in the love poems is the beloved's, as opposed to the principal speaker, who is the poet. Her voice is a source of life to him: it initiates the creative dialogue that will fill him to a state of utter completion:

> Y de pronto tu voz, tu voz cayendo
> en el centro de mí
> me hizo sentir la vida...   (ll.84-6)

Her voice has brought him to self-discovery; it has allowed him to find his own voice, his poetic identity.[38]

Through the love relationship the poet draws closer to the biological force of procreation: through intimacy with the beloved's 'otherness' he perceives her latent creative powers as indistinguishable from her role as muse, source of his own creative powers. In a celebration of timeless, inexorable creativity - whether artistic or biological - Salinas alludes to a supreme, non-verbalised "voz":

> Voz nunca servidora
> de lengua alguna, si de sus palabras
> sólo son los teclados
> donde tocas tu eterna melodía.
>
> (ll.19-22, Vocación, Todo, p.711)

It is precisely his awareness of the omnipresence of unvoiced creativity that inspires Salinas to articulate. Just as he did in an early poem of the same title, "Vocación", *Seguro azar*, he professes here, in this later poem from *Todo más claro* the need to express the unexpressed.

> Pero bien se sentía
> que todo era subirme poco a poco,
> por tu voz, a su más: que es este cántico.   (ll.32-4, p.712)[39]

This latent creativity invades his consciousness and is brought to light in the poet's song.

> Alma arriba, alma abajo, vas y vienes,
> cantando y recantando   (ll.42-3)
> te oigo a ti, omnipresente, fidelísima
> Vienes y vas.   (ll.60-1, p.712)

The voice of creation comes and goes, is absent as well as present, yet mysteriously ever-present. It is as though the condition of absence were simply the poet's inability to hear; the voice is ever-audible to those who are attuned.

> va ligero
> por las venas del ser hacia la entraña
> que su correr es mi razón de vida.
> Y eres mi sangre misma, si se oyera.
>
> (ll.70-3, Vocación, Todo, p.713)

In Salinas's later work, the pronoun "tú" is no longer addressed solely in the context of love, but can be read as a broader definition of 'otherness'; all life that inspires the poet. For this reason he speaks of a "razón de vida" in line 72, rather than a "razón de amor". The life-force that flows in his veins is the poet's song, his verse, his identity, inspired by the presence of the other, this "tú", which is so frequently (though not exclusively), embodied by the beloved.

The poet is not alone in defining himself by his ability to speak. The whole Hebraic-Hellenic tradition of Western Europe rests on the assumption that humanity differs from the rest of nature because of the ability to articulate. And yet, poets and philosophers alike lament the inadequacies of language, claiming that vital qualities such as subjective feeling, have no accurate verbal expression. It is ironic that this kind of experience, the highly subjective emotional experience of love that is so resistant to verbalisation, should enable this poet to find his most memorable voice.[40] The end of a love relationship, and the withdrawal of love, threatens to end the poet's poetic dialogue; with the beloved, with himself; like a conversation suddenly cut off in mid-stream -[41]

> Y cuando nos separen
> y ya no nos oigamos,
> te diré todavía
> . ¡Qué pronto!
> ¡Tanto que hablar, y tanto
> que nos hablaba aún!
> (ll.25-30, ¿Hablamos, desde cuándo?, *La voz*, p.286)

The sad irony here, is that once out of earshot, the poet cannot even pass on this simple observation to the beloved.

The following lines from an early love-poem in *Seguro azar* draw together the various thematic threads pursued in Salinas's poetic treatment of separation and absence: "los adioses" as encounters rather than partings; the inversion of dawn from a setting for separation to one of unification; the beloved's presence manifest in her voice as Logos, the source of all creation -

> Con tu palabra última

- adiós -
anoche encadenaste
la noche a tu silencio.   (ll.1-4)
hasta que tú, con la primera palabra
de tus labios de hoy
- adiós - crees el día.   (ll.13-15, Dominio, *Seg.*, p.122)

The spectre of silence hovers around these poems. It is the antithesis of the poet's dialogue with the beloved, and with all creation, denying the possibility of self-realisation through dialogue, and is invariably associated with a melancholy condition of absence. If the poet's life is a dialogue, then the absence of 'otherness', deprives him of the oxygen of discourse:

El aire ya es apenas respirable
porque no me contestas:
tú sabes que lo que yo respiro
son tus contestaciones. Y me ahogo.
          (ll.1-4, *Largo*, p.530)

Silence for Salinas is a fate comparable only with death, which aptly, is probably the only area of human experience to lie outside the realms of discourse and articulation. The discovery of the individual voice, the poet's self-invention through self-expression, hinges on the presence of otherness, most commonly apprehended and poeticized in the love experience.

The overlapping of the qualities of song, speech and love in a poem entitled "Presente simple", indicates the inseparable nature of the elements of poetry and love in the poet's mind.

Ni recuerdos ni presagios:
sólo el presente, cantando.

Ni silencio, ni palabras:
tu voz, sólo, sólo, hablándome. (ll.1-4)

sólo el amor, sólo amando.   (l.16, *Confianza*, p.805)

Every act of speech, like love, brings the poet closer to self-knowledge: but, like love, his expression must be reciprocated if it is to grow. A single voice in the void of absence creates nothing new - but only repeats itself in the manner of an echo. His work is therefore a dialogue with the all that exists beyond the boundaries of his own consciousness. In the present continuous acts of singing, speaking, and loving, beloved and poetry are eternally fused in a process that must be sustained in the here and now. This is the poet's hunger for presence in the present.

NOTES

Chapter III

1. In Jacques Derrida's analysis, inherited Western thinking and culture is logocentric by nature, requiring not only a centre, but a centre that is occupied by the presence of an absolute being or value. Historically, this presence has been given many names, as he outlines in the following passage from "Structure, Sign and Play in the Discourse of the Human Sciences".

> Successively, and in a regulated fashion, the centre receives different forms and names. The history of metaphysics, like the history of the West, is the history of these metaphors and metonymies. Its matrix... is the determination of Being as *presence* in all senses of the word. It could be shown that all names related to fundamentals, to principles, or to the centre have always designated an invariable presence - *eidos, arche, telos, energeia, ousia* (essence, existence, substance, subject) *aletheia*, transcendentality, consciousness, God, man, and so forth.

Jacques Derrida, "Structure, Sign and Play in the Discourse of the Human Sciences", trans. Alan Bass, in *Writing and Difference*, Routledge and Kegan Paul (London, 1978), pp.278-295.

2. This letter is quoted in Guillermo de Torre's article, "Pedro Salinas en mi recuerdo y en sus cartas", *Buenos Aires Literaria*, No.13 (1953), pp.87-96.

3. The displacement of the creative production of primary texts by that of secondary, discursive material, is the inevitable outcome of geographic exile in the opinion of George Steiner.

> Hermeneutic unendingness and survival in exile are, I believe, kindred... On the one hand there is a sense in which all commentary is itself an act of exile. All exegesis and gloss transports the text into some measure of distance and banishment... On the other hand, the commentary underwrites - a key idiom - the continued authority and survival of the primary discourse. It liberates the life of

meaning from that of historical-geographical contingency. In dispersion, the text is homeland.

This schism between poetic and creative output is evident in the earliest years of Salinas's exile (1936-42). However, as Marichal points out, the eventual outcome of inhabiting a literary homeland is an intensive exploration of the poet's cultural heritage, and the ultimate fusion of purpose and content in his poetry and prose of the 1940s. The coincidence of theme and tone in Salinas's critical and creative writings during this period can be read as an indication that the poet had acquired a significant degree of personal 'entereza' in his life. (See Marichal p.73) For this reason, Salinas's collection of essays *El defensor*, described by Marichal as "el fiel transunto del hombre entero", presents us with the same 'persona' or voice that speaks through Salinas's later poetic works; we encounter the same breadth of subject-matter, the same inclusivity - from subjective emotion to social commentary - in both the discursive and creative works of this period: "Esa misión fue realizada por el poeta en sus obras del exilio: y así, el creciente enraizamiento en la tradición literaria y espiritual de España permitió a Pedro Salinas encontrar su voz más universal". See George Steiner, *Real Presences*, Faber & Faber (London/Boston, 1989), p.40, and Juan Marichal, *Tres voces de Pedro Salinas*, Chapter III, "La voz universal del exilio", Ediciones Taller (Madrid, 1976), p.85.

4. Pedro Salinas, *Reality and the Poet in Spanish Poetry*, John Hopkins Press (Baltimore, 1966), p.3.

5. Birute Ciplijauskaite, *La soledad y la poesía española contemporánea*, Insula (Madrid, 1962), p.212.

6. This letter was written by Salinas on receipt of the proofs of an article by his friend, entitled "Con Pedro Salinas", which was subsequently published in *Clavileño*, (No.11). The extract quoted is reproduced in Dámaso Alonso's, "España en las cartas de Pedro Salinas," in, *Del siglo de oro a este siglo de siglas*, Gredos (Madrid, 1962), pp.154-162.

7. Pedro Salinas, *La poesía de Rubén Darío*, Seix Barral (Barcelona, 1975), p.165.

8. Pedro Salinas, *Jorge Manrique o tradición y originalidad*, Seix Barral (Barcelona, 1974), p.210.

9. Pedro Salinas, *Jorge Manrique o tradición y originalidad*, p.211. As in Note 8.

10. The double-edged nature of memory is recognised by Salinas in his discussion of the work of Garcilaso de la Vega:

By evoking, by recreating in his soul the image of the lost one, the poet fulfills a double function: he creates for himself the illusion of having once more what he never again will have; and then he makes us feel the great value and loss of what has past.

Pedro Salinas, *Reality and the Poet in Spanish Poetry*, pp.88-9. As in Note 4.

11. In the much-cited poem "Vocación", from *Seguro azar*, a poetic manifesto is set down as the poet's need to participate in an ongoing process of creation: "un mundo sin acabar / necesitado, llamándome...(ll.21-2) / que ponga lo que le falte" (ll.24, p.110).

12. Pedro Salinas, *Reality and the Poet in Spanish Poetry*, (as in Note 4), p.3.

13. In her Introduction to *Cartas de amor a Margarita, 1912-15*, Solita Salinas points out that her father's extended 'noviazgo', conducted by correspondence, elicited a supreme exertion of imagination from the young poet: "Las cartas del joven Salinas son una ensoñación continua del vivir de su novia en Argelia". She draws a telling parallel between this necessity to visualise another world - one that is unknown to him, and Salinas's subsequent vision of a "trasmundo".

... Y esa separación de los enamorados (que tanto lamenta) le obliga a hacer un esfuerzo imaginativo que le transporta a un mundo no vivido por él; y que será, más adelante, una de las características de su poesía.

Cartas de amor a Margarita, 1912-15, Alianza Tres (Madrid, 1984), p.15.

14. Stephen Gilman sees temporary absence as a re-vitalising principle in the love relationship. Moreover, it instils in the reader, as in the lovers, a desirable degree of tension, driving us ever forward from one 'poem', or fragment of the love cycle, to the next.

Los poemas en que la persona amada está ausente se alternan con tal rapidez que parece que el poeta premeditadamente inclina al lector a no forjarse una trama... Hay aquí un enigma sin solución (o por lo menos sin una solución fácil o predeterminada) que ayuda a mantener una tensión y expectativa continuas según salimos de un trozo de poesía sin título y comenzamos otro. El misterio del amor, a la vez completo e incompleto... encuentra aquí su contrafigura de misterio formal.

Stephen Gilman, "El proemio a *La voz a ti debida*", in *Pedro Salinas*, ed. A. P. Debicki, El escritor y la crítica, Taurus (Madrid, 1976), pp.119-20.

15. The quotation is taken from Carta III (Madrid 1912), in Pedro Salinas's, *Cartas de amor a Margarita, 1912-15*, p.36. As in Note 13.

16. This practice of creating absence seems to have been initiated by Salinas during his courtship with Margarita. Solita Salinas writes in the Introduction to *Cartas de amor a Margarita, 1912-15*: "...estos novios se escribían aún durante el único mes del año que pasaban juntos, 'al acabar de vernos, como si estuviéramos lejos...'". (As in Note 13, p.14)

17. These interjections, withholding the inevitable moment of departure recall Juan Ramón Jiménez's poem of that title - "¡Adiós!".

> ¡Ahora!
> > El sol se pone...
> > > ¡Adiós!
> - El que te lleva soy yo -
> ¡Adiós! ¡Adiós!
> > > Di, ¿te alejas?
> ¿Vienes hacia mí?...¡No llegas!
> ¿No llegarás?
> > (ll.1-8, *Estío*, No.8, p.211)

and again in "Víspera",

> ¡Adiós! ¡Adiós! ¡Adiós a todas partes aun sin irnos,
> y sin querernos ir y casi yéndonos! (ll.17-18),

J. R. Jiménez, *Diario de un poeta recién casado*, No. 25, *Segunda antolojía poética*, ed. Leopoldo de Luis, Austral (Madrid, 1983) p.229.

18. On reading J. G. Cummins' assessment of the "aubade" in the Western European tradition, we can deduce that Salinas, with characteristic multiplicity of perspective, draws on almost every historical application of the dawn motif.

> The theme of dawn (sunrise, cock-crow, awakening), is a factor in both the traditional lyric and the medieval courtly lyric, and the possibility of interaction between the two cannot be discounted. In the court lyric, especially in French, the 'aubade' is a minor facet of the courtly convention, often involving the separation of the illicit lovers in face of the threat of discovery. Separation is only one side

of the alba theme in the traditional lyric; quite commonly dawn is the time of meeting or arrival, or of the awakening of one lover by another.

J. G. Cummins, *The Spanish Traditional Lyric*, Pergamon, (Oxford, 1977), pp.57-8.

19. In *El defensor*, Salinas alludes to Plato's definition of love as "un estado intermedio entre poseer y no poseer" (p.74), reflecting the general inter-relatedness of absence and presence in his own work. There is a specific kind of "estado intermedio", however, between absence and presence, where spatial definitions are broken down, and which echo Jiménez's lines:

a ti, que no llegaste a mí, aun cuando corriste,
y a quien no llegué yo, aunque fui de prisa
- ¡qué triste espacio enmedio! -   ("Víspera", ll.23-5)

J. R. Jiménez, "Diario de un poeta recién casado", *Segunda antolojía poética*, p.229. As in Note 17.

20. One example already alluded to is "La memoria en las manos", *Largo lamento*, pp.469-71, where memory is evoked as being very tangible, for example: "Hoy son las manos la memoria" (l.1).

21. Robert Havard makes some penetrating observations on Salinas's idiosyncratic deployment of antithetical terms:

Salinas's whole purpose is to destabilise language, in its lexicon, its syntax and its rhetorical resources. Supreme amongst destabilising devices is the paradox or conceit... In the conceit, two contradictory ideas - matter/weightlessness, presence/absence - are held in a state of continuous opposition and their interaction has a decidedly unsettling effect upon the words' connotations and readers' method of linguistic apprehension.

I would suggest that the process of semantic destabilisation is brought even further, so that this state of "continuous opposition" is so utterly "unsettled" that distinctions break down, and antonym is converted into equation. See Robert Havard, *From Romanticism to Surrealism. Seven Spanish Poets*, Chapter V, "Pedro Salinas. The Poetics of Motion", University of Wales Press (Cardiff, 1988), pp.182-3.

22. Salinas expounds on this early theory of the indistinguishable natures of absence and presence in *El defensor*, so that not only the conditions themselves fuse, but absent and present parties are also swathed in the homogenous mists of separation: "distancias y ausencias son tinieblas, y envuelven por igual al presente y al ausente". Pedro Salinas, *El defensor*, Alianza Tres (Madrid, 1984), p.74.

23. In his essay, "Defensa de la carta misiva y de la correspondencia epistolar", Salinas admits that the very act of communication by writing renders the correspondents immaterial: "en el trato epistolar, los dos interlocutores están descarnados, por decirlo así, desmaterializados". (*El defensor*, p.65. As in Note 22) This phenomenon of immaterial presence is a fundamental characteristic of Salinas's correspondence with Margarita Bonmatí between 1912 and 1915. During long periods of separation the lovers needed to believe in the reality of a "traspresencia" that would allow them to experience a sense of togetherness; in order to accommodate their circumstances it would have to exclude physical presence. There are numerous examples of this non-physical togetherness in Salinas's letters to Margarita in this period: "Margarita, no me separo de ti un minuto..."(Carta LVI, p.159); "Verás como no me he separado de ti, como estoy a tu lado, sombra tuya..."(Carta LXXXI, p.216); "Sigo tan contento... por ti, por ti, aun estando sin ti, ya ves, aun estando separados..."(Carta LV, p.157). See *Cartas de amor a Margarita, 1912-15*. As in Note 13.

24. The point is neatly captured in a later poem "Lo inútil", whose title is equally applicable to the beloved and/or the poet's craft: the former provides the inspiration for the latter, without which the poet could not achieve self-realisation. This desired otherness can only be calculated as: "exacta-mente lo que me falta" (ll.67-8, *Todo.*, p.751).

25. That very 'entereza' that the poet seeks is projected onto the figure of the beloved as early as 1914, when Salinas tells Margarita that the quality he most loves her for - "... es, Margarita, ese maravilloso sentido que tienes de la vida completa y entera" - an indication that she is perceived as the source of what he most desires. Carta LV, Madrid 1914, *Cartas de amor a Margarita, 1912-15*. As in Note 13.

26. Leo Spitzer's infamous article on *La voz a ti debida*, "El conceptismo interior de Pedro Salinas", *Revista Hispánica Moderna*, VII (1941), postulates that the only existence granted the beloved by these poems is that of the poet's internalised image of her; an idea, a concept, rather than a flesh and blood person.

> Cosa curiosa, hasta la mujer amada es negada por nuestro poeta; no conozco poesía de amor donde la pareja amorosa se reduzca hasta tal punto al yo del poeta, donde la mujer sólo vive en función del

espíritu del hombre y no sea más que 'un fenómeno de conciencia' de este.

Robert Havard, among many others, contests this assertion. He insists upon the biographical 'reality' of the beloved of Salinas's love poetry, and assiduously seeks out pictorial and circumstantial details of a 'real' woman in *La voz a ti debida*, which, he suggests, can only be read accurately in the context of a particular illicit relationship in Salinas's life coinciding with the poems' composition -

> 'A single muse, a single tone', was Salinas's comment on Garcilaso. Similarly, of vital importance is Salinas's consistency of detail, particularly with regard to her youth. His preoccupation with this is as conclusive evidence of her presence as his *dolor* in the later poems.

The only physical characteristics that Havard is able to extract from the text however, are more generic than particular. They deal solely with the beloved's youth; Havard deduces twenty as a possible age. While the absence of personal detail is, as Havard points out, very much in keeping with the secrecy surrounding the Courtly tradition, the very archetypal nature of her youth is also so typical of this tradition as to undermine the effectiveness of the argument. "Consistency of detail" may just as validly grow from recognisable literary type, as from a 'real' person. See Robert Havard, "Pedro Salinas and Courtly Love. The beloved as 'amada' in *La voz a ti debida*: woman, muse and symbol", *Bulletin of Hispanic Studies*, LVI (1979), p.130.

27. "Salvación por el cuerpo" provides an apt example:

> Cómo nos encontramos con el nuestro
> allí en lo otro..,   (ll.129-30)
>   ...jubiloso
> nacer, por fin, en dos, en la unidad
> radiante de la vida, dos."
>   (ll.142-4, *Razón de amor*, p.422)

28. Although by no means a feminist, some passages of Spitzer's article on *La voz a ti debida* do expose the common phenomenon of gender-bias at work in the male portrayal of the female.

> La mujer será tan puramente pasiva que ningún indicio de su amor pueda prestar materialidad a su persona, más tenue que la de Laura... (p.39)

and again,

> como la amada no está vista más que por los ojos del poeta que la
> escruta para conocerse a sí mismo, es, por lo tanto, como uno de los
> términos de una comparación persistente, un elemento del concepto
> fundamental sobre el que reposa esta poesía. (Spitzer, p.56. As in
> Note 26).

29. Pedro Salinas, *La poesía de Rubén Darío*, p.63. As in Note 7.

30. As in Note 7.

31. Dámaso Alonso accepts the view that a literary, archetypal representation of
woman can somehow capture the identity of real women; I would contest his use
of the term "personalidad" in this context as misleading. Salinas does not convey
the personality of the beloved, but only certain archetypal qualities which she
symbolises for the poet.

> Aquellas variantes dentro de un tipo, llevaban hacia una
> consecuencia que es la que triunfa ahora en *La voz a ti debida*; una
> sola personalidad llena de variaciones y matices. En esta amada del
> último poema de Salinas se concentran y resumen todas aquellas
> anteriores.

Dámaso Alonso, *Del siglo de oro a este siglo de siglas,* Gredos (Madrid, 1962),
p.138.

32. Pedro Salinas, "El nacimiento de Don Juan", *Ensayos completos, Vol. III*,
Taurus (Madrid, 1983), p.133.

33. Salinas's letters to Margarita (1912-15) demonstrate his need of a literary as
well as a sentimental relationship. The terms of endearment chosen by the young
poet for his beloved are essentially literary and archetypal: she is repeatedly evoked
as "la mujer", "la esposa" (after Juan de la Cruz's *Cántico espiritual*), and even
"Ella" complete with capital 'E'. The extract reproduced below is from a letter
written in 1914, where Salinas reflects on a recent trip to Asturias, and conjures up
a pastoral idyll of a home in the countryside with his beloved/muse. Woman and
nature (as is so often the case), fuse into an archetypal expression of all that is pure
and wholesome.

> Yo soñaba en hacer una casa, allí, frente al mar, entre las manzanas;
> y pensaba en lo grato de retirarse allí con la mujer amada, a solas

con Ella y con el mar... Y yo veía mi vida límpida, clara, transparente, como agua de peñas, a solas con dos bellezas, de la Naturaleza y de la Esposa. (Carta XLIII, Madrid 1914), *Cartas de amor a Margarita*, 1912-15. As in Note 13.

34. The most thorough proponent of this interpretation is Alma de Zubizarreta who makes the following assessment of the importance of the love relationship in the development of Salinas's dialogue with the reality he inhabits:

> Trazada la evolución del proceso dialógico de la poesía de Salinas, se revelaba significativo un extenso número de poemas dirigidos a un tú personal: la amada; y se apreciaba que tal diálogo alcanzaba su máxima vitalidad después de la primera apertura del poeta a las cosas y de su primer encuentro consigo mismo.

Alma de Zubizarreta, *Pedro Salinas: el diálogo creador*, Gredos (Madrid, 1969), Chapter III "La Amada", p.121.

35. Rupert Allen assesses the creative force of the anima, discovered through the love relationship -

> With the poet's passing from the beloved herself to contact with the feminine unconscious comes the awakening into creativity, and with this we arrive at the original meaning of the muse. It is difficult to exaggerate the importance for poets of the woman as muse.

Rupert C. Allen, *Symbolic Experience: A Study of Poems by Pedro Salinas*, The University of Alabama Press (Alabama, 1982) p.66.

36. J. F. Cirre points to the anomalous relationship between any reading of the love cycle as a dialogue between "yo" and "tú", and the actual "yo"-centred perspective offered by the poems.

> Hay un perpetuo díalogo entre el "yo" - amante - y el "tú" - amada. Diálogo raramente directo. Casi siempre rememorado o supuesto desde el ángulo del "yo". "Yo" que persiste en negar la visión objetiva del tú, y de los ambientes y circunstancias que lo acompañan para encastillarse en una pasión subjetiva por lo absoluto, independiente de formas y presencias. Nos hallamos ante un universo inmanente que sólo el poeta es capaz de percibir.

J. F. Cirre, "Pedro Salinas y su poética", *Homenaje a Rodríguez Moniño*, Editorial Castalia (Madrid, 1966), pp.91-7.

37. Writing to Margarita from Paris in 1915, with a sense of poetic vocation somewhat clearer in his mind than previously, Salinas first defines their relationship as a dialogue, and secondly, explains how this dialogue with the beloved allows him to address his innermost self: "para mí, este hablarte ilimitadamente es como mi posibilidad de definirme, de formarme a mí mismo". (Carta LXXIX, Paris, 1915) *Cartas de amor a Margarita, 1912-15*, p.209. As in Note 13.

38. In 1914, Salinas writes to Margarita expressing his sense of satisfaction at having found his own poetic form - "es, sí, verso libre" - adding that he owes this discovery to her - "Margarita, ya sabes tú lo que he contado en ella, tú me la has sugerido, a ti te la debo, como debo todo a ti" - so rehearsing the eventual title of *La voz a ti debida*, and celebrating the role of the beloved as muse. See Carta XLIII, Cartas de amor a Margarita, 1912-15, p.134. As in Note 13.

39. Salinas's use of the term "cántico" here, is probably a tribute to the work of Jorge Guillén, whose *Cántico* celebrates all creation.

40. Despite the difficulties he encounters in his quest for a language of love, and a means of communicating intense emotional experience, Salinas ultimately holds great faith in the ability of language - not only to describe empirical reality, but to create its own reality. Thus, he is rather sceptical of the whole question of ineffable experience.

> Me aconsejo a mí mismo una cierta precaución ante eso de lo inefable. Puede existir lo más hermoso de un alma sin palabras, acaso. Pero no llegará a tomar forma humana completa, es decir, convivida, consentida, comprendida por los demás.... Hasta lo inefable lleva nombre: necesita llamarse inefable. No. El ser humano es inseparable de su lenguaje. (*El defensor*, p.283. As in Note 22).

41. The prospect of the beloved's absence fills the poet with an acute awareness of his own inarticulacy. Again Salinas seems to echo the voice of Juan de la Cruz, who reproduces the stammering inarticulacy of separation in his *Cántico espiritual*: "Y déjame muriendo / un no sé qué que queda balbuciendo". See Juan de la Cruz, "Cántico espiritual" (Verso 7), in *The Poems of John of the Cross*, ed. Roy Campbell, Pantheon Books (London, 1951), p.16.

Chapter IV
Suma y Cero
Avoiding the Void.

Much of Salinas's later work is framed by the concepts of "suma" and "cero". These terms encapsulate for the exiled poet two opposing tendencies in humanity - both collectively and individually. The "suma" of a human life, or of a civilisation, is comparable with Salinas's frequently stated ideal of 'entereza'. It represents a sum total, an apogee of human endeavour and human consciousness. "Cero", on the other hand, represents a lack of fulfilment, an absence, whether of the beloved or of a purpose for life itself. Ultimately, the "cero" motif in Salinas's later poetry comes to symbolise death, the greatest void of all. Against the ominous political backdrop of World War Two, the thematic emphasis of Salinas's poetry shifts from the exploration of 'otherness' in intimate, personal relationships, to the broader relationship between the individual and society, as socio-political concerns are expressed explicitly.

Salinas's awareness of humanity's inherent duality, the dual capacity to create and destroy, is inextricably linked with his growing unease throughout the 1940s, as to the direction (or lack of it) taken by scientific research. In the period from 1937-47, when Salinas was engaged in writing *El Contemplado*, *Confianza*, *Todo más claro* and the essays collected in *El defensor*, the latter tendency of destruction seemed dominant. Modern methods of warfare, especially the increasingly deadly use of aerial bombardment in World War Two, threatened the survival of the "suma" of European civilisation. The "blockbuster" bomb was deployed for the first time in 1942. "Terror" or "pattern-bombing" had become a feature of the war in Europe, with all too dire results in Hamburg and Dresden. Salinas's poetic response to this new and terrifying reality took shape in a lengthy poem called "Cero", written in 1943, which points up the dread efficiency of modern weaponry. The works of centuries are destroyed in the apocalyptic vision offered by this poem, heralding the devastation to be brought by the A-bomb.[1]

Scientific advancement seemed to have lost sight of the purpose of evolution as the preservation of the species, and had now devised a means of total self-destruction. How could this void be avoided? How could humanity ensure the continued evolution of the species? Salinas perceives the problem as not only intellectual but ethical. The solution he offers in his poetry is the restoration of "la entereza del hombre", where the individual lives both in touch with himself, and with the 'other' as embodied by people, things and the natural environment. Urban life was already undermining communication between individuals, and without a coherent sense of community there could be no sense of temporal continuity. How could the urban citizen of the 1940s feel in any way connected with the lives of those before him in the past, those to come after him in the future, when there was so little contact with those surrounding him/her in the present? The increasingly mechanized nature of modern life also put distance between man and nature, which this poet regards as the supreme model of continuity and co-operation. Salinas points up an inherent irony in the disengagement of science from nature, the growing alienation from its 'roots' in Natural Philosophy. So many scientific principles are drawn from the observation of natural processes: there is still, his poetry suggests, much to be learned from nature.

These intellectual, social, and ethical concerns are reflected in the evolution of Salinas's poetry from the *intimismo* of his love lyrics in the 1930s to his poetry of the 1940s, particularly *Todo más claro*, which addresses collective, social and moral issues. The poet himself acknowledged this trend in his work in 1951, when he addressed an audience in Wellesley College on the subject of his debt to the United States of America, saying "Creo que ha sido más bien lo urbano y lo social lo que ha encontrado reflejo en mi poesía".[2] Political events of the late 1930s and 1940s - the rise of fascism, a Civil War in Spain fired by an absolute incompatibility of ideologies and political interests, and the Second World War, brought dramatic changes to the experiences and aspirations of the Western consciousness. These changes are reflected in Salinas's poetry, not only in its thematic content but equally in its poetic expression. The sheer weight of contemporary historical event renders the pursuit of a purely 'personal' and private artistic response unsatisfactory for this poet. It is interesting at this point to refer back to Salinas's letters to Guillén in the 1930s, and compare his response to the tremendous build-up of political pressure in Spain at that time, with his later reactions in the 1940s.

> ... estoy sintiendo que España llega a un punto en que todos los propósitos personales van a ser superados, lo mismo los del rey que los míos. Y eso es lo que me indigna por dentro. (20.2.31.)[3]

The expression of indignation at the intrusion of politics into the poet's personal life, qualified in another letter as his "vida espiritual", is compatible with the intensely personal nature of Salinas's poetic output during the 1930s.[4] His love cycle is *intimista* in tone, certainly metaphysical in content, and verging on the transcendental in its expression. However, by the 1940s, the degree of political tension experienced by the poet in Spain in the lead-up to the Civil War, was now manifest in an enormous area of the globe engulfed in a World War. The individual's feelings of indignation at such an 'intrusion' become increasingly difficult to sustain. What we read in the poems collected in *Todo más claro* is a new kind of indignation that is directed, not at politics itself, but at the rise of a certain kind of political philosophy which is clinical, aggressive and materialistic. There can be little doubt that there is a strong connection in Salinas's mind between this mode of thinking, and the problems arising from mass, technologised society. There is an overwhelming sense of *desengaño* in *Todo más claro*, of disappointment in the spiritual vacuum of urban existence, and disillusionment with the application of new areas of knowledge opened by science.

The provision of an ethical solution to the threat of the void is vital, but for the poet striving to define himself in an endangered civilisation, so too is a poetic solution. In the later poems especially, the presence of the void seems to intensify the poet's awareness of the "suma", the wealth and variety of the world he inhabits, just as the threat of the beloved's future absence heightened his appreciation of presence in the love cycle. As demonstrated in Chapter Three, the poet-lover's instinctive response to the threat of the beloved's absence, was to invoke her memory, so creating the sensation of presence, in the hope of somehow warding off the dreaded void of absence. Now, as a poetic defence against the obliteration of the "suma", Salinas invokes the processes of accumulation that give us a sum total of Western civilisation.

From his earliest works, a fascination with mathematical rules and theories is prevalent. Mathematics alone cannot order chaos, but they provide coherent systems to define it, and so harness the enormity of the "suma" to the limited scale of human conception and comprehension. However, by the time *Todo más claro* is composed, mathematical principles are no longer perceived as an attractive metaphor for evolution and progress. Moreover, mathematics emerges as an entirely unsuitable method for describing the "suma" of human experience, which for Salinas includes metaphysical as well as physical considerations. Mathematics is primarily the scientist's tool serving the express purpose of measuring the empirical world. Like many philosophies, science claims unique truth, advocating that future projections be based on empirical observations of the past. Herein lies the paradox and the source of Salinas's *desengaño*, for science in the 1940s appeared to threaten the existence of any future -

> Conozco la gran paradoja: que en los cubículos de los laboratorios, celebrados templos del progreso, se elabora del modo más racional la técnica del más definitivo regreso del ser humano: la vuelta del ser al no ser.[5]

The equation of knowledge and evolution has become problematic: knowledge without direction, without ethical guidance can be anti-evolutionary.[6] Salinas's response, both ethically and poetically, is to propound the sanctity of aspiration: the belief that creativity of any kind should be motivated by a desire to generate further creativity. In the shadow of atomic warfare, the notion of completion, of finality, has become philosophically, politically, and poetically suspect. Salinas therefore presents the desire to project, as vital to continued evolution, with the motto "vivir, seguir, querer seguir viviendo" (l.156, "Pasajero en museo", *Todo*, p.707). It is not completion that the individual and collective humanity should strive for, but continuation.

Time is a vital source of integration in Salinas's poetry, connecting past, present and future. The present is a "suma," or sum of past and present, and its value can only be gauged by future developments. Evolution is effected through the accumulation of experience and knowledge in time. For Salinas, motion itself is life: because time is uni-directional, inexorably thrusting forward, it is perceived by him as progressive.[7] This is a singularly post-Darwinian viewpoint, as it is only in the light of Darwin's theory of evolution that the concept of change has entered into the Western consciousness as synonymous with progress. In both his verse and prose works, Salinas frequently alludes to Jorge Manrique's telling metaphor of human life as a river, which captures so concisely time's relentless motion.[8] However, the perspective of the modern poet is radically different. Jorge Manrique wrote within a Christian, man-centred Universe, where time existed only in relation to the life of the soul, whose real element was not found in this life but in the next. Time, in Manrique's intellectual and philosophical context, runs not on, but out. Salinas, on the other hand, writes from a secular perspective, where the passage of time is not proof of the transience of human life, but of its continuation, so that time becomes a source of confidence, inspiring feelings of security:

> Tiempo divino que llegó a ser tiempo
> poco a poco, mañana tras su aurora,
> mediodía camino de su véspero,
> estíos que se juntan con otoño,
> primaveras sumadas al invierno.
> (ll.42-6, Cero V, *Todo*, p.781)

It is the measured sum of its component days and nights: our calendars are mapped out in the secure knowledge that one year is the sum of four seasons. Time is 'divine' because it promises the indefinite continuation of this sequential process; it appears to be infinite, because we have no experience of its stopping. Humanity has evolved through time, but Salinas delights in the idea of time itself evolving over a protracted period, "... poco a poco," (l.43). In *El Contemplado*, time is personified so that -

> Tarda noches la noche en ser auroras,
> la luz se hace despacio.
> (ll.19-20, *Var.* VI, "Todo se aclara", *El Cont.*, p.622)

Nothing is instantaneous in creation: evolution is a long and arduous process, quite the antithesis of the Biblical six-day version. In this account, light does not shine forth at the flick of a divine switch, but emanates slowly from the darkness. The felicitous physical result of time's prodigious industry is the "suma" of the world we inhabit: past potential is fully realised in the present, a point demonstrated by the image of the rose in "La nube que trae el viento" (*Confianza*) -

Mira:
aquí tienes la rosa,
ayer cerrada, hoy abierta. (ll.66-8, *Confianza*, p.798)

These teleological patterns in nature reflect time's tireless creativity: the
simultaneous embodiment and realisation of the bud in the flower, the material
manifestation of the past in the present. Evidence of the past is present everywhere
in Nature, but perhaps the most effective example chosen by Salinas is that of the
very bedrock underfoot -[9]

En una piedra está
la paciencia del mundo, moderada despacio,
Incalculable suma
de días y noches...
(ll.14-17, La memoria en las manos, *Largo*, p.469)

The physical formation of the world we have inherited is the product or "suma" of
millennia of change. A geological expression of time seems particularly apt: the
strata visible in the rock face serve as a constant reminder of the time-scale of the
evolution.[10]

Whether in nature or art, current creativity is inevitably influenced by the
creations of the past. For Salinas, time is the crucial link between the created,
empirical world and human creativity; it is essentially the medium in which both
take shape:

Y así, con lentitud que no descansa,
por las obras del hombre se hace el tiempo
profusión fabulosa. Cuando rueda
el mundo, tesorero, va sumando
- en cada vuelta gana una hermosura -
a belleza de ayer, belleza inédita.
(ll.52-7, Cero III, *Todo*, p.775)

Again, the nature of evolution is characteristically slow, "con lentitud", but sure,
"que no descansa". As the passage of time occasions the earth's continuous

creativity, it simultaneously accumulates, "va sumando" the fruits of humanity's creative faculties.

Material treasures, man-made and natural, are not the only inheritance of the past. Time also accumulates the less palpable gems of collective experience. In his commentary on originality and tradition in the works of Jorge Manrique, Salinas defines tradition as the knowledge that links past, present and future. He stresses the importance of what is unconsciously absorbed, not consciously learned, but residual in the collective memory. There is more to tradition, he argues, than "influencias", "precursores" and "fuentes":

> Todos estos son factores parciales, agentes menores de una realidad mucha más profunda, de mayor complejidad biológica: la tradición.[11]

The term "biológica" is deliberate and provocative, reinforcing the notion of tradition as primarily instinctive, and only then, intellectual.[12] Collective knowledge seems to create its own momentum as it passes from one generation to the next: the individual constitutes a link in this chain effect, making up the whole, or "suma". As the momentum gathers pace, the bulk of knowledge being transmitted from one generation to the next increases; in this way, knowledge can be seen to be accumulated in time, and by time. In *El defensor*, Salinas describes this self-perpetuating body of knowledge as a sea, made up of the many waves of individual consciousness.

> Históricamente, el ser individual en su grupo, en su generación, es una onda, empujada por miles de ondas que vinieron antes, y a su vez impulsa a las que le van a seguir, todos en el caudal común de lo humano.[13]

The limitless capacity of the sea for self-generation makes it an especially appropriate analogy. No matter how vast the volume of water, how strong the swell, no wave is ever overtaken by the tide, but retains its place in a perfectly coordinated sequence. In the same way, each individual has his/her place as contributor to, and recipient of tradition, and can never be overwhelmed by the weight of too much knowledge. No one individual is ever required to know everything, nor, in Salinas's view, need we ever aspire to omniscience, because - "Todo lo sabemos entre todos" (*El defensor*, p.167). This point of view appears to put collective, before individual knowledge: "Lo que yo no acerté, otros me lo acertaron", (ll.67-8, "En un Trino", *Confianza*, p.795). Salinas is sufficiently confident in collective experience to perceive it as a source of consolation. If, in one lifetime, he cannot live out every experience to its maximum potential, those unfulfilled experiences will eventually be realised by others. Thus, the emphasis is non-egotistical, remaining with the experience rather than the self. Even in the intimacy of love, the poet trusts -

> Que en algo, sí, y en alguien,
> se tiene que cumplir
> este amor que inventamos
> sin tierra ni sin fecha
> donde posarse ahora:
> el gran amor en vilo.
> (ll.20-5, Lo encontraremos, sí.., *La voz*, p.324)

This brand of consolation is distinctly secular: for the Christian poet the faith in an afterlife compensates for the transience of this one. Salinas, however, derives consolation from the knowledge that life itself continues, in a way that is rather reminiscent of Unamuno's conception of an "intrahistoria". His 'credo' is less subjective than the Christian because it apprehends the importance of life outside the self, and indicates a collective understanding of immortality. In such instances, Salinas seems to relinquish his desire for personal eternity, identifying instead with the continuation of the collective. Salinas acknowledges his contribution to a collective consciousness that transcends the individual's experience, without transcending the boundaries of this world: his life, although mortal, forms part of a self-perpetuating process, and can therefore be read as a life that exists "en vilo".[14]

The quest to integrate with a greater whole, whether nature or society, can be read as part of the overall quest for 'entereza'. Salinas perceives himself as just one of the waves in a sea of literary tradition; an 'integer', and an integral, vital part of the whole. He describes, in his book on Jorge Manrique, how the artist interacts with the past:

> Asimismo la tradición, el conjunto de sus obras, se ofrece como una serie de objetivaciones magistrales de la experiencia humana, y en su repertorio el poeta elige los que más desde dentro le llaman, y las emplea a su talante, fiando el triunfo o el fracaso de la obra que emprende al acierto de su motivo combinatorio y al grado de su potencia integradora.[15]

Elective affinity draws the poet, writing in the present, to the works of others who have preceded him. The success or failure of the work depends on the poet's ability to combine and integrate what he has read with what he is about to write, so that the tide of tradition may flow unhampered and enriched from the past, through the present and into the future.

Whether knowledge is consciously or unconsciously acquired, whether in the literate or illiterate mind, the dominant means of transmitting information has historically been language. If the accumulation of knowledge goes to make up a "suma" of tradition, then language is the means of communicating that knowledge. Echoed here, is Antonio Machado's famous motif of "palabra en el tiempo", indicating that any form of self-expression is temporally defined, but linguistic expression especially, as the medium itself is profoundly subject to the changes wrought by time.[16] Language evolves in time; the semantic value of words is accumulated in time and will vary according to social and historical context. In "Camino del poema" (*Todo más claro*), voices from the past are audible to the poet, carried by language across the centuries: he 'hears' them in the written words

of Garcilaso de la Vega, "aquel Doncel de Toledo" (1.43); San Juan de la Cruz,
"aquel monje de la oscura / noche del alma" (ll.45-6); and Miguel del Cervantes,
"el que inventó a Dulcinea, / la de la Mancha" (ll.47-8). Language also preserves
resonances of everyday speech, the language of pursuits humbler than poetry:

> Bocas humildes de hombres
> por su labranza,   (ll.33-4)
> Hombres que siegan, mujeres
> que el pan amasan...
> (ll.41-2, Camino del poema IV, El verbo, *Todo*, p.664)

A whole non-literary heritage is recorded by language too - spoken and sung in
words that have accompanied men and women in their labours over the centuries.
These songs and verses are lasting reminders of the cultural continuity that
language nurtures. In the same poem, Salinas advocates the anti-esoteric theory
that words are, "Cada día más hermosas por / más usadas" (ll.27-8, p.663) - that
their value lies in the accumulated meaning that is acquired by extensive usage.
Salinas has little faith in the notion of 'literary language' as the rare and unusual.
Rather than seek out an esoteric and ornate lexicon, he attaches value to
commonplace language, an approach that is extremely compatible with his ideas
on the presence of poetry in even the most everyday surroundings, and his choice
of some very mundane objects as poetic subjects in his early poems. Salinas is not
a poet who sets out to dazzle us with neologisms or with studied lexical postures:
his art lies in the revelation of new meaning in familiar words, and the restoration
of original, forgotten resonances. Or, to use the poet's own analogy of words as
currency, he refrains from coining many new words but appreciates the real value
of those grown grubby and dull from handling.

> Se ennegrecen, se desdoran
> oros y plata;
> 'hijo', 'rosa', 'mar', 'estrella', nunca
> se gastan.
> (ll.29-32, Camino del poema IV, El verbo, *Todo*, p.663-4)

Despite the frequency with which such words change hands/lips, they are inexpendable and inexhaustable. Each word is renewed as it is uttered by another tongue. It would appear that in linguistic, as in evolutionary theory, the present is indeed the sum of the accumulated past. Salinas even applies the mathematical processes of aggregation and multiplication to the writing of poetry:

> Every poem is a sum, the finding of a single number in which the rest are indeed included but no longer recognisable, raised to a single result.[17]

In another essay, Salinas goes as far as to describe his poetic ideal as "una aritmética fantástica", where the act of reading a poem enriches reader, poet and poem:

> Esto quiere decir que el poeta, al hacer vivir a otros lo que ha vivido él, multiplica a sí mismo.[18]

The poet expresses his experience in a poem, but its communication to others adds the readers' perceptions to the original experience, thereby enriching both the poet and his poem:

> ...en suma, se ha verificado la mágica operación de la poesía, la multiplicación de la capacidad de sentir, de entender, de vivir un momento todo.[19]

In other words, the formula: Poet + Poem + Reader = more than the sum of its composite parts. This is the magical element of Salinas's "aritmética fantástica"; the capacity of language to generate its own meaning.[20]

Salinas pursues his "aritmética fantástica" as he sets out to absorb the sum total of his cultural and natural inheritance. To this end, he not only resorts to the verbal expression "sumar", but also to the nominative and adjectival forms of "la suma" and "sumo/a". For example, in "Amor, mundo en peligro," (ll.118-9, *Largo*, p.493), the lover exclaims, "¡... esta suma / de aciertos que es la tierra!". The mathematical coherence of the many processes of aggregation evident in the physical environment, suggests that the world is, in fact, the correct solution to a mathematical equation; a "suma de aciertos". It is only a short semantic step from this association between "suma" and precision, to Salinas's most frequent application of the term "suma", to denote apogee:[21]

> Colmo, tensión extrema,
> suma de la belleza
> el mundo...
> (ll.15-17, Afán, *Fáb.*, p.197)

The "suma" here not only represents a sum total but a paragon. Various equations of a qualitative as well as a quantitative nature emerge. The equation of "la suma" with perfection occurs in several poems, such as -

> tan acorde con tu techo,
> como si estuvieses ya en
> en tu sumo, en lo perfecto.
> (ll.4-6, *Var.* XI, *El Cont.*, p.635)[22]

A strong association also emerges between "sumo" and "mediodía". This is achieved when syntactic juxtaposition suggests a compound noun of "sumo mediodía". An example of this compound is the "Fiera luz, la del sumo mediodía" (l.30, "Cero III", p.774), where the light at midday is consummate, more intense than at any other time, as the sun shines directly overhead.

> A las doce el sol, ajusta
> las cuentas de la mañana
> y hace la suma total:
> mediodía.   (ll.27-30, Los otros, *Confianza*, p.818)

The motion of the clock hands reflect the arched progression of the sun until it reaches its "suma" or zenith. The clock hands point directly upwards to meet the sun's beams travelling directly downwards; they connect to express an apogee of light and symmetry.

Salinas's experimentation with mathematical processes is one outlet for his urge to encompass 'all reality' in his work: numbers extend to infinity and offer infinite variation. They also provide scope for Salinas's ludic intelligence, as he invents his own mathematical formulae, ignoring conventions of mathematical association. The arithmetic rule of categories is frequently turned on its head, as Salinas combines incompatible phenomena to form an all embracing "set" of his own device.[23] This revolutionary "set" stresses the similarities rather than the differences between quite separate aspects of experience, from phenomena to feelings, and illustrates a process of integration at work in Salinas's poetry that brings together previously unconnected realities in one, all-encompassing "suma". Most of the phenomena selected for these poetic calculations are drawn from nature, with the occasional "máquina", and the vast terrain of human emotion is also ploughed for examples. The dominance of natural phenomena in this stylistic trait reflects nature's own resistance to vacuums, and its function in Salinas's poetry as a symbol of 'entereza'. In keeping with his poetic concept of an "aritmética fantástica", nature tends to form whole entities that have more than the sum of the parts, by means of ordered grouping, and in much of his poetry Salinas could be said to mimic this holistic trend. In the following extract from "Cero", we see Salinas's efforts to hold back the encroaching void by accumulating experience: "estíos que se junta con otoño, / primaveras sumadas al invierno (ll.45-6, Cëro V, p.781)". The poet adds summer to autumn, spring to winter, to reach the total of "tiempo divino" (l.42, p.781). This example illustrates how, while defying arithmetic conventions of association, Salinas consistently deploys the verb "sumar" as though he were in fact complying with them. Only the unquantifiable nature of the actual phenomena added together subverts this apparently logical process. Otherwise there is nothing in the poet's tone - no irony, no qualifications - to draw our attention to the disparity between the logic of the mathematical formula applied, and the illogical nature of its linguistic application; springs cannot be added to a winter and produce a semantically coherent result.

The verb "multiplicar" is employed with the same ingenuousness as "sumar". In *La voz a ti debida*, the poet-lover, in vain, seeks the beloved in the realms of "la duda", when in fact she resides,

> En el vértice puro
> de la alegría alta,
> multiplicando júbilos
> por júbilos, por risas,
> por placeres.
> (ll.22-6, Te busqué por la duda.., *La voz*, p.311)

- a formula that defies numerical logic, the multiplication of rejoicings by laughter and pleasure, but one which highlights love's capacity to produce happiness. The inexhaustible reserves of love are regularly evoked by this motif of multiplication. The aptly titled "Sí, todo con exceso ...", is just one example:

> A subir, a ascender
> de docenas a cientos
> de cientos a millar...(ll.1-3)

The poem enacts a numerical crescendo from dozens to a thousand. But love requires more inventive, imaginative expression, since quantity alone will not suffice: "Tablas, plumas, y máquinas, todo a multiplicar..." (ll.11-12) - miscellaneous objects are drawn into the all-embracing ledger that adds up to "el amor". The cumulative process presses on, caress crowding caress, until the lovers' embrace culminates in a volcanic climax, "caricia por caricia / abrazo por volcán", (ll.13-14, Sí, todo con exceso, *La voz*, p.252).

Nature repeatedly emerges in this poetry as a symbol of the positive "suma" of creativity and as antithetical to the man-made void represented by the bomb in "Cero". It displays an inimitable propensity for multiplication, and Salinas exploits this prolific growth in the imagery of *El Contemplado*, where he evokes the glorious accumulation of colour that spreads over the sea's surface at sunrise, in terms of a flowering spring meadow -

> Blancas vislumbres, flores fugacísimas
> florecen por las campas,
>
> de otro azul. Si una espuma se deshoja
> - pétalos por la playa -
>
> se abren mil; que el rosal de donde suben
> es rosal que no acaba.
> (ll.17-22, *Var.* II, Primavera diaria, *El Cont.*, p.614)

As one rose-tinted wave breaks, scattering its foam-petals, a thousand more appear and the effect is multiplied ad infinitum. The "Primavera diaria" of sunrise on the water, where each wave is flushed to the hue of a rose, resembles a magical, ever-flowering rose-tree.

Nature's compulsive multiplication is not always expressed as an inevitable, teleological process, but at times emerges as an exertion of will, a restless dissatisfaction with seeming perfection and an urge to create more and more:

> La luz, unidad del alba,
> se multiplica en destellos,
> lo que fue calma es fervor
> de innúmeros espejos
> que sobre el faz del agua
> anuncia su encendimiento.
> (ll.50-5, *Var.* XI, El poeta, *El Cont.*, p.636)

Nature's desire for self-expression is insatiable: the sea can change dramatically from one moment to the next, from smooth calm to a dazzling mirage, as the water swells into motion. Similarly, love ensures its own continuation through its ingenious powers of self-invention, and Salinas celebrates love's remarkable ability to regenerate itself in a myriad of forms in *Razón de amor-*

> Vive de beso en beso

redondo, como el mar
se vive de ola en ola,
sin miedo a repetirse. (ll.41 4, p.400)

Kisses multiply like waves, each one unique, each one part of a neverending sequence -

Suma, se suma, suma.   (ll.52)
seguro a no acabarse:
toca
techo de eternidad.
(ll.55-7, ¡Pasmo de lo distinto!, *Raz*., p.400)

Infinitely creative, love's progeny is its own re-creation.

Mathematical processes serve the poet as a useful metaphor for the inexorable creative processes he observes without, in nature, and within himself, in the love experience, and in his own creativity. He does not confine his poetic manipulation of the processes of accumulation to the use of the verbs "sumar" and "multiplicar". Salinas also combines enumerated nouns with the conjunction "y", to produce an effect of accumulation. The creative and procreative implications of this pseudo-mathematical technique in the context of the love experience are self-evident: self-perpetuation and reproduction. It seems apt, therefore, to draw on a term used by Salinas in his critical work, *La poesía de Rubén Darío*, "la y copulativa".[24] An exercise in this coupling technique can be found in "¡Ay, cuántas cosas perdidas!" (*La voz a ti debida*), where, as the title suggests, the poet accumulates a litany of phenomena he believed lost to him by the passage of time. When he meets the beloved, she miraculously restores the past and all its "cosas perdidas":

Y por perdidas las nubes
que yo quise sujetar   (ll.9-10)
Y las alegrías altas
del querer, y las angustias
de estar aún queriendo poco,

    y las ansias
    de querer, quererte más.   (ll.13-17, p.234)

The "y" conjunction is used extensively in this poem, and plays a significant part in the unfolding of its theme. The build-up of the "cosas perdidas" in lines 9-17, ("y" appears in ll.9, 13, 14 and 16), is balanced by the retrieval of "los tiempos y las espumas, las nubes y los amores," in ll.31-32.

Conjunctions can serve as bridges, both literally and figuratively, spanning semantic and emotional distances. This point becomes immediately apparent on reading "Los puentes", where the lovers are connected by many kinds of bridges: letters, familiar pronouns, tears, all contributing to better communication. The syntactic deployment of the "y" conjunction is interesting: the "y" in this instance rarely connects clauses within a sentence, as may be expected, but is more often situated at the beginning of a sentence. This creates the impression that each sentence is semantically linked to the previous one; the "y" acts as a "puente", even where no particular semantic link is evident. The technique is quite uncharacteristic of Salinas's customary spartan syntax, where conjunctions tend to be minimised, and therefore attracts the reader's attention in a self-conscious reinforcement of the accumulation theme.[25]

Throughout Salinas's love-cycle, the conjunction "y" unites and integrates, suggesting an ideal existence of infinite possibilities, all simultaneously realisable. The effect of accumulating love need not be expressed by the piling up of enumerated nouns, however, but can link one noun, repeatedly, regenerating it, as is the case in "Los puentes": "otro y otro y otro" (l.67), and above, "amor y amor y amor" (l.87).[26] In this way the poem presents a qualitative rather than a quantitative assessment of love, which is not so much the sum of many "things", as the sum of its own capacity for self-perpetuation.

Mathematical terminology, formulae, numerical progressions, all hold an undeniable attraction for Salinas in his quest to capture the world's "suma" in his poetry. Nonetheless, it is important to distinguish between this fascination with arithmetical processes, and a belief in the veracity of their conclusions. In his early poetry Salinas seems to indulge an ingenuous, almost childlike attraction to the symmetry and precision of numbers. As his work progresses, however, the charm of these mathematical processes of accumulation pales, as he becomes increasingly attentive to, and critical of, the quality of those things being accumulated. Disenchantment is the dominant tone where accumulation occurs in *Todo más claro*, as Salinas responds to the growth of materialism and the diminution of idealism in his immediate environment of North America in the 1940s.

The attraction of numeracy is still irresistible in an early poem such as "Números", where the counting of money is chosen over counting the stars. The night sky offers too vast a scale of constellations for the poet to read, it is incomprehensible to him: "Tenías abecedario / innumerable de estrellas" (ll.1-2). Not so the "cuentas" being settled at the table beside him:

Más bellas que los luceros
fúlgidas, cifras y cifras,
cruzaban por el silencio,
puras estrellas errantes,
señales de suerte buena
en largas caudas de ceros. (ll.10-15)

The observer of the night sky feels dwarfed by its immense scale; he prefers a human scale to that of the heavens; the settling of monetary accounts can be conducted with manageable ciphers; it is a task that falls within the boundaries of human conception - "¡qué constelación perfecta / tres por tres nueve!" (ll.17-18, *Seg.*, p.129). The multiplication of three by three is perfect in its precision, and is perfectly accessible to the human mind in its predictability, unlike the unquantifiable sum of the stars. Albeit with a measure of irony, the poet's view of numbers is still innocent in this early poem. They are as yet uncontaminated by materialist values, but this is a perspective that will alter quite radically in

Salinas's poetry between the composition of *Seguro azar* (1924-28) and *Todo más claro* (1937-47).

By the time "Escorial II" appears in *Fábula y signo* (1931), the numerical assessment of empirical reality has already become rather ambivalent - the poet's response to the outstanding symmetry and perfection of the monastery of San Lorenzo is: "En vez de soñar, contar" (1.1). So measured is the scene that his eyes and mind are sated, overwhelmed by its precision. There is no need to dream or imagine; this is perfection. Yet there is still a naive appreciation in the tone here, reminiscent of a child's counting-rhyme,

> Yo te quiero a ti, y a ti,
> y a ti.
> A tres os quería yo.   (ll.9-11)

The poet cannot resist the temptation to add up the numerical elements of the scene to find a total:

> Haré una raya
> para ir sumando; seiscientos
> doce, más cinco, más tres,
> más doce.
> ¡Qué felicidad igual
> a seiscientos treinta y dos!
> En abril, al mediodía
> cuenta clara.   (ll.16-23, Escorial II, *Fáb.*, p.196)

But so measured is the scene, so precisely defined, that instead of being inspired to create, he instead calculates; "en vez de soñar, contar". This numerically quantifiable "account" contrasts quite sharply with the spirit of Salinas's later poems where numerical calculations no longer serve as an adequate means of measuring human perception. Here, the pleasure extracted from the scene is expressed as exactly equal to the total of windows and clouds it contains. This poem "Escorial II", therefore, seems antithetical to Salinas's theory of an "aritmética fantástica", where the sum total is always equal to more than a

composite of parts.[27] A point further stressed in an essay where he cautions, "...
¡Pero cuidado! ¡que la suma no son los sumandos!".[28]

These contrasting perspectives are divided chronologically by twenty years:
"Escorial II" appeared in 1931, while the paper, "Deuda de un poeta" was delivered
in 1951, after the socio-political impact of the Spanish Civil War, and the Second
World War. Salinas's approach to mathematical quantification is already
problematic in *Fábula y signo*, indicating a possible shift in perspective even this
early. While "Escorial II" seems to celebrate the monastery's calculable "cuenta
clara", the poems "Jardín de los frailes", and "Escorial I" from the same volume,
offer a more ambivalent evaluation of the question of arithmetical calculation. A
transitional phase between the initial allure of numbers in Salinas's early poetry,
and later disenchantment, is discernible in the love poems of *La voz a ti debida*,
and *Razón de amor*. When confronted with the dilemma of computing the "suma"
of the beloved, Salinas acknowledges that arithmetic rules are quite inappropriate
to this task. The norms that govern the rest of existence do not apply to the
beloved; nothing is to be gained from adding her past life to her present; the sum
of what she has been and done will not, in this case, provide an answer to the
poet's question of "¿cómo eres?", which is essentially qualitative rather than
quantitative: "sumar acción con sonrisas, / años con nombres, sería ir perdiéndote"
(ll.13-14, Yo no necesito tiempo.., *La voz*, p.238). An interesting variation on the
function of numerical progression is presented in *Largo lamento*. In this case,
accumulation impoverishes where it had previously enriched. One year is added to
the next, but the sum total is depressingly little from the point of view of the
lovers, who require an endless lifespan to live out their love -

> ¡Cuánto nos falta por fuera!
> ¡Qué tiempo tan corto, el nuestro
> cuando el mundo nos lo cuenta! (ll.1-3)

If they are to quantify their lives purely numerically, there is little joy to anticipate:

> Qué futuro tembloroso,
> incierto, si se le mira
> con la mirada aritmética
> que cree que el porvenir
> es un año más un año,
> y así todos,
> hijos de la misma pena. (ll.7-13, *Largo*, p.555)

The poet-lover rejects the numerical quantification of his life because it limits any potential creativity to the reproduction of predetermined "hijos de la misma pena". Likewise, the result of the processes of accumulation in Salinas's poetry deteriorates gradually from a final sum of pleasure, to one of "pena" or anguish.

This association of negative feelings with the process of accumulation first emerges in the love cycle, becoming prevalent in *Todo más claro* where the obsessive materialism of contemporary society is dramatised in "Contra esa primavera". The compulsion to collect and hoard possessions, is extended to the accumulation of negative emotions and experiences. Crowds of people await the official coming of spring, weighed down by their emotional baggage of monotony and misery:

> Gran gentío aguarda ...
> ... con sus maletas, llenas
> de ahorros
> - rutina, tedio, niebla -,
> penosamente acumulados,
> en siete u ocho meses, día a día. (ll.22-9, *Todo*, p.755)

In a hopelessly materialist, urban setting, even lovers limit their own happiness by their insistence on quantifying it in material terms. "Error del cálculo" is a particularly anecdotal poem where Salinas dramatises the "romantic" encounter of lovers who cannot communicate outside the realms of concrete, calculable existence. Modern-day cynicism, urban sophistication and a fear of emotional revelation cause the would-be lovers to flee -

> ...la selva virgen donde vivimos
> en busca de ese sólido asfalto de los cálculos,
> de las cifras exactas, inventores
> de una aritmética de almas que nos salve
> de todo error futuro.   (ll.54-8, p.741)

The realm of emotion is a veritable jungle where the urban lovers feel vulnerable, prey to the uncontrollable primal forces of passion. They yearn for the sterile security of a concrete, quantifiable world where risks can be calculated. The only relationship they can offer one another is the collective accumulation of material clutter:

> Si juntamos tú y yo los capitales
> que hemos atesorado
> a fuerza de sumandos extrañísimos:
> sortijas, discos, lágrimas y sellos...
>   (ll.135-8, *Todo*, pp.744)

The urge to "sumar", at this point in Salinas's poetry, is decidedly suspect, indicating a hoarding mentality that is incompatible with the generous, procreative nature of love, as presented in the love cycle. The insertion of tears amongst the collections of rings, records and stamps, suggests that none of these possessions can alleviate underlying unhappiness; that each of the potential lovers hides a secret collection of suppressed anguish.

Salinas's deployment of the "suma" motif in his first three volumes of poetry and in the love-cycle, can be described as a stylistic device aimed at emphasising nature's accumulated riches and the seductive power of numbers. However, in his work of the 1940s, both the function and tone of this motif are transformed. His interest in the concept of a "suma" is now more thematic than stylistic, as he stresses the importance of accumulated learning and tradition as a means of resisting the threat of the void posed by war. It may be worth bearing in mind that by 1945 the "suma" of human existence was threatened by a new force of elimination. The scientific development that created the atomic bomb, like

all other knowledge accumulated in time, was uni-directional: knowledge can only be passed on, there is no way of turning the clock back, no way of un-learning what was too well learned at Nagasaki and Hiroshima. Moreover, this knowledge was not life-enhancing, but life-denying, seeming to break with Darwin's melioristic theory of human progress through evolution. With the invention of the bomb, evolution no longer seemed inevitable, but totally random. Humanity now seemed more possessed by, than in possession of knowledge, capable in an instant of reducing amassed history to a "cero".[29] This sense of an entire species treading the brink of unbeing, could only intensify the individual's appreciation and consciousness of his/her own threatened being. The psychological price of humanity's progressive removal from a man-centred Universe, is an increasing sense of marginality in an uncaring world. The existential doubts that plague the "Hombre en la orilla", suggest the very tenuous nature of the legitimacy of human presence on earth. The poems in *Todo más claro*, overall, focus on the individual's sense of crisis as part of a collective that is hurtling towards a gaping void. Salinas confronts the void in "Cero", the final poem in the collection, and grapples with the nature of absolute nothingness. The epigraphs to the poem remind us not only of the omnipresence of the void, but of man's historic and fatal fascination with the sources of his own destruction, in whatever guise.

> Y esa Nada, ha causado muchos llantos,
> Y Nada fue el instrumento de la Muerte,
> Y Nada vino a ser muerte de todos.

Attributed to Quevedo, this "Nada" is death, the great leveller that indiscriminately reduces everything to a singular void. Machado updates the source of destruction: the new God is rationalism, followed in the blind faith that it will lead to progress.

> Ya maduró un nuevo cero
> que tendrá su devoción.[30]

Unlike the aggregation of numbers or objects, the aggregation of nothings will not create a "suma", but simply a greater void. The reductionist impact of the bomb is immediate: one moment obliterates millennia of painstaking evolution:

> Lo que era suma en un instante es polvo
> ¡Que derroche de siglos, un momento!
> (ll.64-5, Cero V, *Todo*, p.782)

In Darwin's theory of evolution natural selection directs the species inexorably towards physical and intellectual perfection, so that progress is as inescapable as the passage of time. Salinas's earlier poetry appears to comply with this optimistic reading of human history. However, in the later poem "Hombre en la orilla", the relentless pressing forward of time inspires fear, not hope.

> Porque el momento que viene,
> ese que se va a pasar
> en un momento, detrás
>
> acarrea otro, y ése
> otro...   (ll.89-93)
> Muchos, terrible unidad   (l.96, Hombre en la orilla II, p.689)

Time is truly uni-directional, as its flow can neither be stopped nor reversed: "¿Redropaso? ¿Hay redropasos?" (l.111), "¿Desandar? ¡Puro embeleco! / Siempre se va hacia adelante" (ll.120-1, *Todo*, p.689).

The bomb undoes time's work as centuries of accumulated thoughts and endeavours are decimated. Time seems to stop dead – "vasto ayer que se queda sin presente" (l.5, Cero III, p.774). Present potential is denied fulfilment in a future, and past developments go unexpressed in the present. There is a profound irony here, for where scientific observation demonstrates that entropy and decay are the results of time's forward motion, Salinas's earlier work portrays time as inherently negentropic, bringing progressive order to the universe and leading to an eventual "suma" of 'entereza'. Entropic imagery pervades the apocalyptic "Cero". Although

222

the repeated allusion to ruins communicates a visual impression of the destruction inflicted by the bomb, Salinas is more concerned with the damages sustained by time, which is reduced to rubble, as the chain of continuity between past, present and future is broken: "No piso la materia; en su pedriza / piso el mayor dolor, tiempo deshecho" (ll.40-1, p.781).[31] The debris surveyed by the poet after the bomb, the "aparentes piedras" of Cero III, are in fact the charred remains of time itself: "Piso añicos de tiempo" (l.52, "Cero V", p.781). And with time, are destroyed the innumerable works perfected throughout centuries of human endeavour, "Hollando voy los restos / de tantas perfecciones abolidas" (ll.34-5, p.781).

All the minutiae and meticulous creations of the past, whether the products of nature or humanity, are indistinguishable in the uniform devastation of the bomb site:

> El Cero cae sobre ellas.
> Ya no se las veo, las muchas,
> las bellísimas, deshechas,
> en ese desgarradora
> unidad que las confunde,
> en la nada, en la escombrera.
> (ll.1-6, Cero IV, *Todo*, p.777).

The highly-evolved artistic consciousness that expresses itself in the pursuit of perfection, is rendered nought. The very desire to create has been broken: "Camino sobre anhelos hecho trizas" (l.53, p.781). Fragments of painstakingly sculpted stone are awash in the debris:

> No tibios, no despedazados miembros
> me piden compasión, desde la ruina:
> de carne antigua voz antigua oigo.
> (ll.3-5, Cero V, *Todo*, p.780)

The broken segments of stone limbs are not in themselves what excite the poet's compassion, but what they represent - the "carne", or flesh and blood artists who crafted them. Their voices ring in his ears, a fellow-artist, witness to the destruction of their common aspirations. The poet picks his way through the ruins, the remnants of an entire cultural heritage that seems to be irredeemably lost. An artist with no heritage, he is orphaned, absolutely alone, "Sigo escombrero adelante, solo, solo." (l.33, Cero V, p.781).

Salinas's generation had lived through two World Wars and the Spanish Civil War; the cine-camera brought terrible images of Guernica, Dresden, Warsaw, Hamburg. So it is scarcely surprising to find such a high incidence of entropic imagery in work of this period. These images are not confined to Salinas's work of the 1940s however, but are also prevalent in the love poems, although the tone with which they are employed in these earlier poems differs dramatically. Ruins here represent a distinctly un-tragic razing of the old order, to make way for the raising up of love's new order; they express hope and optimism. Although these ruins serve as a metaphor for time's destruction, the tone differs radically from that of the later poems. As the ironic title-line of "Amor, amor, catástrofe" indicates, love requires the eradication of the past, and the lovers desire a new world for their love to inhabit; everything must be pristine, unique to them.

> Toda hacia atrás la vida
> se va quitando siglos... (ll.11-12)

And while they seek to erase the past - "borrarse la historia" (l.17) - this is not destruction for its own sake, as love promises a new order to replace the old:

> Vamos
> a fuerza de besar
> inventando ruinas
> del mundo... (ll.32-5, La voz, pp.248-9)

The oxymoron of inventing ruins, where creativity emerges from evidence of destruction, reveals a redemptive purpose in this anarchy. Love will salvage the world from its history, and create a new "trasmundo" in its own image. There is no such redemptive purpose behind the deployment of the destruction described in "Cero".

The numerical value of the cipher 0 in the poem "Cero", refers to the void left by the bomb, and the absence of any order, whether old or new. In addition to this, the morpheme "o", signifying selection, is manipulated by Salinas in *Todo más claro* in such a way that word and number are encompassed in one annihilistic 'signo'. The manner in which this is achieved, is by presenting selection as a source of elimination, a means of preventing 'entereza', and another path to the void.

Salinas's use of elimination by selection, using the disjunction 'o' is in direct contrast with the technique of accumulating with the conjunction 'y'. This equation of selection and elimination is expounded in *El defensor*, in the statement that "Cualquier selección implica denuncia".[32]   The inevitability of sacrificed options in the process of selection is dramatised in "Hombre en la orilla":

> ...Eligir
> es una muerte.
> Pero ¿el muerto, quién será?
> aquéllo, si escojo esto.
> (ll.125-8, Hombre en la orilla II, *Todo*, p.690)

The necessity to choose raises questions as to the nature of human evolution. Salinas's conception of evolution as a cumulative process leading to ultimate 'entereza', tends to overlook the less attractive aspects of evolution by natural selection.   Nature has two faces, creative and cruel: in order to preserve the species, individual lives and phenomena are sacrificed as part of 'natural law'. Unlike abstract mathematical processes, the poet cannot aggregate and multiply experiences ad infinitum in one lifetime.   Human life is limited by time, and he is forced to make choices, which involve sacrificing many possibilities.   Every choice therefore involves elimination, and invokes the void:

No hay escape.
Tan solo por una muerte
tiene salida la O.
(ll.142-4, Hombre en la orilla II, p.691)

The reality of existence is fraught with selection, and only in death is the individual freed of the obligation to make choices. Where the "y" unifies, the "o" divides, introducing an element of competition between alternative options which will either be selected and brought to life, or cast aside, stillborn.[33]

Ahí está:
la que nos vuelve imposibles
las nupcias que más querríamos:
la de la luna y el sol,
la de lo uno y lo otro,
la de la cruz con su cara.
No.
Ha de ser aquello o esto
ha de ser nieve o ardor.
(ll.65-73, Hombre en la orilla II, p.689)

The plight of the anonymous "Hombre en la orilla", is the existential paralysis of the individual in a modern urban setting that offers no guidance or direction other than traffic-lights and signals. Which is the way forward for the human spirit? Transfixed by fear of the frenzied speed of city traffic, he hesitates on the kerb, unable to take decisive action. He is poised on the fine line that divides being and unbeing, forced by circumstance into a position where he must make choices, faced by a terrifying "O" -

A muchos les ha tocado
esta hora atroz,
la del hombre en la orilla:
verse enfrente de la O.
(ll.50-3, Hombre en la orilla II, p.688)

The sensation of growing vagueness about individual identity is fostered by modern mass society, which makes it extremely difficult to develop and live by individual standards. So many choices are available, as the flashing neon advertisements in "Nocturno de los avisos" (*Todo más claro*) brashly demonstrate. Indeed, the individual is faced with more choices than he can reasonably be expected to cope with. The strictly channelled character of urban life has closed off the option of integration. The traffic stops and starts according to rigidly-coded signals. The choices available are unequivocal: red to stop or green to go. But which should the man on the kerb obey? Which will extract him from this limbo? "Gravísima decisión / verdi-rojo, muerte-vida" (ll.33-4, p.693).

On a purely physical level, the options are clearly defined, but the implications of these choices are never explained. There is no guidance of a metaphysical or ethical nature, and for Salinas, this absence of the metaphysical renders life incomplete, obstructing the path to 'entereza'. Salinas's first-hand experience of the mighty North American metropolis has brought only one revelation: he now realises that the appearance of order and precision, the geometric perfection of these cities where architecture and roads meet in perfect symmetry, bears no relation whatsoever to the state of mind of the individual who inhabits it. While the urban traffic-system is perfectly ordered, it lacks an ultimate destination. There is an implicit comparison with Jorge Manrique's river/life metaphor in the opening lines of the poem:

> Este río no es aquél: (l.1)
> Ni hay mar que le esté esperando,
> con la eternidad abierta.
> (ll.15-16, Hombre en la orilla I, p.681)

Traffic circulates, the roads weave labyrinthine patterns; the destination of modern civilisation, and of the modern citizen, is unknown, "....nunca se llega / cuando no hay donde llegar" (ll.21-2, p.681). How can the individual find the authentic path of progress? How can he assess his position if he has no understanding of the world he inhabits?

This poet's response is first to describe the world before attempting to evaluate his place in it. Measurement, whether represented by aggregation or multiplication, is nonethless the most precise means of describing matter available to the poet, and Salinas's attitude to it *per se*, is certainly not negative.

> Preciosa es entre todas la noción de la medida, certero camino hacia la verdad. Las ciencias progresan al compás del arte de medir; de medir cada vez mayor y con más precisión.[34]

By measuring the Universe, describing it in numbers, science imposes on it a comprehensible structure and order. There is a strong semantic link between the ability to reason, and the abilty to count. In Roman Antiquity the noun "Rationalis" signified an accountant, or auditor. The common etymological root of these mental processes indicates a strong philosophical link between these urges to measure and understand the universe. In Salinas's early poetry, especially *Seguro azar*, the novelty of technological advancement is evident: by the 1920s, electricity in the home was possible, and motorcars were more accessible than before. Salinas's attitude to these novelties differs little from his general enthusiasm for life. He is not in awe of modern technology; rather he adopts a playful tone, as he sets about possessing the trappings of modern urban life, making them his own, by measuring the dimensions of their speed and power. In the exotic setting of the "Far West" of North America, Mabel, "la caballista" gallops along in some heartstopping chase: "¡Qué viento a ocho mil kilómetros!" (l.1, *Seg.*, p.121); speed and motion are a source of playful speculation. The enraptured tone seems to parody the openmouthed wonder of cinema-goers in the 1920s at these early "special effects", probably created with a crude wind-machine. The estimated speed is quite startling - eight thousand kilometers per hour. The hyperbole is deliberately childlike, demonstrating a total lack of comprehension of the measurement of velocity, and may well reflect the average age and attitude of the 1920s matinée western-buff.

There is a stark contrast in tone beween this playful parody of measured velocity and the more serious satire of "Hombre en la orilla". Here, too, the speedometer is consulted: as Mrs. Morrison drives to her appointment at the beauty salon, she accelerates faster and faster, in an attempt to swallow up the past, and somehow recover her youth.

> ¡De prisa, hacia las cuatro
> las diez, las doce, las cien mil sin cuenta,
> horas, devueltas al pasado, una
> por una a cada vuelta de las ruedas! (ll.53-6, *Todo*, p.682)

The presentation of speed in "Far West" involves a suspension of disbelief, a willing and harmless deception. By way of contrast, Mrs. Morrison's self deception that she can cheat the progress of time through sheer speed, is insidious and pathetic.

The most ambivalent presentation of measured existence in Salinas's poetry arises in an early poem, Escorial I (*Fábula y signo*), and could be said to represent a turning-point in his attitude to measured definitions -

> Está hecho,
> se puede medir, exacto,
> mayor que el ansia y el vuelo. (ll.6-8, p.190)

The tone is flat and emotionless. But is this a statement of fact, devoid of value or opinion? "El ansia" is the impulse that drives the artist - whether poet or architect - to create. "El vuelo" conveys the artist's desire to transcend, to rise above the transient nature of life and find some form of immortality through self-expression. Both of these are abstract nouns, they are immaterial qualities and thus immeasurable. The calculation presented in the poem is, therefore, flawed; the Escorial cannot be quantified as greater than the unquantifiable.

Of course only physical, concrete phenomena are measurable, and these, for Salinas, only represent one half of a whole, integrated view of reality and the self.

Without the immeasurable, the immaterial, the metaphysical, 'entereza' will continue to elude the individual and society. As the poet observes the growing cultural domination of materialistic values in the United States, so his approach to measured realities alters. The ultimate measurable commodity to figure in Salinas's poetry is money, which equals the exact value stated on its face and serves no other purpose than to measure the monetary value of given commodities; its sole function is as a means of quantification. Certain early poems illustrate an attraction to exact "sumas" and fixed quantities that is characteristic of Salinas's work at this time:

> Etiquetas de los precios,
> sin más ni menos, exactas,
> acabando con las dudas,
> allí en los escaparates. (ll.31-4, Nivel preferido, *Seg.*, p.147)

The precision with which monetary value is established seems to offer security. The "etiquetas" are consumer customs, unwritten rules dictated by market forces - not determining socially acceptable or unacceptable behaviour - but acceptable or unacceptable prices.

In "Moneda" (*Fábula y signo*), the poet holds tightly to the coin in his pocket on a foggy December evening. The fog swathes everything in doubt; distance is contorted; space becomes immeasurable. While in his pocket -

> Moneda
> con un número invencible
> por la duda o por la niebla... (ll.14-16, *Fáb.*, p.184)

- the coin remains unchanged, inalterably fixed at its minted value. There is nothing relative about its worth: so absolutely quantified and quantifying, it seems to banish all doubt and insecurity.

The initial attraction of the security of monetary quantification diminishes progressively for this poet. By the 1940s, writing "Civitas Dei" (*El Contemplado*, pp.640-6), Salinas is highlighting the failings rather than strengths of money as a means of measuring reality. Where its qualities of precision and constancy had been predominant, it now emerges as a metaphor for greed and hypocrisy. In this way, he contrasts the earth-bound city - "la gran ciudad de los negocios, / la ciudad enemiga" (ll.23-4) - unfavourably with the "Civitas Dei", its reflection in the sea of San Juan, whose "riqueza es la luz, / la sin moneda" (ll.11-12). In the monetarist city, we are told that -

> En Wall Street banqueros puritanos
> las escrituras firman
>
> para comprar al río los reflejos
> del cielo que está arriba.   (ll.121-124, p.645)

- but what the bankers fail to see is that money cannot fix a value on what is not for sale. The very phrase "banqueros puritanos" is loaded with irony, indicative of the hypocrisy that governs the enemy city. The devout bankers negotiate for salvation by purchasing a piece of heaven reflected in the rivers below, in the conviction that they can meet any price.

> El tiempo ya no es tiempo, el tiempo es oro,
> florecen compañías
>
> para vender a plazos los veranos,
> las horas y los días.
> (ll.39-42, Civitas Dei, El Cont., pp.641-42)

Time is capital, bought and sold; a commercially viable commodity: a man's value is estimated in terms of productivity levels and time worked. Salinas's later work communicates an absolute repudiation of the ethos of "la ciudad enemiga", the materialist citadel of modern capitalism. The theme is developed further in *Todo más claro*, and one poem, "El cuerpo fabuloso", weaves an elaborate metaphor of fate as a stock exchange. With the Wall Street crash still a relatively recent event, the analogy is very apt, as it highlights the absolutely arbitrary nature of both financial speculation and fate. Salinas points to the folly of modern man, who endeavours to predict his future as though life were a monetary investment:

> por esos turbios cielos del periódico
> las bandadas diarias de las cifras,
> cotizaciones de la bolsa, diosas,
> dueñas de los destinos, decidiendo
> que el precio de la dicha - (ll.23-27)
> sea más accesible que otros años... (l.31, *Todo*, pp.736-7)

Capital is the new Goddess, and the public are more than willing to believe that their investment will be rewarded by the new nirvana of wealth. If an economic system of human design can wreak such havoc in men's lives as did the Wall Street crash, there is little reason for men to fear the workings of external forces such as fate. The new religion is speculation, and spiritual aspirations have been replaced by a craving for riches.

Salinas's quest for 'entereza' precludes an acknowledgment of the metaphysical, and it is therefore significant that so little of the subject-matter of his poetry is quantifiable. Immeasurable entities such as "el amor", "la amada", and "el contemplado", inspire a large portion of his work. Salinas is drawn to subject areas whose value is relative and variable, whether the vast scope of human emotion explored in the love cycle, or the infinite changeability of the sea of San Juan. Fascinated by the methods and processes of definition, Salinas finds himself in a world where little is definable. Love is perhaps the supreme example of this. Because it exists "más allá de" time and space, it cannot be measured according to the dimensions of the physical world. Love seeks its own "trasmundo", un-charted, uninhabited, pristine, and the poet-lover explores the disorientating and reorientating effects of love in the poem, "Extraviadamente / amantes, por el mundo":

> ...Los mapas, falsos,
> trastornando los rumbos,

> juegan a nuestra pérdida
> entre riesgos sin faro.   (ll.97-22, *La voz*, p.254)

The old rules no longer apply, and the lovers, who belong to a different sphere of experience that cannot be reduced to scale, will learn nothing from maps. They can even present a danger to lovers foolish enough to try to orientate themselves in the "trasmundo" by the maps of the "mundo" they have left behind. No scale has been devised that is elastic enough to contain love, which dwells in uncharted domains because its parameters cannot be delineated, cannot be reduced to a mathematical scale. The poet-lover therefore refuses to subject his feelings to conventional techniques of evaluation. Nothing about the love experience can be numerically quantified; neither its sorrows nor its joys.

> Lo que nunca he podido averiguar
> aunque he hecho muchos cálculos en láminas
> de lagos, con las plumas de los cisnes
> es el número
> necesario de lágrimas
> para poder pasar sin miedo alguno
> donde queremos ir.   (ll.81-7, Los Puentes, *Largo*, p.465)

Salinas substitutes numerical calculation for the conventional use of objective correlative. However, not even with the aid of these exquisite and highly original measuring implements, (lake-water and swan-feathers), can the lovers calculate the possible sum of their feelings. The prerequisite number of tears to be spilt before they stop fearing the power of their own love, and proceed to the "trasmundo", is an unknown sum.

Despite the fact that numbers extend to infinity, even they can be exhausted by the lovers' resources. Love is metadimensional, even transcendental, occupying levels of experience that numbers cannot hope to apprehend. Emotions have no weight, cover no distance, occupy no physical space.[35] Numbers tell us nothing of their quality, and are of little use to the poet in the realms of subjective feeling, as they habitually drain the reserves of numeracy.

> Hay que cansar los números. (l.15)
> Que se rompan las cifras
> sin poder calcular
> ni el tiempo ni los besos.
> (ll.25-7, ¡Sí, todo con exceso!, *La voz*, pp.252)

The quest for the beloved "tú" in Salinas's poetry has received fairly exhaustive commentary.[36] The beloved eludes definition as surely as love does. Prismatic and ever-variable, her quintessential self (sometimes evoked by Salinas as her "alma"), cannot be pinned down. The more the lover knows her, the more inaccessible she seems to be. The quest acts as a generating motor, impelling the lover along a tantalising route of self-discovery, in the discovery of the 'other'. Salinas explores various methods of defining the beloved. Language fails, as does visual portraiture, and inevitably, numerical computation.

> descubriste los términos
> de todo lo numérico,
> el vacío del número.
> (ll.110-12, Pareja, espectro, *Largo*, pp.454)

The title of "Lo inútil" from *Todo más claro*, while addressed to the beloved, could just as easily refer to poetry. Salinas deploys an "intimista" feminine personal pronoun, reminiscent of Bécquer's *Rimas*, so maximising the poem's potential implications. The poet needs his anti-utilitarian muse. The material world is personified as a melancoly accountant who has missed the vital element in balancing his accounts:

> Innecesaria pura, puro exceso
> tú, la invisible sobra de la cuentas
> que el mundo va echando,
> contable triste...   (ll.56-9, p.750)

The beloved is the missing incalculable element without which the sum of the poet's life is incomplete; through her he achieves 'entereza'. Salinas cleverly enacts the process of completion, the final touch, through the hyphenated enjambement of "exacta-mente":

> ...tú, la demasía, tú la sobra
> en estos cortos cálculos del suelo
> eres, en una altísima
> celesta matemática...   (ll.62-5)
> ... exacta-
> mente lo que me falta   (ll.65-8, pp.750-1)

The beloved's value can only be measured subjectively in terms of what she represents to the lover; any attempt at a quantitative calculation is meaningless.

Apart from love and the beloved, "el contemplado", the sea of San Juan, is another of Salinas's great immeasurables. It is empirically observable; its depth can be gauged numerically as can its volume; from one point of view, the sea is no more than a body of so many square miles of water. Yet it is deemed by Salinas to be an immeasurable commodity. *El Contemplado* was written between 1943 and 1944, directly inspired by Salinas's daily visual dialogue with the sea of San Juan. From this prolonged proximity to the sea, the poet evidently concludes that it is never the same on two consecutive days nor even two consecutive moments. There is no norm, no measured reality other than the perceived sea of the here and now. Infinitely variable, with more facets than even the beloved, there exists no more apt a symbol for dynamic process than a body of water in perpetual motion. The waves serve as a kinetic reminder of nature's continuity; *natura naturans*.

> Se hunden las cien, las mil, las incontables
> figuras cristalinas;
>
> de una en otra, evadiéndose... (ll.51-3, Var. X, p.634)

It is interesting to note that while Salinas delights in the indefinable and immeasurable nature of even the empirical world, his poems reveal a continuous striving after definitions. He is at times enticed by the accuracy and stability of numerical description, at times repelled by the fixed vision of reality it offers. Salinas's chosen term for mathematical definitions is "las cifras". His relationship with these ciphers evolves from a poem such as "Números", from *Seguro azar*, where numbers still denote a pristine innocence, to "Nocturno de los avisos" in *Todo más claro*, where they measure the spiritual vacuum of modern urban life, and the impossibility of integration with 'otherness' or personal 'entereza' in this environment. Whether attracted or repelled, Salinas is always fascinated by numerical computations and always highly conscious of his own complex relationship with "las cifras". This self-awareness is amply demonstrated by his discussion of numeracy as a modern sociological phenomenon in *El defensor*:

> el vocablo matemático, muy particularmente para aquellos que no saben toda la complicación, misterio y hermosura de la matemática, es el tribunal supremo de todas las causas.[37]

Salinas is suspicious of the absolute faith placed in statistics and numerical tables by contemporary Western society, as the individual looks to numbers for demonstrable, fixed answers. They are the Supreme Court of modern society because they are perceived as a source of absolute and unquestionable truth. He acknowledges their "hermosura" - their abstract perfection, but he is equally aware of their complexity, or what he calls their "misterio", a hint that they may not be as transparent nor even as objective as they at first appear. Numerical description, like verbal, is open to manipulation. Nonetheless, the modern citizen chooses to define himself and his circumambient universe in numerical terms.

> El ser humano contemporáneo tiende a realizarse en el número, por donde quiera que se mire, la forma que en él toma la lucha con el destino es la de una pugna con los números.[38]

Much of Salinas's work demonstrates the shortcomings of numerical denomination, whose relevance is limited to the material world. Numbers cannot provide answers to non-material questions and cannot describe non-empirical levels of individual or collective experience -

> ...el fenómeno del número, la gran tarasca de la cantidad, personaje descollante de nuestro tiempo. Pero es hija legítima de nuestro tiempo, y como tal es imperativo aceptar su realidad y hacerle cara.[39]

Salinas's experimentation with mathematical processes is his way of confronting and forging a relationship with this phenomenon. It is, equally, a poetic quest for new metaphors, new "objective co-relatives" to describe the changing world in which the poet lives and writes. Ultimately, "las cifras" fail to provide an apt metaphoric expression for the essentially subjective experiences that figure in so many of his poems.[40] They give no insight into the non-material realms of experience, and ultimately, they fail to provide coherent solutions to the social, collective problems of the age addressed by Salinas in his later works. While appearing to offer absolute measures of demonstrable truth, "las cifras" soon become a source of disillusionment. By the 1940's, the old Gods were dead: the reality of two World Wars seriously undermined the notion of an ordered Universe - whether that order be divine or scientific. According to Salinas, the craving for certainties in modern civilisation would not be met by numeracy nor any other scientific tool. It seemed by this time, that the human intellect could measure and comprehend all material reality, while what remained unexplained and incomprehensible was a purpose to the existence of the Universe and humanity's place in it. Salinas's poems indicate that in his judgement, the precision and accuracy of measured reality is of little assistance in reaching the ontological goal of 'entereza'. The salient tone of *Todo más claro* is disappointment with the course taken by Western civilisation: intellectually, because knowledge had become a source of destruction, and ethically, as older 'spiritual' values were replaced by rampant materialism. (In this respect, it is important to note that Salinas distinguishes between "materialism" and material reality - "las cosas" of the world that figure so consistently his poetry as a source of delight and stimulus). However, he observes in his later poems that society has reduced the value of much phenomena to that of a monetary estimate, and that a personal, intimate relationship with matter has become increasingly difficult for this reason. The poet can only conclude that while the ciphers that so captivated his youthful imagination may accurately quantify matter, and that this accuracy is as durable as marble, they impart little meaning or significance, "esa marmórea exactitud, la cifra, / poco ilumina" (ll.17-18, *Todo*, p.674).

The street numbers of New York in "Nocturno de los avisos" exercise a form of intellectual and spiritual slavery over the city's inhabitants who follow these numerical progressions in a state of blind faith, with no thought as to what they signify or where they may lead. A measured life has the appearance of security; it is clearly defined. Just as the long straight avenues of New York's street grid seem to extend eternally, these numerical sequences give the impression of leading to a total.[41]

> ¿Marca es de nuestro avance hacia la suma
> total, esclavitud a una aritmética
> que nos escolta...   (ll.17-19, p.717)

What do these numbers signify? What do they measure? Where the individual once charted his life in the years that took him from first breath to last, he now looks for his identity in street numbers.

> ¿O son, como los años, tantas cifras
> señas con que marcas en la carrera
> sin señales del tiempo, a cada vida,
> las lindes del aliento ...?   (ll.23-6)
> ¿Llegaré hasta qué número? (l.30, p.717)

The numbers are tantalising, as they extend further and further along the street, but can they live up to their promises? Will they add up to eternity, or does the sheer length and rectitude of the avenue create an optical illusion? - "Infinita a los ojos / y toda numerada" (ll.12-13, *Todo*, pp.717-720). Where he was previously attracted by the promise of infinitely progressing numbers, the poet now pales, confronted by the enormity of numerical expression. However vast their scope, numbers do not point the way to personal fulfilment or 'entereza' because they fail to take account of non-material values. This same theme, the quest for signs or ciphers that will answer his existential questions, receives an ironic treatment in "Civitas Dei" (*El Contemplado*). In "la ciudad enemiga", the future will henceforth be predicted by arithmetic, banishing all doubt. Men will no longer be the victims of blind fortune's arbitrary wheel.

> ¡Clarísimo el futuro, ya aritmético
> mañana sin neblinas!
>
> Expulsan el azar y sus misterios
> astrales estadísticas .   (ll.51-4, p.642)

There will no longer be any need for anticipation or imagination; dreams will become obsolete as calculation fulfills every human need: "Lo que el sueño no dio, lo dará el cálculo" (l.55, p.642).

Equally ironic is Salinas's treatment of the quandary faced by modern-day lovers in the significantly titled "Error del cálculo" (*Todo más claro*, pp.740-5). The lovers' calculations are inaccurate because they attempt to quantify love in material terms. They invest in love and expect to collect emotional returns in much the same way as invested money gathers interest.

> ... Sí, sí, si calculamos
> que mi alma puede resistir un peso
> de treinta días cada mes, o al menos,
> de siete días por semana, entonces ...(ll.69-72)
> ... las cifras esas cuya suma

si es que contamos bien tiene que ser
la eternidad o poco menos. (ll.82-84, p.742)

In this way, Salinas points up the rather desperate nature of the search for
emotional security in the modern world, the longing for material security, and the
confusion of the two. The would-be lovers lack the emotional confidence to take
the vital step of revealing their innermost feelings, which they themselves can only
conceive of as a "cifra".

Ninguno de los dos nos atrevemos
a aventurar la cifra deseada
ni el sí que comprometa   (ll.142-4, p.744)

They are assisted, however, by the timely and fortuitous intervention of an angel
whose annunciation is somewhat cramped by modern architecture. Feathers flying,
the angel stumbles into the hotel lounge after entangling his wings in the revolving
doors (the scene recalls the comic routines of the silent movies of which Salinas
and his Generation were avid fans in the 1920s). Characteristically, Salinas injects
humour into even the most serious of moments. The angel bears a grim message
and all calculations for the future are swept aside as,

...Lo incalculable
se nos posa en las frentes, y nosotros
lo recibimos, mano en mano, de rodillas.   (ll.151-3, p.744)

Like a sacramental blessing, the lovers receive life's greatest immeasurable, death
itself. All their exacting predictions for the future are banished as the angel leads
them to Charon, the oarsman, and they cross the river that divides life from death:

... al otro lado
una alcoba, en la costa de la muerte,
nos abrirá un gran hueco
donde todos los cálculos se abisman.   (ll.165-8, *Todo*, pp.745)

In the absence of real control over individual or collective destiny, modern man finds solace in "los cálculos" and "las cifras". Not even science can predict the future, but it can at least explain the past and the present and so provides a sense of orientation. If life is a process of accumulating knowledge and experience in time, the questions inevitably arise - when is the final calculation made? When is the definitive total computed? And what will it be?

> ¿Vale la pena haber llegado al número
> seiscientos vientisiete?
>> (ll.100-1, Nocturno de los avisos, *Todo*, p.719)

For Salinas, the assessment of reality must embrace more than the numerically measurable. It is a continuous process that occupies an entire lifetime. He discovers his own identity by exploring his relationship with the reality he inhabits.

> Reality, the life that surrounds and limits us, that gives to the individual the measure, at once tragic and magnificent, of his own solitude and of his creative possibilities.[42]

Reality offers both infinite potential and defining limitations: on the one hand, it offers the ready-made definitions of the empirically observable world, and simultaneously, a myriad of potential creations. The nature of the poet's work, as argued by Salinas's essays in *Reality and the Poet in Spanish Poetry*, will to a large extent depend on how he relates to this reality, and which of these aspects he perceives as dominant; potential or definition. The perspective of a Jorge Manrique or a Calderón de la Barca as described in Chapter Two, "The Acceptance of Reality", stresses the limitations of this life and looks forward to a limitless, ideal life after death. But what of the twentieth century poet? How is he to reconcile the reality he inherits with that which is latent in his own imagination? Salinas puts forward the theory that, "the poet has as his object the creation of a new reality within the old reality".[43] Accordingly, he is drawn to a perception of reality that has more to do with the creative process than the creation of a finished product.[44] This is particularly true in the historical context of the Second World War, where all notions of finality were contaminated by the reality of genocide.

Salinas seems to share the Romantic concept of the creative impulse as a spiritual, as well as an aesthetic aspiration. It is the striving to create that leads the artist to a state of enlightenment. Through self-expression, he reaches an understanding of himself, the world and his place in it. The senses and the imagination respond to 'otherness', inspiring the poetic impulse, but it is the anticipation of continued creativity that sustains the endeavour. It is the infinite longing for perfection and not its attainment that ensures that a sum total is never reached. This is not only vital to the individual artistic impulse - but to the collective desire to see life continue.[45] Salinas's poetry, while seeking out new metaphors and new ways of describing reality, ultimately shies from definitive accounts, whether numerical or linguistic, because they constitute an end of creativity, a death. What emerges from this is a growing distrust of experience that is framed, defined - whether physically or figuratively.

Geometric forms such as squares and rectangles display the characteristics of restriction and delineation: by framing experience, they confine it. One of the earliest examples of these framing devices is the big screen in "Cinematógrafo" (*Seguro azar*). The poem opens with a blank screen; the projector starts up: "saltó el mundo todo entero / con su brinco primaveral" (ll.15-16). But this entire world of potential, full of primal energy, is cheated by the enclosure of the four-sided screen.[46]

> La tela rectangular
> le oprimió en normas severas,
> le organizó bruscamente
> con dos líneas verticales,
> con dos líneas horizontales.
> (ll.17-21, Cinematógrafo, *Seg.*, p.133)

Once definition is established by the rectangular image on the screen, infinite potential is lost; the "entereza" of the world is sacrificed to a norm.

Framed paintings are the subject of "Pasajero en museo" (*Todo más claro*), whose inhabitants Salinas observes, the "criaturas salvadas" (1.2) from the ravages of time, they exist in an extra-temporal state, contained in gilded cages, a starkly preserved moment. Framed outside time, they have no reality beyond that of the museum walls:

> Allí detrás estáis amurallados
> en resplendor estático, frontera
> de la paz y la lucha, duros brillos
> que os guardan, rectángulos dorados.   (ll.60-3)

Salinas's choice of adjectives is clearly pejorative in the value-system that has evolved in his poetry up to this point. While these framed images may have escaped the fate of mortal beings, their immortality is, ironically, of a limited kind; resigned to the boundaries of its frame.[47]

> la vida que se para es lo inmortal,
> la que acepta su marco.   (Pasajero en museo, ll.101-02, *Todo*, pp.705-6)

These framing devices illustrate that in Salinas's eyes, reality cannot be truly represented according to strict mathematical rules, either with 'cifras', or with the spartan and orderly appearance of geometric perfection.

Maps also attempt to define the world in measured proportions: what they offer is an abstraction, a geometric, schematic version of empirical reality. The poet's rejection of a charted interpretation of the world is established early in his poetry:

> Abierta de par en par
> la vida por unas páginas
> enormes, verdes, azules,
> servicial, lisa, esquemática,
> atlas...   (ll.6-10, p.146)

From a vantage point of 1,100 metres he surveys the landscape; everything is reduced to measured scale from this perspective; a utilitarian, numerically coherent system. Salinas goes on to declare quite unequivocally that his "Nivel preferido" is not the vantage-point that renders the world a map, but street-level, in an inhabited, recognisable landscape of human proportions: "abajo, allí a media hora" (l.21), "En la calle hirviente, clara..." (l.35, *Seg*., p.146).

We return to the distancing effect of the bird's-eye view in "Cero", with more grim implications. The task of the pilot who must drop the A-bomb is not, after all, so daunting. The immense height from which he surveys the earth renders it a flat, two-dimensional pattern:

> ¿Mundo feliz? ¿Tramas, vidas,
> que se tejen, se destejen,
> mariposas, hombres, tigres,
> amándose y desamándose?
> No. Geometría. Abstractos
> colores sin habitantes,
> embuste liso de atlas.   (ll.13-19)

From such a distance, dropping the bomb will be an abstracted, mechanical act. There is no evident connection between the suffering on ground level and the pilot's view from above that dwarfs the plight of the individual: "Y a un mapa distante, ¿quién / le tiene lástima?" (ll.26-7, Cero I, *Todo*, p.769). Wars are planned on maps, strategies are formed, national boundaries arranged and rearranged, regardless of the thousands of lives implicated; the bomb is dropped on just such an abstract conception of reality as this "mapa".

When Salinas's poetry is read as a whole, what emerges is a preference for the unknown, unfinished, incipient, over definition.[48] Having sought the "suma" - the total consequence of experience - through various mathematical processes, the poet concludes in "Lo inútil" that "el sino de la vida es lo incompleto", (l.70, p.751). Reality has no cipher, no definition, because it is an ongoing process. The very essence of human life is the anticipation of further life, as the dynamic verbal expression of "Pasajero en museo" demonstrates: "vivir, seguir, querer seguir viviendo" (l.156, p.707). The present can only find expression in the anticipated future, just as the past is realised in the present. Today's aspirations are tomorrow's creations. Life, and the desire to live, become synonymous. This impatient consciousness of an incipient future is central to Salinas's conception of reality: "The poet is born into a world that is already made.... And yet at the same time constantly to be made".[49] The world is empirically evident and measurable, and yet it is also unrealised and therefore incalculable. The natural environment demonstrates this point quite clearly: what we perceive in nature is the fulfilment of past seasons and the simultaneous germinating of the next -

> No canta el mirlo en la rama,
> ni salta la espuma en el agua:
> lo que salta, lo que canta
> es el proyecto en el alma.   (ll.1-4, p.409)

This is why nature figures so predominantly in *Confianza* as a symbol of wholeness and 'entereza', while in *Todo más claro*, technology is increasingly associated with destruction and the void. Anticipation and projection are a vital part of nature's grand design, where existing life nurtures and engenders future life: "Perfección casi imposible / de la perfección hallada" (ll.10-11, p.409). The achievement of perfection must appear to be a possibility, otherwise man would not strive to attain it. Yet perfection must also stay just out of reach, perpetually inspiring, perpetually inviting:[50]

> en el beso que se da
> se estremece de impaciencia
> el beso que se prepara
>   (ll.12-14, No canta el mirlo... *Raz.*, p.409)

Even the simplest and most spontaneous of gestures, a kiss, carries in it the promise of another. No action or creation occurs in isolation, such is the inescapably sequential nature of reality.

Incomplete experience is by definition unknown and mysterious. This is an added attraction for Salinas who delights in all novelty. It also justifies his own artistic participation in the revelation and realisation of new creations. As poet and creator, Salinas sees no place for himself in a world already completed - a reality that is perfectly proportioned, with neither excess nor shortfall, denies the poet his vocation:

> Está bien, mayo, sazón.
> Todo en el fiel. Pero yo...
> Tú, de sobra. (ll.10-12, Vocación, *Seg.*, p.110)

The frustration of the poetic impulse is re-enacted by the interruption of line l.11. There is no apparent need for individual contributions to this self-fulfilling and perceivable reality -

> Cerrar los ojos. Y ver
> incompleto, tembloroso,   (ll.16-17)
> un mundo sin acabar
> necesitado, llamándome   (ll.21-2)
> que le de la perfeccion.   (l.25, *Seg.*, p.110)

However, within the poet's imagination awaits a world of tremulous latency, to which he can contribute; the world that he requires - "necesitado" - in order to define himself.[51] Herein lies an interesting paradox. While Salinas abhors the void, and resists it in his work through various devices of accumulation that aspire to encompass a final "suma", this same aspiration requires that there be a void which the poet can fill. As the poem "Vocación" illustrates, if all reality is replete or 'entero', there is no place for individual creativity, no possibility of the individual's achieving 'entereza' through self-expression. This paradox is outlined

quite clearly by Antonio Machado in the guise of Abel Martín, when he points to
the inseparability of all creativity and the void.

> ... es el amor mismo o conato del ser por superar su propia
> limitación quien las proyecta sobre *la nada* o *cero absoluto*, que
> también llama el poeta *cero divino*, pues, como veremos después,
> Dios no es el creador del mundo, según Martín, sino el creador de
> la nada.[52]

And indeed, Martín expands upon the nature of creativity and its relationship with
the void in a sonnet:

> Cuando el *ser que es* hizo la nada y
> reposó, que bien lo merecía, ya tuvo
> el día noche, y compañía tuvo el
> hombre en la ausencia de la amada.
> ¡Fiat umbra! Brotó pensar humano.
> Y el nuevo universal alzó, vacío,
> ya sin color, desustanciado y frío,
> lleno de niebla ingrávida, en su mano.
> Toma el cero integral, la hueca esfera,
> que has de mirar, si lo has de ver, erguida.
> Hoy que es espalda el lomo de tu fiera,
> y es el milagro del no ser cumplido,
> brinda, poeta, un canto de frontera
> a la muerte, al silencio a al olvido.[53]

To gloss Martín's creed in terms of Salinas's poetry: "el ser que es", the supreme
creator, invents - not the world - but the void. However he also invents man,
who, inspired by this "milagro del no ser cumplido", this constant process of
completing, is compelled to create. He must, with his own creative powers, bring
light to the darkness - "¡Fiat umbra! Brotó pensar humano" - and as Salinas's love
poems illustrate, he must draw on his imaginative powers to fill the void left by the
absence of the beloved. The void, therefore, to Abel Martín, did not pose a threat,
but was filled with promise, potential, a "niebla ingrávida" reminiscent of those in

Bécquer's poetic trances or *ensueños*.[54] And he challenges the poet to confront the void, to possess it, to take up the task of creativity, of filling vacuums.

While Salinas's own poetic creed, as outlined in *Reality and the Poet* and "Vocación", is wholly compatible with this philosophy, his perception of the void is inevitably influenced by historic events in his lifetime. It is therefore difficult for him to conceive of a "cero" as being "integral", rather than disintegrating. As indeed, for all his appreciation of "lo incompleto", his song will never invoke those three great expressions of the void listed by Martín in his sonnet: "la muerte, el silencio, y el olvido". If anything, these three represent what Salinas sees in all of his writings as the most negative aspects of the void. This is why the desire to transcend physical death is expressed in the love-cycle by a conception of eternal incarnation. Similarly, in his later work he expresses belief in the need to stimulate the individual life-force in order to ward off the threat of death posed by the bomb. The importance of communication in his work demonstrates a desire to overcome silence, to reach out and strike up a dialogue with all 'otherness'; to enter into the great articulation and 'cántico' that reality represents for him, as it does for Guillén. And the ultimate threat of " el olvido" underlying so many poems, conjures up the fear of lost love, and with the absence of love, the loss of self, oblivion. While differing from Machado in his poetic approach to the void, Salinas is obviously very aware of the inherent duality of "la nada", of its potential as a vacuum awaiting creativity, as well as its destructive aspects. In this sense, a distinction can be made between Salinas's use of the "Cero" motif in a socio-political context, where it symbolises the arbitrary destruction of war, and his rather Creacionista appreciation of the void as a poetic stimulus, a positive symbol of creative potential.

In the new genesis described in Martín's "Al Gran Cero", we see how a true Miltonic inversion directs the powers of creativity away from the creator towards the creature. It may be profitable at this point to consider Salinas's treatment of

248

the creator-creature relationship in this light. The old reality, which is not yet complete or 'entero', inspires a creative response in the artist who then creates new realities. In the act of creating, the artist declares a state of simultaneous connectedness with, and autonomy from, the reality he inhabits. He is inspired by it, but must direct his energies away from it and towards his own inventions, in order to realise himself fully, and find his own 'entereza'. In the same way, the artefact is dependent on the artistic imagination, but in the process of realisation, wins autonomy from its creator. This highly self-conscious poet is fully aware of the paradoxical situation from which he writes: only by not finishing the designed product, by preserving it in a state of incompletion, can the artist secure absolute control over his creature. This is suggested as a mock-serious poetic option as early as *Seguro azar*:

> Un ocio
> tan hondo que yo ya sé
> que lo tengo empezado
> se cumple en el no acabar,
> su sinfín tiene perfecto,
> no se ve, ya de tan claro.   (ll.17-22, Quietud, *Seg.*, p.120)

The poem is riddled with apparent paradoxes and needs to be read in the light of the poet's overall value-system, which establishes incompletion as an ideal of unending creative potential. The equation of completion and perfection in the poem "Vocación" (l.4), "perfecto el mundo, completo", suggesting a sated reality requiring no intervention from the poet, is here reversed to an equation of perfection and incompletion; "su sinfín, tiene perfecto" (l.21).

Once any creative act is completed, the product is released from the artist's nurturing hands and takes on a life of its own. For this reason, there is a perpetual loneliness attached to the act of creating, as described by "Soledades de la obra" (*Seguro azar*).

> Voy a hacer (¡Qué mío es

lo que voy a hacer!)
Estoy haciendo (¡Qué mío!)
Ya está hecho. Míralo.
¡Cuidado!
El hacer, enajenar,
quedarse solo, de hacer. (ll.1-7, p.137)

Out of loneliness the artist creates, and in creating he is returned to loneliness. Salinas explores the inevitable sense of loss experienced by the artist in the transition from the process of creating to the finished product.

This rather playful treatment of creature-creator relationship in Salinas's early work is replaced by a much more sombre tone in his work of the 1940s. The resistance to termination evident in the later poems is clearly connected with the political background of World War Two. The concept of finality in the public mind is now painfully associated with the death-toll of wartime, with 'final solutions', and with the threat of apocalyptic destruction. An interesting shift in tone is again evident in Salinas's treatment of a recurring theme: in the poems of the 1920s the concept of termination presents a purely aesthetic paradox, as he creates in order to fill the void, and in completing his work is returned to that same void. Whereas in his later works the threat of termination acquires political connotations and is closely linked with the negative, wartime "Cero" motif.

It would seem that for Salinas, the ideal state of unrealised perfection can only survive the duration of the actual creative process. As a finished product emerges, the ideal "suma" of infinite possibilities of what it might have been, but is not, is banished to the void. Limitless potential can only exist in the artist's imagination. The eventual creation will represent an "o", just one selected definition of the whole original idea: this is the tragedy of the framed pictures of "Pasajero en museo", whose 'entereza' is sacrificed to fixed form. The poem embodies the great paradox of self-expression: by realising an ideal, the poet redeems it from an uncommunicated state in his own mind, to a state of communicated, perceived reality. However, the price to pay for this salvation, is that all realisation involves definition, and all definition diminishes.

Paradoxically, the completion of a project seems to smother the spark of invention that inspired it. Another example of this is the symmetry of the Escorial: "Está hecho / se puede medir, exacto" (ll.6-7). Salinas finds the monastery-palace oppressive: like the perfect completed world of "Vocación", it leaves no room for invention and overpowers the urge to create with its scale and geometric perfection. So the poet's frustrated desire to participate in a creative process is projected onto the product itself when he comments - "De estar tan hecho / Ya se le acabó el querer" (ll.21-2, *Fáb.*, p.190). The completion of the Escorial has suppressed aspiration and as a result has produced a piece of architecture of a peculiarly sterile symmetry. The artist's desire to capture all the potential of a project is an unrealisable aspiration. An ideal balance of possibility and reality is, however, borne out by "el contemplado", the sea of San Juan. Significantly entitled "El poeta", Variación XI of *El Contemplado* puts forward the sea's continuous activity as a model for the poet's own aspirations.

> Pero tú nunca te quedas
> arrobado de lo que has hecho;
> apenas lo hiciste y ya
> te vuelves a lo hacedero.   (ll.22-5, El poeta, p.635)

The sea never experiences the solitude experienced by the poet who is, ironically, orphaned by his own creations. Its immense creative capacity ensures constant reproduction. "El contemplado", the sea, serves as a symbol of sustained aspiration and continuous creation; it is at once product and process, creator and creature.

The completion of any project contains a deeply rooted ambiguity for Salinas, which is captured in the epigraph to *Presagios* -

> Forjé un eslabón un día,
> otro día forjé otro
> y otro.

> De pronto se me juntaron
> - era la cadena - todos.   (p.51)

The "suma", or total of the creative process is presented here as a chain, which can be interpreted as either a positive interlinking unit, or a negative restrictive implement. Salinas resists the completion of any process for the same reason as he resists the calculation of any sum total; both require definition, both imply the termination of creativity and a possible commencement of entropy. One total, one product, can only present one perspective, whereas Salinas's conception of 'entereza' involves an unsummable total of human perspectives, whose plurality can only be preserved in the process of germination.

> El invento es siempre asombroso, participa, dentro de lo humano, de
> la chispa del milagro; la cosa inventada ya significa una leve
> disminución con respecto al invento.[55]

The finished product fails to fulfil all the potential of the original inspiration. Significantly, it also acquires an autonomous identity, quite independent of the poet, and this very autonomy, the miraculous invention of an independent life, can become the source of catastrophe. The passage continues -

> ...y luego llega la catástrofe, el uso que se hace de la cosa inventada,
> que nos hace maldecir del invento, blasfemar del milagro: la bomba
> atómica. Porque ese es el hecho trágico del mundo moderno: las
> cosas se han desmandado. Ya no las manda su inventor, el hombre;
> son ellas las que empujan, como malos pastores, por el mundo, a los
> rebaños humanos.

The atomic bomb is the Frankenstein's monster of the twentieth century. The creator no longer controls his creatures but is instead controlled by them. In creating the atomic bomb the human intelligence has created the instrument of its own potential downfall. The act of creation itself is corrupted and converted into an act of self-destruction; the "suma" of evolution reduced to a "cero". The explanation offered by Salinas for this conversion is that human knowledge no longer acknowledges either a source, nor an ultimate goal.

> Hoy día hay también una especie de actitud burlona y escéptica ante eso que yo llamo normas, que antes llamaban ideales, que también se llaman virtudes, y sin embargo, no hay momento histórico quizás en que más necesario haya sido el restablecimiento de las normas de vida.[56]

In the absence of ethical guidance as derived from ideal rather than material values, knowledge is easily manipulated and can contribute to the terrible void of "Cero". By the time Salinas was writing these essays, modern science had become the perceived source of absolute truth. The canonical version of science posits an objective reality that is universally perceived and whose quantification is expressed in the language of mathematics. The authority of science has grown from the universalistic claims of the Enlightenment: that experimental science is true because it is verifiable by experience and calculation. This is clearly putative for Salinas, whose poetry undermines any such notion of an objective, universally perceived reality. Calculation too is value-laden, and the creature of socio-economic influences; the only absolutely quantifiable commodity according to Salinas, is money. From the point of view of this poet, science had failed to measure or explain the individual's perception of reality, and he repeatedly expressed his indignation that it could dominate both man and nature with the indiscriminate threat of the bomb.

When new possibilities are presented by scientific advancement, they demand intellectual and philosophical re-orientation. Salinas confronts these changes in the twentieth century world, he looks for new definitions with which to integrate new realities into his poetry. Attracted by the novelty of recent inventions, he seeks appropriate metaphors with which to assimilate them. Mathematics is the language of science, so the poet raids this area of expression in order to frame and describe the technologically advanced urban society he inhabits in the 1940's. Inevitably, the advent of atomic weaponry in the 1940s must affect the poet's subjective view of the world and his role in it. How should the artist live and create in the shadow of the void? What is the way forward for "el hombre entero": a thinking, feeling and conscious entity. In the essays collected in *El defensor*, Salinas directs the reader to the classical Western tradition as he has inherited it through its literature. While a lover of matter, he denounces materialist society - materialist, not just in terms of the acquisition of wealth, but in its denial of the existence of the non-material, the ideal, and its unwillingness to integrate physical amd metaphysical aspirations. In *El defensor*, Salinas recommends a return to the humanist disciplines of reading and reflection, as a means of self-betterment. He champions eternal aspiration, rather than achievement. If science and the new Gods cannot show humanity the way to progress, Salinas reminds the reader of older, more instinctive sources of knowledge, of atavistic impulses which may point the way to avoid the void. From the debris left by the bomb in "Cero IV", a symbol of hope and redemption emerges in the shape of a "bajel pétreo" (ll.37, p.778) reminiscent of accounts of early Christian saints who made miraculous voyages in boats hewn of stone, delivering the "Good News" to new territories. The "bajel" also recalls the traditional icon of the Church as a ship of faith - an interpretation re-inforced by this evocation of stain glass and illuminated manuscripts in the lines : "Naves de salvación con un polícromo / velamen de vidrieras, y sus cuentos"(ll.47-8, p.778). The passengers in the boat, however, are not early Christian saints or monks, but the fragmented sculpted images of pre-Christian, Classical deities: "Mármol, que flota porque viste de Venus" (l.49). The passage can be read as an exercise in syncretism, where the ancient classical and Christian traditions come together in a "suma" of the Western civilisation, to convey a unified message of hope and an antidote to the void. Salinas looks back nostalgically to the Gods of the past. The actual names of these deities are unimportant: whether pantheist or monotheist, their importance lies in the message they offer of regeneration, the continuation of cultural tradition, and continued life.

When the bomb drops in "Cero", it seems to interrupt time irrevocably, stopping it in its tracks. The "suma" of accumulated knowledge and tradition are reduced to a uniform devastation. Yet even in this grim image of all-engulfing oblivion, Salinas finds some hope.

> Armadas extrañísimas de afanes;
> galeras, no de vivos, no de muertos,
> tripulaciones de querencias puras,
> incansables remeros...   (ll.60-3, Cero IV, *Todo*, p.778)

Like a counter, time flicks back to - OOOO - , as past and present are obliterated. But perhaps this can be interpreted as new beginning as well as an end, where the untiring "remeros" of Salinas's poetry - hope and aspiration - can steer humanity to a better future.

Notes

Chapter IV

1. The omnipresence of the void is highlighted by Julian Palley, whose study of Salinas's poetry *La luz no usada*, opens with a Prologue which suggests that it is the desire to penetrate the void of the unknown that impels the poet to self-expression: "Todo poeta verdadero procura entrar en ese trasmundo, lo desconocido, la nada". Palley goes on to describe the poem "Cero" as the "síntetis final y más angustiosa de la idea de la nada". An alternative interpretation is offered by Villegas, who examines the nature of the void in the context of Salinas's love poetry and concludes that the void is not represented by the unknown, but by the too-familiar: "La nada no está concebida aquí como lo que hay más allá de la muerte, sino como el vivir cotidiano, banal". See Julian Palley, *La luz no usada*, Colección Stadium 55, Ediciones de Andrea (Mexico, 1966), p.7, and Juan Villegas's essay "El amor y la salvación existencial en dos poemas de Pedro Salinas", in *Pedro Salinas*, El escritor y la crítica, ed. A. P. Debicki, Taurus (Madrid, 1976), pp.129-141.

2. Pedro Salinas, "Deuda de un poeta" in *Ensayos completos, Vol. III*, ed. Solita Salinas de Marichal, Taurus (Madrid, 1983), p.436.

3. This letter, among others from the period, is reproduced in Christopher Maurer's article, "Sobre 'joven literatura' y política: cartas de Pedro Salinas, y de F.G. Lorca, la Guerra Civil", in *Estelas, laberintos, nuevas sendas. Unamuno, Valle-Inclán, García Lorca, La Guerra Civil*, Co-Ord. Angel de Loureiro, Anthropos (Barcelona, 1988), p.303.

4. See Salinas's letter to Guillén (6.6.30), p.300. As in Note 3.

5. Pedro Salinas, Preface to "Todo más claro" in *Poesías completas*, ed. Solita Salinas de Marichal, Seix Barral (Barcelona 1981), p.655.

6. The same perceived threat of aimless knowledge is expressed by F. G. Lorca in *Poeta en Nueva York*:

> La luz es sepultada por cadenas y ruidos
> en impúdico reto de ciencia sin raices. '

"La Aurora", ll.17-18, *Poeta en Nueva York*, Lumen (Barcelona, 1976), p.49.

7. Robert Havard places great importance on the concept of motion in Salinas's poetry. He discerns a dual philosophical influence in this respect: firstly Henri Bergson, whose theory that language has an "in-built tendency to solidify" Salinas shared; and secondly, Ortega's theory of perspectivism, which gave him insight into the "motion-based nature of reality". Havard neatly concludes:

> From this dual metaphysical source flowed his characteristic interest in spontaneity, randomness, chance, freedom, irrationality and illumination, all of which may be conveniently condensed into the equation: motion=vitality.

Robert Havard, *From Romanticism to Surrealism. Seven Spanish Poets*, Chapter V, "Pedro Salinas. The Poetics of Motion", University of Wales Press (Cardiff, 1988), p.143.

8. "Nuestras vidas son los ríos / que van a dar en la mar / que es el morir". Jorge Manrique, "Coplas a la muerte de su padre", in *Cancionero*, ed. Augusto Cortina, Clásicos Castellanos (Madrid, 1975), p.90.

9. This geological expression of time opens a new perspective on the initial poem of Salinas's first collection, *Presagios,* where the humble "Suelo" evokes more than contemporary, material reality - it is the sum total of an entire heritage.

10. Salinas revives this geological analogy in his study of the poetry of Jorge Manrique, where he considers the impact of past literary achievements on contemporary writers.

> Podemos afirmarnos orgullosamente en nuestro presente, con la misma certidumbre con que se ahinca los pies en el suelo. Pero conviene no olvidar que ese trozo de superficie que pisamos es la apariencia última de capas y capas terrenas, obra de millones de años: nuestro piso existe, por ellos y sobre ellos; y aunque las oculta a la mirada, las contiene a todas, a todas las presupone.

Pedro Salinas, *Jorge Manrique o tradición y originalidad*, Seix Barral (Barcelona, 1974), p.104.

11. See Pedro Salinas's, *Jorge Manrique o tradición y originalidad*, Chapter IV, "La valla de la tradición", pp.103-104. As in Note 10.

12. See also, Alan S. Bell's "Pedro Salinas's challenge to T. S. Eliot's concept of tradition", in *Revista de Estudios Hispánicos*, University of Alabama Press, No. 1, XL (September 1967) pp.43-52. Bell elaborates on Eliot's theory that tradition must be consciously acquired, and compares it with Salinas's concept of tradition, which allows for residual memory, unconsciously inherited.

13. Pedro Salinas, "Defensa del lenguaje" in *El defensor*, Alianza Tres (Madrid, 1984), p.290.

14. The original title given by Salinas to a selection of poems from *La voz a ti debida*, published in *Cuatro Vientos* (February 1933), was "Amor en Vilo".

15. As in Note 10, pp.121-122.

16. Antonio Machado, "De mi cartera" No.1, *Nuevas canciones* CLXIV, *Poesías completas*, ed. Manuel Alvar, Austral (Madrid, 1982), p.298.

17. *Reality and the Poet in Spanish Poetry*, Chapter IV, "The Escape From Reality", John Hopkins Press (Baltimore, 1966), p.104.

18. "Palabras previas a una lectura de su poesía" (Wellesley College, Mass., 1937), in, *Ensayos completos, Vol. III*, Taurus (Madrid, 1983), p.432.

19. "Palabras previas a una lectura de su poesía". As in Note 18.

20. For Salinas, reality is always more than the sum of material elements; the individual's perception of it is a vital contributory factor. Likewise poetry is governed by principles of subjective perception as reality, so that -

> si ese niño se equivoca
> y dice: cuatro y dos siete,
> al ver cruzar unas nubes;   (ll.15-17)

> todo es adrede,
> el mundo algo quiere.   (ll.21-22, Adrede, *Confianza*, p.821)

21. It is broadly accepted that the close friendship between Salinas and Guillén extended to a shared enthusiasm for, and familiarity with, each other's work, with an inevitable degree of mutual influence. In *Cántico '28*, Guillén seems to echo Salinas's fascination with numeracy in his use of terms such as "sumas", as for example in the poem "Bosque y bosque", where he evokes his experience of a starlit wood as a "suma":

> los sumandos frondosas de la tarde,
> ¡Prolija claridad: uno más uno!
> Son en la suma de la noche ceros.
> No los ceros solemnes de la nada:
> Anillos para manos de poeta
> Que alzarán un gran bosque sobre bosque.
> (ll.1-6, Bosque y bosque, *Cántico '28*, p.55)

All the trappings of mathematical accumulation are here: "sumandos", the addition of "uno más uno" and the total "suma". Jorge Guillén, *Cántico '28*, ed. Víctor Pozanco, Ambito Literario (Barcelona, 1978).

22. So closely linked are these two terms, "sumo" and "mediodía", that even when the midday motif is deployed without the qualifier of "sumo", it invariably recalls the same value associations of apogee and paragon:

> desde cenit total
> mediodía absoluto (ll.7-8, ¡Qué día sin pecado!, *La voz.*, p.250)

> las voces en la cima
> del cántico, los altos
> mediodías del alma   (ll.33-5, El dolor, *Raz.*, p.428)

23. The universally accepted rule that 1 apple + 1 apple can be combined to give a sum of 2 apples, but that 1 apple + 1 pear must remain distinct, as two discrete entities, is defied in the processes of aggregation in Salinas's work. This tendency is described as an "error of categories" according to classical logic and metaphysics.

24. Commenting on an extract from Darío's *Poema de otoño*, Salinas notes:

> Estos versos están estilísticamente construidos a base de la vuelta
> constante de la conjunción copulativa "y", la cual aparece en ella
> doce veces. Logra el poeta por medio de este recurso reiterativo
> que enlaza dolor con dolor sin dejar resquicio, un efecto de
> acumulación abrumadora.

Pedro Salinas, *La poesía de Rubén Darío*, Chapter VIII, "Divina psiquis, dulce mariposa", Seix Barral (Barcelona, 1975), p.180.

25. Examples of this may be seen in lls 13, 22, 23, 40, 47, 58, 69, 103, 106, 114, 127, 133, 153 and 153, 162 and 163, "Los Puentes", *Largo lamento*, pp.463-468.

26. Salinas judges the effect of "la y copulativa" in Darío's work to be one of crushing accumulation, as one "dolor" crowds the next (see Note 25). In his own work, however, he deploys the same conjunction to accumulate love's happiness. The result is not crushing despair, but an inspired faith in love.

27. See Pedro Salinas, "Deuda de un poeta", in *Ensayos completos, Vol. III*, ed. Solita Salinas de Marichal, Taurus (Madrid, 1983), p.432.

28. Pedro Salinas, "Lo que debemos a Don Quixote", *Ensayos completos, Vol. III*, p.54. As in Note 27.

29. George Steiner gives an interesting philosophical interpretation of the predominance of the concept of the void in modern thinking:

> The enigma of nothingness haunts the inception of cosmological and philosophical thought in the Western tradition. The void and the abyss are eschatological concepts throughout religious mysticism and the theological speculations which, as in Pascal, have their mystical source. But it is only in recent philosophy, in Heidegger's *Nichtigkeit*, in Sartre's *le néant*, a variation on Heidegger, that the concept of absolute zero becomes almost obsessive. Whereas in common grammar, in the logic that articulates, the negation of negation generates a positive... it now produces a final nothingness, a midnight of absence.

George Steiner, *Real Presences*, Faber & Faber (London/Boston, 1989), p.133.

30. The epigraph is taken from Machado's *Proverbios y cantares*, XXXIV.

> Ya maduró un nuevo cero.
> que tendrá su devoción:
> un ente de acción tan huero
> como un ente de razón...

Antonio Machado, *Poesías completas*, ed. Manual Alvar, Austral (Madrid, 1982), p.272.

31. This kind of entropic imagery is also pervasive in Alberti's *Sobre los ángeles* (1929), externalising his feelings of disorientation. Alberti transfers his inner feelings of vulnerability, of being under assault, onto the external cityscape, to produce an apocalyptic vision of toppling citadels. Many examples can be drawn from "El cuerpo deshabitado":

> Y se derrumban murallas
> los fuertes de las ciudades
> que me velaban.
>
> y se derrumban las torres,
> las empinadas
> centinelas de mi sueño.   (ll.17-22)
>
> Tú, caída,
> tú, derribada,
> tú
> la mejor de las ciudades.   (ll.98-101)

Salinas's application of similar images of ruined cities is less introspective, and more concerned with the destruction of universal values. The difference in perspectives illustrates a shift in emphasis from a largely Freudian, "yo"-centred poetry of the 1920s to the expression of collective concerns in the 1940s. In his book *Teoría de la expresión poética*, Gredos (Madrid, 1970), Carlos Bousoño describes post-war Spanish literature as being characterised by a new "realismo". The crisis experienced by Alberti in the 1920s was that of the individual psyche victimised by society. In the 1940s, not only the individual, but society at large, was threatened by extinction.

32. "Defensa de la lectura", *El defensor*, p.167. As in Note 13.

33. Even in his cumulative theory of tradition, Salinas acknowledges the inevitability of selection: "Porque la tradición es una suma tan enorme que no hay individuo capaz de usarla en toda su enormidad", and he affirms "la obligación de elegir". See Pedro Salinas, *Jorge Manrique o tradición y originalidad*, Chapter IV, "La valla de la tradición", p.114. As in Note 10.

34. "Defensa de la lectura", *El defensor*, p.115. As in Note 13.

35. Robert Havard has pointed out that the "trasmundo" of the love experience bears all the hallmarks of Bergson's "pure durée", a perpetually changing and continuous present that is free from the restrictions of time and space. See Robert G. Havard, "The Reality of Words in the Poetry of Pedro Salinas, *Bulletin of Hispanic Studies*, LI, (1974), pp.28-47.

36. Some examples are:
Dámaso Alonso, "La poesía de Pedro Salinas, desde *Presagios* hasta *La voz a ti debida*", in *Del siglo de oro a este siglo de siglas*, Gredos (Madrid, 1962), pp.126-167.

Stephen Gilman: "El proemio a la voz a ti debida", in *Pedro Salinas: el escritor y la crítica*, ed. A. P. Debicki, Taurus (Madrid, 1976), pp.119-27.

Robert G. Havard: "The Reality of Words in the Poetry of Pedro Salinas", *Bulletin of Hispanic Studies*, LI (1974), pp.24-47; and, *From Romanticism to Surrealism. Seven Spanish Poets*, Chapter V, University of Wales Press (Cardiff, 1988).

Julian Palley, *La luz no usada*, Chapter V, Colección Studium 55, Ediciones de Andrea (México, 1966).

Alma de Zubizarreta, *Pedro Salinas: el diálogo creador*, Chapter III, Gredos (Madrid, 1969).

37. "Defensa de la minoría literaria", *El defensor*, p.236. As in Note 13.

38. "Defensa de la lectura", *El defensor*, p.119. As in Note 13.

39. "Defensa de la lectura", *El defensor*, p.119. As in Note 13.

40. Salinas's application of the term "cifras" is reminiscent of Bécquer's "Rima I":

> Yo sé un himno gigante y extraño
> que anuncia en la noche del alma una aurora,   (ll.1-2)

> Yo quisiera escribirle, del hombre
> domando el rebelde mezquino idioma   (ll.5-6)

> Pero en vano es luchar; que no hay cifra
> capaz de encerrarle...   (ll.9-10)

Further evidence of disenchantment with the quantification of experience is present in "Rima IV":

> Mientras la ciencia a descubrir no alcance
> las fuentes de la vida
> y en el mar o en el cielo haya un abismo
> que al cálculo resista,

> Mientras la humanidad siempre avanzando
> no sepa a do camina...   (ll.13-18)

Rimas, like Salinas's poetry, is written against a backdrop of great scientific advancement. Newton's law of gravity gave the Romantics a mechanical explanation of the Universe: the heavenly spheres lost some of their music and much of their mystery. Bécquer, like Salinas in *Todo más claro*, perceives this advancement as ultimately aimless. See Gustavo Adolfo Bécquer, *Rimas*, ed. José Pedro Díaz, Clásicos Castellanos (Madrid, 1975), pp.11, & 18-19.

41. Salinas refers to the strong visual impact that New York's Avenues had on him, when he arrived in the USA in 1936, in "Deuda de un poeta", *Ensayos completos, Vol.III*, ed. Solita Salinas de Marichal, Taurus (Madrid, 1983), p.437.

> Yo, no hacía mucho tiempo había dejado la ciudad de Sevilla, una de las ciudades más intricadas, en donde las calles se cansan a los veinte metros de seguir el mismo camino y se van por otro lado: son calles tortuosas, intricadas; y despúes de andar por ellas, sorprende enormemente lo rectilíneo de las calles americanas, esa inflexibilidad rectilínea que da la sensación de que la calle no se acaba...

42. *Reality and the Poet in Spanish Poetry*, Chapter One, "The Reproduction of Reality", p.3. As in Note 17.

43. "The Reproduction of Reality", *Reality*, p.3. As in Note 17.

44. This reluctance to establish a fixed definition of experience is reminiscent of Machado's maxim that: "No se define en arte, sino en matemática - allí donde lo definido y la definición son una misma cosa". See Antonio Machado, "Prólogos a páginas escogidas", *Poesías completas*, ed. Manual Alvar, Austral (Madrid, 1982), p.67.

45. Juan Marichal makes this connection between the life-urge and the urge to create very clear: "Porque, muy probablemente, para Pedro Salinas en los museos se veía literalmente aquella "profusión fabulosa" de obras que encarnaban la "negación del morir", que eran, en verdad, la perenne ansia de vida de sus autores". Juan Marichal, *Tres voces de Pedro Salinas*, Ediciones Betancor (Madrid, 1976), p.82.

46. It may be interesting to compare Salinas's use of such framing devices with that of the Creacionista poet, Vicente Huidobro. Where for Salinas, the enclosed geometric form of the square confines experience, and is deployed with negative connotations in his poetry, Huidobro theorised that the imposition of such geometric forms onto experience had, in fact, a positive effect of reducing it to human scale. In his essay, "El Creacionismo", Huidobro explains the title of his 1917 volume, "Horizon Carré": this explanation takes the form of a poetic manifesto, compressed into four points, the first of which is -

Humanizar las cosas: Todo lo que pasa a través del organismo del poeta debe coger la mayor cantidad de su calor. Aquí algo vasto, enorme, como el horizonte, se humaniza, se hace íntimo, filial, gracias al adjetivo CUADRADO. El infinito anida en nuestro corazón.

Vicente Huidobro, "El creacionismo", reproduced in E. Caracciolo Trejo's *Vicente Huidobro y la vanguardia*, Gredos (Madrid, 1974), p.49.

47. One of the epigraphs to this poem is taken from John Keats' "Ode on a Grecian Urn". Given the subject matter of both poems, it could be said that Salinas's "Pasajero en Museo" constitutes a poetic response to the Romantic poet's musings on the nature of mortality. Where Salinas clearly opts for "la gran mortalidad", Keats's position is altogether more ambivalent as he sustains the tension between frustrated aspiration and the preservation of promise.

Fair youth beneath the trees, thou canst not leave
thy song, nor ever can those trees be bare;

Bold lover, never, never canst thou kiss,
Though winning near the goal - yet, do not grieve;
she cannot fade, though thou hast not the bliss,
Forever wilt thou love, and she be fair. (ll.15-20)

John Keats, "Ode on a Grecian Urn", *The Poems of John Keats*, ed. Jack Stillinger, Heinnemann (London, 1978).

48. Carlos Feal Deibe comments on this preference for process over product in *La poesía de Pedro Salinas*, Gredos (Madrid, 1965), pp.56-59.

49. "The Reproduction of Reality", *Reality and the Poet in Spanish Poetry*, p.3. As in Note 18.

50. The same motivating aspiration is essential to the process of writing, as Salinas outlines in a letter to Margarita as early as 1914.

el poeta debe sentirse contento por su obra hecha, pero no considerarla nunca completa, total, y por lo tanto no sentir el pleno orgullo de la vida realizada en la obra. Ya ves, las palabras últimas de Goethe, 'Luz, más luz', lo que revelan de aspiración de anhelo todavía.

Cartas de amor a Margarita, 1912-15, ed. Solita Salinas, Alianza Tres (Madrid, 1984), p.124.

51. González Muela's interpretation of "Vocación" is rather literal: "Si para Guillén lo importante es la vista, para Salinas lo es el tacto, con los ojos cerrados". This interpretation of Salinas's inward gaze implies a sensible hierarchy, where the sense of touch presides over that of sight, and rather deflects from the main thematic content of the poem. In effect the poet is overwhelmed by the perfection of empirical reality, and so turns his vision inwards to tune in to his own creative resources. See Joaquín González Muela, "Poesía y amistad: Jorge Guillén y Pedro Salinas", in *Pedro Salinas*, ed. A. P. Debicki, El escritor y la crítica, Taurus (Madrid, 1976), pp.197-203.

52. Antonio Machado, "De un cancionero apócrifo", CLXVII, *Poesías completas*, p.319. As in Note 44.

53. As in Note 44, pp.324-5.

54. An example of this positive state of hazy *ensueño*, where the imagination is released, is Bécquer's "Rima VIII":

> Cuando miro el azul horizonte
> perderse a lo lejos,
> al través de una gasa de polvo
> dorado e inquieto;
> me parece posible arrancarme
> del mísero suelo
> y flotar con la niebla dorada
> en átomos leves
> cual ella deshecho   (ll.1-9)

G. A. Bécquer, *Rimas*, pp.26-7, as in Note 40.

55. "Don Quixote en presente", *Ensayos completos, Vol. III*, p.76. As in Note 2.

56. "Lo que debemos a Don Quixote", *Ensayos completos, Vol. III*, pp.60-1. As in Note 2.

Conclusion

The dominant themes in Salinas's poetry survive both geographic dislocation and the maturing process of personal and poetic evolution. These themes persist, even where tone and style may radically differ: the importance of dialogue and communication; the emotional and philosophical need for the individual to seek self-realisation through knowledge of 'otherness'; the fear of absence, of death and the void; the encounter and loss of love; and a stubborn resistance to the concept of a fixed or defined reality, both thematically and stylistically. 'Entereza', the central theme of Salinas's work, encompasses all of these. "La reconquista de la entereza del hombre" represents more than a quest for personal fulfilment: it is a theme that is inextricably linked with the times in which this poet lived. For this reason, it has been necessary in the course of this study to look beyond the boundaries of Salinas's creative writings, and consider the historical circumstances in which he wrote. After all, this poet's life spanned the most turbulent years in twentieth century history. The growing sense of crisis in the West in the 1930s and '40s was at once profoundly personal - an existential awareness of alone-ness - and at the same time intensely communal, as the inherited orders of tradition and Western civilisation could not prevent another World War. A crisis of confidence, both private and public, was inevitable, and exacerbated the individual's sense of vulnerability and isolation.

In his personal and poetic quest for 'entereza', Salinas strives to bridge the gap between self and world opened by philosophy, psychology, and the historical events of this century. No poet is limited to one path in his / her pursuit of this state of integration, and effectively, Salinas follows up two of the routes open to him. One of these (the most commonly discussed), is the bid to merge with 'otherness' by dissolving self-consciousness; a quest for ecstasy or oblivion. This tendency peaks in the love poems and *El Contemplado*, where the 'otherness' sought by the poet, the desired object of fusion, is embodied by the beloved and nature respectively. How successful this bid to lose the self is, or indeed is intended to be, remains questionable. The reader is always aware of Salinas's poetic identity, his voice, and at times even suspects that the sea of San Juan and the beloved may, after all, be no more than internally developed abstractions of the poet's, as opposed to real 'otherness'. This suspicion stems from the fact that even when Salinas is most adamant about his surrender to the 'other', it is his voice we hear, not that of the beloved or the sea; it is his presence that occupies the poem. It is a tribute to his skill that we allow ourselves to accompany him down this path, willing partners to his ingenuity, even when unconvinced that we will arrive at the promised destination. For all the apparent mysticism of his love poetry, Salinas is in fact less interested in oblivion and loss of self, than in redefinition. The destination of this particular route is an expansion of the self rather than any escape from it, a transformation rather than a loss, as the poet seeks communion with the 'other' through novel, and frequently surprising relationships. It is Salinas's *intimista* voice that resounds here, as he addresses "las cosas" of the world, the beloved, and nature. This is the voice most readily recognisable as Salinas's. However it is not his only voice. There is more than one route leading to poetic and ontological 'entereza': the coming together of self and world can also occur through the possession of external reality. Although perhaps not consciously, this is a process initiated by Salinas's metaphoric appropriation of artefact in *Seguro azar* and *Fábula y signo*. Significantly, this path to 'entereza' has implications that extend beyond the innovative relationships forged in Salinas's earlier works between the poetic consciousness and "las cosas". It is this method of achieving 'entereza' that gains prominence in Salinas's later work, embracing external reality of a less palpable character, the realm of human action, of history. As Salinas identifies increasingly with the collective destiny of society, his poetry expresses at a similar rate an urge to arrogate and absorb the historical world. The "Suma" of Western civilisation and culture is therefore of paramount importance in *Todo más claro*, which, together with the poem "Civitas Dei", best exemplifies his concern with the self in relation to society. Here, a different poetic voice surfaces: no longer intimate, this is a public voice; no less ironic than the other, although here the irony is more melancholic than mischievous.

The kind of critical attention received by Salinas's poetry has been directed almost exclusively towards his most 'personal' poetry, especially the collections *La voz a ti debida* and *Razón de amor*, which are unanimously lauded as his best. While their many qualities have been highlighted, this has never been done in the overall context of Salinas's poetic canon. These love poems demonstrate an emotional, psychological and intellectual depth that is quite exceptional. Reading them alongside any of his other collections, the reader must conclude that here, in the love cycle. the poet finds his most resonant, memorable voice, and we are prompted to ask why this should be? Why should this personal, confidential, almost confessional voice, ring more true than any other? What is it that makes this poet's skills so compatible with the *intimista* tone and setting of love? Comparison with an alternative poetic voice may illuminate the issue. The poems contained in *Todo más claro*, for example, are inspired by Salinas's relationship with a collective entity, society, and subsequently we find a poetry with less emotional force. For Salinas, it appears that the intensity of a one-to-one relationship cannot be sustained within group relations. The contrasting degree of emotional force in these collections is matched by the relative expressive impact of each. This is partly the result of a dramatic shift in tone that occurs between the love-cycle and *Todo más claro*. In his love poetry, we see Salinas at his most open and inventive linguistically, as he mines the physical and metaphysical depths of the love relationship and explores every linguistic possibility of expressing subjective, 'personal' experience. There are no moral boundaries or limitations imposed by his subject-matter: theme and expression convey discovery and adventure, a sense of novelty and freshness that is appropriate to the sensation that love re-creates the lovers and their world anew. The poems of *Todo más claro* have none of this freshness, either in tone or expression. The temporal realm they inhabit has not been subject to any glorious transfiguration, as we move from the sparkling, primordial "trasmundo", to a present threatened by conflict and sepulchral silence. Reading *Todo más claro*, one is struck by the disappearance of that most striking feature of the love poetry, its rich, semantic ambiguity: while the thematic resistance to definition persists in Salinas's rejection of a measured reality - as illustrated in Chapter Four - the emotional mood of these poems is quite different, and commands a mode of communication that is altogether more direct. No longer the savoured, bittersweet agonies of temporary absence, no longer the prolonged conceptual play of the love poems (itself a langorous metaphor for love-making). The poet's tone is now predominantly indignant and disenchanted: history presses, lending an air of urgency to this work. These factors, in turn, instil in the poet the desire to communicate a moral message, and only a few years after the composition of the love cycle, seductive conceits seem a luxury of the distant past.

Salinas's later poems demonstrate this poet's increasing tendency to identify with 'otherness' in the shape of society, and to seek 'entereza' through contact with a community. This, in turn, leads him to address a wider audience than previously.[1] His later work is coloured by this compulsion to impress upon as many people as possible, the importance of the non-material humanitarian values that he saw as the last hope of Western civilisation; this explains the evangelising tone of some of these poems.[2] The poetry of *Todo más claro* is not Salinas's best, but nonetheless, it merits some critical attention, if only because an awareness of this public voice can enhance our appreciation of the private. These are, after all, two facets of the same poet's work: they serve as a reminder of his complexity, and the complexity of the times in which he lived.

If Salinas's Spanish poetry is preoccupied with finding 'entereza' in intimate relationships, in his American works there is a patent need to explore the potential for integration with the collective, on a social plane. This becomes a vital part of the on-going quest for 'entereza', for self-knowledge, and characterises Salinas's work in the 1940s as poet, essayist and critic. The historical reality of the Spanish Civil War, apart from the obvious divisions it wrought in Spanish society, has created an unfortunate chronological rift in the study of modern Spanish literature. Academic curricula and research commonly fall into periods such as 1898-1936, or classifications such as 'Pre-Civil War Poetry', or 'The Post-War Novel'. Salinas did not stop writing in 1936, but he did stop writing in his native environment, and this is an important and relatively unexplored factor in the emergence of a 'public' voice in his poetry. It is highly significant that Salinas's most acclaimed poetry was written in Spain, prior to 1936 and to the commencement of his long exile. During this period he lived, worked, and fully participated in Spain's political culture, completely integrated with the living reality of Spanish society. Yet it is principally in the poetry written in exile that a public voice develops, when Salinas was based in North America, conscious of his own social, cultural, and linguistic displacement.[3] The shadow of absence that stalked the love-cycle and his personal life in the 1930s, now darkens his whole sense of social identity as an exile.

In the light of Salinas's commitment to the principle of 'entereza', his writings of the 1930s raise fundamental doubts about the extent to which he was able to integrate his poetry with other areas of his life. Seen in the overall context of his life and works, the love-cycle begs an intriguing question, and that is why a man who was certainly not apolitical, should produce poetry of such a personal tenor at a time of political crisis in his environment? Why, in the 1930s - an extremely tense period in Spanish history - did Salinas's public voice not emerge? As the outbreak of Civil War became more and more probable, so the relationship between the poet as individual, and as a responsible and politically aware citizen of Spanish society, became increasingly painful. What was his role? Could these two aspects of his life be integrated? At this stage, it seems that a public voice was not possible for Salinas, and as a private and shy individual, he did not seek one. Until recently only speculation was possible on this subject, but the publication of Salinas's letters to Guillén, who was in Oxford in the 1930-31 period, reveals Salinas's attitude to this complex relationship between poet and politics.[4] He abhorred, in life as in art, the inherent oversimplification of Cartesian dualities: in his politics as with philosophy and language, he was loathe to be defined as adhering exclusively to one camp or another. In the instance of Spanish politics in the early 1930s, this would have meant aligning himself with one half of a pair of binary opposites soon to lock in deadly combat due to the extremity of their ideological incompatibility. The values that form the bedrock of this poet's work are founded on a fundamental belief in the interdependence of opposites. Accordingly, he refused to join any political party, calling himself a "republicano sin fé, antimonárquico convencido".[5] Card-carrying politics was not for him, because party politics, by definition partial, could never express the entire range of an individual's political feeling or identity.

In the letters to Guillén we sense a growing dismay at the dangerous polarisation of ideologies in Spain at this time; the "división de las gentes en derechas e izquierdas con el peor espíritu de partido y de banda".[6] His criticism is directed most vehemently against his colleagues, writers and intellectuals who had joined in the fray. Following Ortega y Gasset's article in *El Sol* (14 March 1931), which invoked Napoleon's famous words "Hoy el destino es político", Salinas writes to Guillén in anger -

> ...los escritores españoles no admiten más distinción que ésta: los que están con la reacción y los que están con la revolución. La política es el verdadero gas asfixiante de nuestros días.[7]

It appears that for Salinas, the harsh reality of politics was not compatible with his standards of personal integrity: he did not lack commitment to the model of the Republic, but had absolutely no faith in certain "republicanos", whom he described as "grotescos, encerrados en el Ateneo y forjándose una república del salón y de los pasillos".[8] Comments such as these suggest that Salinas's objection to "la política" was motivated less by separatist individualism, than by a suspicion that the republicanism professed by many Spanish intellectuals was lacking in political integrity, and had more to do with opportunism, personal ambitions, and internecine feuds. All of which led him to conclude - "La política. Formidable concentración de asnería, de bajeza, de cuquería, de estupideces y mala entraña".[9]

In the face of such evident repulsion at the political activity of the day, are we to conclude that Salinas's production of love poetry in the 1930s represents a retreat from the pressures of public debate into the intimacy of one-to-one dialogue, where the individual can speak freely, without fear of misrepresentation? Does this period in the poet's life represent a split in the psyche between public and private, an inability to integrate different facets of his personality, a failure to achieve 'entereza'? Is the love poetry an attempt to preserve some level of privacy in his life, a defensive reflex, to prevent the invasion by the public and political into every area of his consciousness? One thing emerges very clearly from the letters to Guillén: that as far as this poet was concerned, current political circumstances did not allow for the free and total expression of the self. Perhaps such 'entereza' of expression was what most interested Salinas in the 1930s. If this is the case, then the composition of the love-cycle at this time was not so much a retreat from the external, public world, a denial of what was happening outside the cosy reassuring realm of the "trasmundo", as an attempt to emphasize Salinas's basic philosophy on his own terms. Through his expression in the love-cycle, Salinas attempts to convey a philosophical alternative to the opposition of ideologies, a counterbalance to the weight of historical evidence suggesting that such extremities of opposition would inevitably end in mutual destruction. From this perspective, the love relationship now reads as a metaphor for the mutual dependence of opposites. Salinas's love poetry provides a defiant model of 'entereza': it asserts the importance of difference, and welcomes ambivalence in the face of political dogmatism. In this respect it can be said that even this most 'private' of poetry addresses public issues, and that the aims of his most *intimista* love poetry and the more socially conscious *Todo más claro* coincide.

Personality plays a part in the pace of evolution of Salinas's most dominant poetic voices. Again, the poet's correspondence is revealing: from the letters to Guillén, Christopher Maurer rightly concludes that Salinas's political activities were deliberately low-key, unpublicized, and that he saw this as a private area of his life.[10] This natural reserve is also evident in his letters to Margarita Bonmatí during their courtship. In this instance the young Salinas declares that poetry occupies a purely private area of his consciousness - "Y es que la poesía... tiene algo de íntimo y delicado que no gusta de la publicidad excesiva; que se resiente con el conocimiento público".[11] This reluctance to accept that his poetry could ever acquire the aspect of published literature - the dread of 'going public' - is not dissimilar to Salinas's feelings about politics. Of course, by 1923 he had overcome his artistic prudishness and had begun to publish, extending his readership from Margarita exclusively, to a more extensive audience. Can we then surmise that by the 1940s Salinas had outgrown his self-image as a poet of purely private subject-matter, striking a more open, public chord in *Todo más claro*?[12]

The orientation of this poetry is best described as social rather than political, a distinction Salinas himself was at pains to make in his book on Rubén Darío. Examining what he sees as the Nicaraguan poet's most important sub-theme (love being the dominant theme), he states:

> La poesía social es la originada por una experiencia que afecte al poeta no en aquella que su ser tiene de propio y singular, de inalienable vida individual, sino en ese modo de su existencia por el cual se siente perteneciendo a una comunidad organizada, a una sociedad, donde sus actos se aparecen siempre como relativos a los demás.[13]

This initial, comprehensive definition is then sub-divided into four categories of social poetry. Firstly, there is "el modo histórico", exemplified in Salinas's own work by his awareness of being a part of a literary tradition, a collective "suma". The second category outlined is "el modo nacional" or identification with nation. Of the four classes of social poetry he describes, this is probably the least represented in Salinas's work. Perhaps this is due to a process of political disillusionment in the 1930s with the "pueblo español", who, in Salinas's eyes fell into two equally unattractive groups: the first comprising those who, ostrich-like, ignored the political situation of their country, and whose apathy opened the way for political extremists.[14] And the second, those whose intransigence and blind dogmatism pushed the country further towards Civil War, the historical reality of which denied any coherent concept of nationhood. The third category of social poetry delineated is "el modo político", and here, Salinas registers his strong objections to the misapplication of this term to denote any poetry of social relevance.[15] Finally, we come to "el modo humanitario", transcending all geographic and ideological boundaries, where the poet is concerned with no less than "los hombres del universo". At this point, Salinas's definition of what constitutes social poetry becomes impossibly comprehensive. Once we begin to trade in terms as all-embracing as this, any commentary ceases to be socially relevant and acquires metaphysical ramifications. This tendency to equate society with humanity lies at the heart of the perceived weaknesses of *Todo más claro*, which deals with problems and dilemmas very specific to a concrete society - that of the United States in the 1940s - but does not address these problems on social terms, as most of us would understand them. Perhaps the underlying problem here is that Salinas's core philosophy of 'entereza' - while embracing modern psychological notions of personal integration - is more rooted in traditional spiritual values than in a strong sense of social realities. The solutions offered to the concrete problems of rampant consumerism and the absence of human communication in *Todo más claro* are too vaguely metaphysical to counteract the tide of negativity that surges over this collection. Yes, there is an important metaphysical dimension to these poems, which lament the loss of spiritual values in the nightmarish setting of urban America. But the promise of spiritual regeneration fails to address the concrete socio-economic causes of the collective existential crisis outlined in the same poems.

In this respect it is interesting to contrast *Todo más claro* with Lorca's *Poeta en Nueva York*: like Salinas, Lorca found his public voice in the United States, in a state of voluntary exile, and in New York he found a collective, social dimension to his personal malaise of isolation. The crucial difference between these two poet's responses to the city lies in the comparative degrees of success achieved by each in finding an appropriate idiom in which to describe the urban experience. Lorca's stay in New York yields a poetry that is uncompromisingly original, where his idiosyncratic and at times surreal expression successfully captures both a highly personalised vision of the city, and something of its physical reality - with all its socio-economic problems, and racial tensions.[16] By way of contrast, Salinas's expression in *Todo más claro* strikes the reader as tired, and at times even clichéd. In this collection, Salinas strives to capture the "suma" of Western civilisation, but the thematic weight of such an undertaking is at times too heavy a burden for the rather predictable metaphors he deploys, and the unwieldy, rambling form of many of the poems. The "Hombre en la orilla", for example, is a shadowy, abstract symbol of urban man, alienated and out of control; yet this rather slight symbolic figure must carry the burden of all the social problems of Western, urbanised societies. In addition, he must act as the conveyor of the many literary allusions that overcrowd the poem. He is not, we are told, Shakespeare's Hamlet, that "vagoroso doncel"; nor is the "orilla" he hesitates before that of Jorge Manrique's river of life, flowing inexorably towards death ("Hombre en la orilla II", p.688). Salinas's intention in his recourse to literary antecedents is presumably to expose the 'death of tragedy' in modern existence, the absence of any profound sense of destiny that renders life meaningful. But by exposing the relative insignificance of the "Hombre en la orilla" he effectively undermines this already vague and undefined symbolic figure. This is just one example of Salinas's failure in *Todo más claro* to find an appropriate set of contemporary symbols sufficiently original and forceful to communicate his message.

If we persist in this comparison of Lorca and Salinas, another area of contrast that emerges is their respective tones: both are judgmental, but Lorca strikes an orphic, prophetic tone, whereas Salinas's is meditative. These differing tones are partly the logical outcome of differing personalities and ages, but they are also partly due to each poet's temporal perspective. Working from the assumption that Lorca's poems were first drafted between 1929 and 1930, they can be seen as reflecting the actual crisis of the New York he observed, and predicting an impending crisis in the entire capitalist West. Furthermore, these poems proffer an overtly political solution: no less than the overthrow of the capitalist system. Lorca's call for revolution and blood sacrifice pre-dates the reality of Civil War in Spain, of a second World War, and the ultimate irony of his own role as sacrificial offering. Salinas, on the other hand, wrote from the perspective of the 1940s, having seen how one war had deformed and maimed his own country, and how another now plunged a large portion of the developed world into similar chaos and misery. What political solutions remained? *Todo más claro* conveys a loss of faith in a melioristic world, but Salinas's vision of 'entereza' seems to offer no concrete course of action to rectify the situation. In the 1940s the poet responds to a culture that is not only spiritually, but ideologically bankrupt, so that when a poem such as "Cero" invokes the images of ancient deities, urging the reader to turn back to atavistic forces - it is as much a condemnation of the failure of politics to provide hope for the future, as it is an appeal for a return to non-material values.

Despite the differences between these works, a common theme was developed by both poet's responses to the metropolis, namely, the positive role that nature could play as a model of continuity, consolation and hope in this difficult and insecure age. The theme is discernible in *Todo más claro* in Salinas's presentation of a hierarchy within the empirical world, as nature takes precedence over artefact. But it is most fully developed in the collection published posthumously in 1955, entitled *Confianza*, where we find great consistency of theme and evenness of tone. It is from nature's continuous capacity for regeneration that this poet derives consolation and 'confianza'. Here, 'entereza' functions as a much more positive and effective model of harmony and integration than in *Todo más claro*. But then the emotional and temporal context of this collection is very different: the tone here is meditative, the style lyrical. There is a sense of timelessness that is utterly absent from *Todo más claro*, where history and social realities press hard upon the poet. In so many of these poems, "Presente simple", "Parada", "Esta", nature's tireless reproduction seems to offer the hope of some conceivable version of eternity. Serenity is transmitted by the simplest - and for Salinas as for Guillén the most miraculous - natural phenomena: "Soy feliz en un trino / tembloroso de pajaro" (ll.1-2, "En un trino", pp.793-5).

The development of a poetic voice as distinct as that which we hear in the love-cycle is a significant achievement in its own right, and considerably more than is achieved by many published poets. The fact that Salinas went on to experiment with other poetic styles, and sought an alternative voice with which to address a rapidly changing world, indicates a restless creative spirit, and is a measure of the scale of his poetic aspirations. One is reminded of Salinas's definition of poetry as "una aventura hacia el absoluto"; there are no limits.[17] The need to expand, to occupy new artistic spaces and establish new relationships between his poetry and the world, led almost inevitably, to Salinas's experimentation with the kinds of poetry that could be described as public and private. The poetic results of this ambitious undertaking are, not surprisingly, uneven.

The exploration of private and public expression is yet another dimension of Salinas's 'tema vital', the quest for 'entereza', as he became increasingly attuned to the poet's complex situation as both single, individual consciousness, and as part of a collective entity or will.[18] The fact that the poet is utterly dependent on language as a means of self-realisation, and for the purposes of bridging the gap between self and world, makes his relationship with his medium particularly complex. "El hombre es uno, y, además, uno de tantos o uno de muchos, y es el poeta el que ha de llevar adelante con insigne dificultad este dual destino".[19] Part of the poet's vocation, then, is to take up the challenge of this tricky balancing-act of social and personal expression.

The essays contained in *El defensor* are overtly social in their declared interests: apart from championing the liberal, humanistic values which provided the philosophical framework of Salinas's life and work, they reveal a special interest in the social functions of language. The fact that Salinas felt a need to compose an essay with the ominous title "Defensa del lenguaje" in the 1940s, shows considerable foresight. Already, he was predicting a crisis in social and individual attitudes to language, in an increasingly technological society. Prior to the advent of the micro-chip, the byte, or the reality of artificial intelligence, he was conscious of a growing culture where numeracy would dominate, going as far as to say - "El ser humano contemporáneo tiende a realizarse en el número".[20] The new order, if not exactly anti-literate, would certainly be counter-literate. Many of the fears Salinas expressed in the 1940s have indeed been realised, and his concerns are shared even today by intellectuals, among them George Steiner, who has described contemporary civilisation as an era of the after-word.[21] All these fears and predictions profoundly influenced Salinas's later writings, and explain the partial sacrifice of form to content, the dispensation with conceptual complexity in the interests of clear, unhindered communication.

A truly representative view of Salinas's poetry requires a reading that will bear in mind the central roles played by both metaphysical and historical concerns in his life and work, and an attentive observation of the organic relationships between poetry and the social, temporal realities that make up its matrix. Salinas's entire poetic production was written in an historical period of repeated collective crises, with quite drastic ramifications for the individual consciousness. Out of his need to re-affirm dearly-held values under threat, Salinas wrote poetry: where the love poetry of the 1930s represents a personal affirmation of his aspiration to 'entereza', by the 1940s he sought a more evangelising kind of expression that he hoped would assist its collective adoption and application. As Juan Marichal so eloquently states, Salinas's common aim as poet and critic was to -

> ...hacer patentes los valores humanos de la literatura española por afán de integración universal: las grandes obras hispánicas podían así contribuir al nacimiento de una auténtica comunidad humana del espíritu.[22]

More than this, Salinas believed that not only could contemporary Western society learn from literature, but that there was a pressing need to relearn and salvage the most basic linguistic skills, which he feared were disappearing. His belief in the healing and inspiring powers of literature was founded on his profound faith in the ability of language to communicate - to bridge gaps and heal rifts. In the final

pages of *El defensor*, in a sub-section suggestively entitled "La palabra y la paz",
he clarifies the social and political relevance of this belief, saying - "No hay duda
de que en la palabra cordial e inteligente tiene la violencia su peor enemigo...", and
he quotes the refrán, "hablando se entiende la gente", continuing -

> La lengua es siempre una potencia vinculadora, pero su energía
> vinculatoria está en razón de lo bien que se hable, de la capacidad
> del hablante para poner en palabras propias su pensamiento y sus
> afectos.[23]

While the Second World War raised many doubts in the minds of
intellectuals and artists as to the real relevance of art or literature in the world,
Salinas's faith never faltered. Europe, the home of the humanities, of benevolent
Hellenism, had become the stage of unimagined self-inflicted suffering. Many
artists concluded, sadly, that art and politics could never be congruent. Salinas,
however, remained optimistic. Confronted by the spiritual and ideological vacuum
of the Second World War, he continued to believe in the redemptive powers of
language, in salvation through the word, with a small but potent w. Of course
language has its failings; Salinas recognised these throughout his career, though
never in a way that indicated defeat. Rather, it posed a challenge. No-one knew
better than this most eloquent love-poet that language could never capture the
essence of subjective experience. The only alternative, however, was silence,
which unlike language will never betray or distort meaning, but which for this poet
would have represented an admission of defeat, a surrender to the ineffable, and
above all a vehicle of despair.

Notes

Conclusion

1. This response also extended to Salinas's prose works, including his literary criticism, which he wrote specifically for a wider audience than is usually expected of this genre. Bruce Wardropper, a colleague, commented in 1952 -

> When the recent brilliant books on Jorge Manrique and Rubén Darío drew the Academic Hispanists' fire because of their inapparent documentation, Don Pedro protested that he had deliberately written them as an essayist addressing himself to the general public.

Bruce Wardropper, "Pedro Salinas" *Modern Language Notes* No.67 (1952), p.72.

2. It is also worth noting that the expression of this impulse brought Salinas more success in his prose works of the 1940s than in his poetry. In his literary criticism and the essays collected in *El defensor* Salinas communicates his message with clarity, force, and considerable wit, a factor which is less evident in *Todo más claro*.

3. The obvious exception here is *El Contemplado*, where Salinas retains the highly personal and intimate character of his love poetry.

4. Extracts from the said letters first appeared in Christopher Maurer's article, "Sobre 'joven literatura' y política: cartas de Pedro Salinas y de Federico García Lorca (1930-35)", in *Estelas, laberintos, nuevas sendas. Unamuno, Valle-Inclán, García Lorca, la Guerra Civil*, Co. Ord. Angel G. Loureiro, Anthropos (Barcelona, 1988), pp.297-319. In 1992 Salinas's *Correspondencia*, edited by Andrés Soria Olmedo, was published by Tusquets (Barcelona).

5. This quotation is taken from a letter to Guillén (2.4.31). See Maurer, pp.304-6, as in Note 4.

6. This extract is taken from the same letter (2.4.31), pp.304-6. As in Note 4.

7. As in Note 4, pp.304-6.

8. Again, Salinas addresses Guillén, describing what he deprecatingly terms "la vidita de Madrid" (6.6.30). As in Note 4, pp.299-300.

9. As in Note 4, p.300.

10. Maurer writes: "En septiembre de 1931, momento en que ha sido nombrado vocal de las Misioneras pedagógicas y de la Biblioteca Nacional, Salinas volvería a insistir en su rechazo de la política de partido, y su apoyo a la reforma cultural. Seguirá colaborando (confiesa a Guillén), 'en lo que no es mera política despreciable, sino actividad concreta, definida y privada'. Actividad privada". As in Note 4, p.308.

11. As quoted by Soledad Salinas in her Introduction to *Cartas de amor a Margarita, 1912-15*, ed. Soledad Salinas, Alianza Tres, (Madrid, 1984), p.26.

12. The intellectual climate in the 1940s may have eased this transition for Salinas. Raymond Williams, literary and cultural commentator, had something to say on the historical ebb and flow of the popularity of literature that can be described as public.

> Most writers' statements for or against 'commitment' are now understandably subjective; it is the fashionable tone of the time, at most levels from serious creation to publicity. By contrast, when 'commitment' became the local name for an old kind of argument, in the 1940s, the fashionable tone was more public - in the atmosphere of the war and the resistance.

Raymond Williams, "Commitment" (1988), in *What I Came To Say (1921-88)*, Hutchinson Radius (London, 1990).

13. Pedro Salinas, *La poesía de Rubén Darío*, Seix Barral (Barcelona, 1975), p.217.

14. In another letter to Guillén, Salinas laments this degree of apathy demonstrated by the electorate:

> Y la gente totalmente al margen, en la más absoluta indiferencia, sin importarles nada que haya actos políticos o no, libertades o no, Constitución o no... (6.6.30). As in Note 4, p.300.

15. "Dicho sea de paso, la costumbre de reservar para este tipo de poesía tan solo el nombre de poesía social se me antoja abusiva e impropia". As in Note 13.

16. Howard T. Young also compares *Todo más claro* with Lorca's *Poeta en Nueva York* and concludes that, unlike Lorca, Salinas fails to capture the essence of urban existence in his poetry -

> A pesar de lo acertado de algunas de las imágenes, no creemos que Salinas logre incorporar la experiencia de la ciudad americana a su poesía. Su reacción fue siempre la de un poeta fino, pero su éxito no fue siempre poético. Cedía a la tentación de moralizar.

I would suggest that Lorca's poems are also overtly moralistic, but that the savagery of his indignation and satire, married to the sheer originality of his expression, renders this a poetic strength rather than a weakness. See Howard T. Young, "Pedro Salinas y los Estados Unidos, o la nada y las máquinas", *Cuadernos Hispanoamericanos*, No.145, XLIX, (1962) pp.5-13.

17. See Salinas's preface to a selection of his own poems in Gerardo Diego's *Poesía española contemporánea, 1931-34*, Taurus (Madrid, 1959).

18. In *El defensor*, he glosses the writings of the sociologist Simmel as follows:

> Cree el sociólogo Simmel que el hombre se halla comprendido en la sociedad y a la vez frente a ella. Pero estas dos caracterizaciones no se dan separadas, aisladas, forman una unidad, y lo propiamente humano es el ser elemento de la sociedad y producto de la sociedad al mismo tiempo. De una parte, el hombre siente plenamente su existencia social, y de otra, plenamente también, su existencia individual...

- and goes on to apply the same principles to language, this time quoting Saussure:

> Este estado en lo social tiene exacto correlativo en lo linguísto. Dice Saussure que la palabra obedece, por un lado, a la coacción, a la presión de la lengua común, y, por otro, a la espontaneidad del espíritu y del corazón del hombre que habla. Lenguaje es colaboración inevitable del ser individual y de la sociedad.

Pedro Salinas, *El defensor*, Alianza Tres (Madrid, 1984), pp.218-19.

19. As in Note 18.

20. *El defensor*, p.119. As in Note 18.

284

21. George Steiner, *Real Presences*, Chapter II, "The Broken Contract", Faber (London/Boston, 1989), p.115.

22. Juan Marichal, *Tres voces de Pedro Salinas*, Betancor (Madrid, 1976), p.107.

23. *El defensor*, pp.325-26. As in Note 18.

Bibliography

Works by Pedro Salinas

(i) Poetry

Salinas, Pedro. *Poesías completas*, ed. Soledad Salinas de Marichal, Seix Barral (Barcelona,1981).

Salinas, Pedro. *Poesías escogidas*, ed. Jorge Guillén, Austral (Madrid, 1982).

_____. *Poesías completas, Vols. 1-4*, Alianza, Prologue by Soledad Salinas de Marichal (Madrid, 1990).

_____. *Poesía*, ed. Julio Cortázar, Libro de Bolsillo, Alianza (Madrid, 1980).

(ii) Prose

_____. *Reality and the Poet in Spanish Poetry*, John Hopkins Press (Baltimore, 1966).

_____. *Ensayos completos, Vols. 1-3*, ed. Soledad Salinas de Marichal, Taurus (Madrid, 1983).

_____. *El defensor*, ed. Soledad Salinas de Marichal and Jaime Salinas, Alianza Tres (Madrid, 1984).

_____. *Cartas de amor a Margarita, 1912-15*, ed. Soledad Salinas de Marichal, Alianza Tres, (Madrid, 1984).

_____. *Correspondencia (1923-51)*, ed. Andrés Soria Olmedo, Tusquets (Barcelona, 1992).

_____. *La poesía de Rubén Darío: Ensayo sobre el tema y los temas del poeta*, ed. Soledad Salinas de Marichal and Jaime Salinas, Seix Barral (Barcelona, 1975).

_____. *Jorge Manrique o tradición y originalidad*, ed. Soledad Salinas de Marichal and Jaime Salinas, Seix Barral (Barcelona, 1974).

_____. *Ensayos de literatura hispánica*, ed. Juan Marichal, Aguilar (Madrid, 1966).

_____. *Literatura española siglo XX*, Alianza (Madrid, 1983).

_____. "El poeta y las fases de la realidad", *Insula*, No.146, XIV (15 January 1959), pp.3 & 11.

_____. "Poesía y voz", *Buenos Aires Literaria*, No.13 (13 October 1953), pp.5-16.

_____. "Siete cartas de Pedro Salinas a Jorge Guillén", *Buenos Aires Literaria*, No.13 (13 October 1953), pp.16-37.

_____. "Poética", *Poesía española contemporánea 1931-34*, ed. Gerardo Diego, Taurus (Madrid, 1959).

Secondary Sources

1. Monographs

Allen, Rupert C. *Symbolic experience: A Study of Poems by Pedro Salinas*, University of Alabama Press (Alabama, 1982).

Almela Pérez, Ramón. *Hacia un análisis lingüístico cuantativo de la poesía de Pedro Salinas*, Murcia University Press (Murcia, 1982).

Cirre, J. F. *El mundo lírico de Pedro Salinas*, Editorial Don Quijote (Granada, 1982).

Costa Viva, Olga. *Pedro Salinas, frente a la realidad*, Alfaguarra (Madrid/Barcelona, 1969).

Feal Deibe, Carlos. *La poesía de Pedro Salinas*, Gredos (Madrid, 1965).

Marichal, Juan. *Tres voces de Pedro Salinas*, Betancor (Madrid, 1976).

Palley, Julian. *La luz no usada. La poesía de Pedro Salinas*, Colección Stadium 55, Editoriales de Andrea (Mexico, 1966).

Stixrude, David L. *The Early Poetry of Pedro Salinas*, Castalia (Princeton/Madrid, 1975).

Zubizarreta, Alma de. *Pedro Salinas: el diálogo creador*, Gredos (Madrid, 1969).

2. Other Books

Alonso, Dámaso. *Del siglo de oro a este siglo de siglas*, Gredos (Madrid, 1962), pp.126-67.

Cabrera, Vicente. *Tres poetas a la luz de la metáfora: Salinas, Aleixandre, Guillén*, Gredos (Madrid, 1975), pp.33-46 & 75-117.

Cano, José Luis. *Poesía española del siglo XX*, Guadarrama (Madrid, 1960), pp.199-204.

_____. *La poesía de la generación del '27*, Guadarrama (Madrid, 1970), pp.52-67.

Cirre, J. F. *Forma y espíritu de una lírica española (1920-35)*, Editorial Don Quixote (Granada, 1982), pp.43-70.

Darmangeat, Pierre. *Antonio Machado, Pedro Salinas, Jorge Guillén*, Insula (Madrid, 1969), pp.110-201.

Debicki, Andrew P. *Estudios sobre poesía española contemporánea. La generación de 1924-25*, Gredos (Madrid, 1968), pp.56-110.

Díez Canedo, Enrique. *Estudios de poesía española contemporánea*, Editorial Joaquín Mortiz (Mexico, 1965), pp.197-204.

Havard, Robert. *From Romanticism to Surrealism. Seven Spanish Poets*, University of Wales Press (Cardiff, 1988), pp.142-199.

Hernández Valcárcel, María del Carmen. *La expresión sensorial en cinco poetas de '27*, Murcia University Press (Murcia, 1978), pp.23-95.

Mayoral, Marina. *Poesía española contemporánea*, Gredos (Madrid, 1973), pp.140-150.

Morris, C. B. *A Generation of Spanish Poets 1920-36*, Cambridge University Press (Cambridge, 1969), pp.82-118.

Onís, Federico de. *Antología de la poesía española e hispanoamericana 1882-1932*, Centro de Estudios Históricos (Madrid, 1934), pp.1074-1085.

Río, Angel del. *Estudios sobre literatura contemporánea española*, Gredos (Madrid, 1972), pp.178-235.

Silver, Philip. *La casa de Anteo. Ensayos de poética hispánica (de Antonio Machado a Claudio Rodríguez)*, Taurus (Madrid, 1985), pp.118-147.

Valbuena Prat, Angel. *Historia de la literatura española Vol. IV*, Gustavo Gili (Barcelona, 1968), pp.646-53.

Zuleta, Emilia de. *Cinco poetas españoles*, Gredos (Madrid, 1971), pp.42-107.

3. Homenajes (Individual articles listed under name of author).

Asomante, No.2 (April-June 1952).
Boletín de la fundación F. G. Lorca, No.3 (June 1988).
Buenos Aires Literaria, No.13 (October 1953).
Hispania, No.2, XXXV (May 1952).
Insula, No.74 (15 February 1952).
Insula, No.300-1 (November-December 1971).

4. Articles and Introductions

Agrait, Gustavo. "Pedro Salinas en Puerto Rico", *Insula*, No.356-7 (1976), p.10.

_____. "A Pedro Salinas", *Asomante*, No.2 (April-June 1952), pp.71-2.

Aguilera, Francisco. "La voz del poeta", *Hispania*, No.2, XXXV (May 1952), p.132.

Alberti, Rafael. "En la muerte del poeta Pedro Salinas", *El Tiempo* (13 January 1952), p.3.

Aleixandre, Vicente. "Pedro Salinas", *Hispania*, No.2, XXXV (May 1952), pp.132-3.

_____. "En casa de Pedro Salinas" in *Pedro Salinas*, ed. A. P. Debicki, El escritor y la crítica, Taurus (Madrid, 1976), pp.43-44.

288

Alonso, Dámaso. "España en las cartas de Pedro Salinas", *Insula*, No.74 (15 February 1952), pp.1 & 5.

_____. "Un poeta y un libro" *Revista del Occidente*, No.98, XXXIII (1931), pp.239-246.

_____. "Con Pedro Salinas", in *Pedro Salinas*, ed. A. P. Debicki, El escritor y la crítica, Taurus (Madrid, 1976), pp.53-60.

Bataillon, Marcel. "Salinas, anacreóntico del siglo XX", *Hispania*, XXXV (May 1952), pp.133-4.

_____. "Pedro Salinas 1892-51", *Nécrologie: Bulletin Hispanique*, No.1, LIV (1952), pp.112-116.

Bell, Alan S. "Pedro Salinas' challenge to T. S. Eliot's concept of tradition", *Revista de Estudios Hispánicos*, University of Alabama, No.1, XL (September 1967), pp.43-52.

Blanco, Tomás. "Estancia en la isla", *Asomante*, No. 2 (April-June 1952), pp.54-63.

Blecua, J. M. "Una charla con Pedro Salinas", *Insula*, No.70 (15 October 1951), pp.2-4.

_____. "El amor en la poesía de Pedro Salinas", *Hispania*, No.2, XXXV (May 1952), pp.134-7.

Bou, Enric. "Salinas, al otro lado del océano", *Boletín de la fundación F. G. Lorca*, No.3 (June 1988), pp.38-45.

Bravo Villasante, Carmen. "La poesía de Pedro Salinas", *Clavileño*, No.21 (1953), pp.44-52.

Canito, Enrique. "Pedro Salinas: profesor en Sevilla", *Insula*, No.74 (15 February 1952), p.5.

Cano, J. L. "Dos cartas de Salinas a Cernuda", *Insula*, No.300-1(November-December 1971), p.12.

Capote, Higinio. "Memoria de Pedro Salinas", *Estudios Americanos*, No.12, IV (January 1952), pp.55-62.

Carpintero, Heliodoro. "Pedro Salinas y Gabriel Miró", *Insula*, No.300-1 (November-December 1971), pp.11-12.

Castro de Zubiri, Carmen. "Recuerdo de Pedro Salinas", *Hispania*, No.2, XXXV (May 1952), p.156.

Ciplijauskaite, Birute. "Oasis en el destierro", *Insula*, No.356-7 (July-August 1976), p.7.

_____. "Salinas 'el atento'", *Boletín de la fundación F. G. Lorca*, No.3 (June 1988), pp.29-33.

Cirre, J. F. "Pedro Salinas y su poética", in *Homenaje a Rodríguez Moñino, Vol. I*, Castalia (Madrid, 1966), pp.91-97.

Correa, Gustavo. "El Contemplado", *Hispania*, No.2, (May 1952), pp.137-42.

Costa Viva, Olga. "Pedro Salinas: exaltación de la realidad", *Revista de la Universidad Nacional de Buenos Aires*, No.3, V (July-September 1960), pp.347-58.

Cremer, V. "Fábula y signo de la poesía de Pedro Salinas", *Estafeta Literaria*, No.399 (1 June 1968), pp.11-12.

Debicki, Andrew P. "La metáfora en algunos poemas tempranos de Salinas", in *Pedro Salinas*, ed. A. P. Debicki, El escritor y la crítica, Taurus (Madrid, 1976), pp.113-117.

_____. "La visión del mundo en la poesía temprana de Pedro Salinas", *Cuadernos Hispanoamericanos*, No.205 (1965), pp.64-80.

Dehennin, E. "Pedro Salinas: Inspiration et effort créateur", *Bulletin Hispanique*, No.2, LX (1958), pp.208-215.

Devlin, John. "Reality and the Poet. Pedro Salinas", *Renascence*, No.24 (1971), pp.102-9.

Díez-Canedo, Enrique. "Fábula y signo", in *Pedro Salinas*, ed. A. P. Debicki, El escritor y la crítica, Taurus (Madrid, 1976), pp.109-111.

Durán, Manuel. "Pedro Salinas y su *Nocturno de los avisos*", *Insula*, No.300-1 (November-December 1971), pp.1 & 21.

Doreste, Ventura. "Claridad y rigor en la poesía de Salinas", *Insula*, No.74 (15 February 1952), pp.3, 10 & 11.

Feal Deibe, Carlos. "La amada de verdad y la incompleta en dos narraciones de Pedro Salinas", *Revista Hispánica Moderna*, XLIV (June 1991), pp.48-58.

Feldbaum, J. "El trasmundo de la obra poética de Pedro Salinas", *Revista Hispánica Moderna*, XXII (1956), pp.12-34.

Fernández Méndez, E. "Pedro Salinas: Quixote moderno", *Asomante*, No.2 (April-June 1952), pp.84-6.

Florit, Eugenio. "Mi Pedro Salinas", *Hispania*, No.2, XXXV (May 1952), pp.146-7.

Frutos, Eugenio. "Ser y decir en la poesía de Salinas", *Insula*, No.39 (15 March 1949), pp.1-2.

Gilman, Stephen. "El proemio a *La voz a ti debida*", in *Pedro Salinas*, ed. A. P. Debicki, El escritor y la crítica, Taurus (Madrid, 1976), pp.119-151.

_____. "América y Don Pedro Salinas", *Hispania*, No.2, XXXV (May 1952), pp.147-8.

Gómez de la Serna. "Novísimos Retratos: Salinas y Guillén", *La Nación* (31 August 1947), Sección Artes/Letras, p.1.

Gómez Paz, Julieta. "El amor en la poesía de Pedro Salinas", *Buenos Aires Literaria*, No.13 (October 1953), pp.55-68.

González Muela, Joaquín. "Poesía y amistad: Jorge Guillén y Pedro Salinas" in *Pedro Salinas*, ed. A. P. Debicki, El escritor y la crítica, Taurus (Madrid, 1976), pp.197-203.

Guillén, Jorge. Introduction to *Reality and the Poet in Spanish Poetry*, John Hopkins University Press (Baltimore, 1966), pp.ix-xxx.

_____. Prologue to *Poemas escogidos*, Austral (Madrid, 1982), pp.11-14.

_____. Prologue to Alma de Zubizarreta's *El diálogo creador*, Gredos (Madrid, 1969), pp.9-19.

_____. "Pedro Salinas: poeta y profesor", *Hispania*, No.2, XXXV (May 1952), pp.148-150.

_____. "Tres poemas de Pedro Salinas", Insula, No.300-1 (November-December 1971), pp.1 & 19.

_____. "Elogio de Pedro Salinas" in *Pedro Salinas*, ed. A. P. Debicki, El escritor y la crítica, Taurus (Madrid, 1976), pp.25-33.

_____. "Poesía de Pedro Salinas", *Buenos Aires Literaria*, No.13 (October 1953), pp.41-54.

_____. "Mientras hubo...", *Insula*, No.74 (15 February 1952), pp.1-2.

Gullón, Ricardo. "La poesía de Pedro Salinas", *Asomante*, No.2 (April-June 1952), pp.345.

_____. "La multiforme transparencia de Pedro Salinas", *Hispania*, No.2, XXXV (May 1952), pp.150-1.

_____. "Salinas el intelectual", *Insula*, No.74 (15 February 1952), pp.9-10.

Havard, Robert, G. "The reality of words in the poetry of Pedro Salinas", *Bulletin of Hispanic Studies*, LI (1974), pp.28-47.

_____. "Pedro Salinas and courtly love. The 'amada' in *La voz a ti debida*: woman, muse and symbol", *Bulletin of Hispanic Studies*, LVI (1979), pp.123-44.

_____. "Meaning and metaphor of syntax in Bécquer, Guillén and Salinas", *Iberoromania*, No.19 (1984), pp.66-81.

Helman, Edith. "Pedro Salinas y la crítica desde dentro", *Revista Hispánica Moderna*, XXXI (1965), pp.222-229.

Lewis de Galanes, Adriana. "*El Contemplado*: el infinito poseído por Pedro Salinas", *Revista Hispánica Moderna*, XXXIII (1967), pp.38-54.

Lida, Raimundo. "Camino del poema. *Confianza* de Pedro Salinas", in *Pedro Salinas*, ed. A. P. Debicki, El escritor y la crítica, Taurus (Madrid, 1976), pp.169-195.

Llorens, Vicente. "El desterrado y su lengua", *Asomante*, No.2 (April-June 1952), pp.46-53.

_____. "Trayectoria poética de Pedro Salinas", *Insula*, No.300-1 (November-December 1971), pp.44-5.

Mainer, J. C. "Pedro Salinas y el lugar del escritor", *Insula*, No.300-1 (November-December 1971), p.8.

Marco, J. "Tensión poética en Pedro Salinas: una aproximación", *Insula* No.300-1 (November-December 1971), p.18.

Marías, Julián. "Pedro Salinas en la frontera", *Hispania*, No.2, XXXV (May 1952), pp.152-3.

Marichal, Juan. Introduction to *El defensor*, Alianza Tres (Madrid, 1984), pp.9-14.

_____. "La poesía de Pedro Salinas", *Letras*, No.74-75, XXXVII (1965), pp.435-6.

Marichalar, Inés de. "El proceso de comunicación en Pedro Salinas", *Prohemio*, No.4 (1973), pp.379-403.

Maurer, Christopher. "Notas" on "Ocho cartas inéditas a F. G. Lorca", *Boletín de la fundación F. G. Lorca*, No.3 (June 1988), pp.12-21.

_____. "Nota Introductoria" to "Pedro Salinas, Miguel Pérez Ferrero y César González Ruano: Defensa y crítica de la antología de Gerardo Diego" (1932), *Boletín de la fundación F. G. Lorca*, No.3 (1988), pp.54-64.

_____. "Sobre 'joven literatura' y política: cartas de Pedro Salinas y de Federico García Lorca (1930-1935)", in *Estelas, Laberintos, Nuevas Sendas. Unamuno, Valle-Inclán, García Lorca, la Guerra Civil*, Co-Ord. A. Loureiro, Anthropos (Barcelona, 1988), pp.217-319.

Morello de Frosch, Martha. "Salinas y Guillén: dos formas de esencialidad", *Revista Hispánica Moderna*, XXVII (1961), pp.16-22.

Morris, C. B. "Pedro Salinas and Marcel Proust", *Revue de Littérature Comparée*, No.44 (1970), pp.195-214.

Múñoz Marín, L. "Testimonio de fe", *Hispania*, No.2, XXXV (May 1952), p.153.

Palley, Julian. "*Presagios* de Pedro Salinas", in *Pedro Salinas*, ed. A. P. Debicki, El escritor y la crítica, Taurus (Madrid, 1976), pp.99-197.

Prat, I. "Formas de continuidad en la poesía de Pedro Salinas", *Insula*, No.300-1 (November-December 1971), p.15.

Quiroga, José María. "El espejo ardiendo", *Cruz y Raya*, No.11 (1934), p.99-116.

Río, Angel del. "El poeta Pedro Salinas", in *Pedro Salinas*, ed. A. P. Debicki, El escritor y la crítica, Taurus (Madrid, 1976), pp.15-23.

_____. "El Contemplado", *Hispania*, No.2 (May 1952), pp.142-44.

Rogers, D. "Espejos and Reflejos in Pedro Salinas", *Revista de Literatura*, No.29 (1966), pp.57-66.

Rosales, Luis. "Dulce sueño donde hay luz", *Cruz y Raya*, No.2 (1934), pp.118-127.

Salinas de Marichal, Soledad. Introduction to *Cartas de amor a Margarita, 1912-15*, Alianza Tres (Madrid, 1984), pp.11-28.

_____. "El primer Salinas", in *Boletín de la fundación F. G. Lorca*, No.3 (June 1988), pp.22-28.

Solana, Rafael. "Salinas, poeta de sí y de no", *Letras de México*, No.32 (1938), p.4.

Spitzer, Leo. "El conceptismo interior de Pedro Salinas", *Revista Hispánica Moderna*, VII (1941), pp.33-69.

Stixrude, David L. "El *Largo lamento* de Pedro Salinas", *Papeles de San Armadans*, No.232, LXXVIII (July 1975), pp.7-36.

_____. "El mundo léxico de Pedro Salinas", in *Aventura Poética*, ed. D. Stixrude, Cátedra (Madrid, 1982), pp.23-53.

Torre, Guillermo de. "Pedro Salinas en mi recuerdo y en sus cartas", *Buenos Aires Literaria*, No.13 (1953), pp.87-96.

_____. "Presencia de Pedro Salinas", *Cuadernos Hispanoamericanos*, No.52, XIX (April 1954), pp.32-38.

Valender, James. "Salinas y Altolaguirre: un poema olvidado y tres cartas", *Boletín de la fundación F. G. Lorca*, No.3 (June 1988), pp.46-53.

Villegas, Juan. "El amor y la salvación existencial en dos poemas de Pedro Salinas", in *Pedro Salinas*, ed. A. P. Debicki, El escritor y la crítica, Taurus (Madrid, 1976), pp.129-41.

Walsh, María Elena. "Pedro Salinas y su triángulo de silencios", *Buenos Aires Literaria*, No.13 (October 1953), pp.109-113.

Wardropper, Bruce. "Pedro Salinas", *Modern Language Notes*, No.67 (1952), p.72.

Young, Howard T. "Pedro Salinas y los Estados Unidos, o la nada y las máquinas", *Cuadernos Hispanoamericanos*, No.145, XLIX (January 1962), pp.5-13.

5. Spanish literature

Alberti, Rafael. *Sobre los ángeles*, Seix Barral (Barcelona, 1978).

Alonso, Amado. *Materia y forma en poesía*, Gredos (Madrid, 1955).

_____. *Estudios lingüísticos: temas españoles*, Gredos (Madrid, 1951).

Alonso, Dámaso. *Poesía española. Ensayo de método y límites estilísticos*, Gredos (Madrid, 1950).

Ballesta, Juan Cano. *La poesía española entre pureza y revolución (1930-36)*, Gredos (Madrid, 1972).

Bécquer, Gustavo Adolfo. *Rimas*, Clásicos Castellanos (Madrid, 1975).

_____. *Rimas y prosas*, Ediciones Rialp (Madrid, 1968).

Blanch, Antonio. *La poesía pura española: conexiones con la cultura francesa*, Gredos (Madrid, 1976).

Bousoño, Carlos. *Teoría de la expresión poética*, Gredos (Madrid, 1970).

Calderón de la Barca. *Obras completas, Vol. I*, Aguilar (Madrid, 1959).

Cano, José Luis. *De Machado a Bousoño. Notas sobre poesía española contemporánea*, Insula (Madrid, 1955).

Caracciolo Trejo. *La poesía de Vicente Huidobro y la vanguardia*, Gredos (Madrid, 1974).

Castro, Américo. *La realidad histórica de España*, Ediciones Porrúa, (Mexico, 1954).

Cernuda, Luis. *Poesías completas*, ed. Derek Harris and Luis Maristany, Barral Editores (Barcelona, 1977).

Ciplijauskaite, Birute. *El poeta y la poesía: del romanticismo a la poesía social*, Insula (Madrid, 1966).

——————————. *La soledad y la poesía española contemporánea*, Insula (Madrid, 1962).

Cruz, Juan de la. *The poems of St. John of the Cross*, ed. Roy Campbell, Pantheon Books (London, 1951).

Cummins, J. G. *The Spanish Traditional Lyric*, Pergamon, (Oxford, 1977).

Díaz-Plaja, Guillermo. *Hacia un concepto de la literatura española: ensayos elegidos, (1931-41)*, Espasa-Calpe (Madrid, 1962).

Encina, Juan del. *Poesía lírica y cancionero musical*, ed. R. O. Jones and C. R. Lee, Clásicos Castalia (Madrid, 1975).

García Lorca, Federico. *Poeta en Nueva York*, Lumen (Barcelona, 1976).

Garcilaso de la Vega. *Poesías castellanas completas*, ed. Elias L. Rivers, Clásicos Castalia (Madrid, 1972).

González Muela, Joaquín. *El lenguaje poético de la generación Guillén-Lorca*, Insula (Madrid, 1955).

Guillén, Jorge. *Cántico '28*, ed. Víctor Pozanco, Ambito Literario (Barcelona, 1978).

——————. *Cántico '36*, ed. José Manuel Blecua, Labor (Barcelona, 1970).

Gullón, Ricardo. *Conversaciones con Juan Ramón Jiménez*, Taurus (Madrid, 1958).

Huidobro, Vicente. *Poesías*, ed. Enrique Lihn, Casa de las Américas (Havana, 1968).

Jiménez, Juan Ramón. *Segunda Antolojía poética*, ed. Leopoldo de Luis, Austral (Madrid, 1983).

Machado, Antonio. *Poesías completas*, ed. Manuel Alvar, Austral (Madrid, 1982).

Manrique, Jorge. *Cancionero*, ed. Augusto de Cortina, Clásicos Castellanos (Madrid, 1975).

Marcial de Onís, Carlos. *El surrealismo y cuatro poetas de la generación del '27*, Ediciones José Porrúa Turanzas (Madrid, 1974).

Morla, Carlos. *En España con Federico García Lorca*, Aguilar (Madrid, 1958)

Morris, C. B. *Surrealism and Spain (1920-36)*, Cambridge University Press (Cambridge, 1972).

Onís, Federico de. *Ensayos sobre el sentimiento de la cultura española*, Residencia de estudiantes (Madrid, 1932).

Quevedo, Francisco de. *Poemas escogidos*, ed. José Manuel Blecua, Clásicos Castalia (Madrid, 1981).

Spitzer, Leo. *Lingüística e historia literaria*, Gredos (Madrid, 1955).

Terry, Arthur. *An Anthology of Spanish Poetry, Part II, 1580-1700*, Pergamon (Oxford/London, 1968).
Torre, Guillermo de. *Literaturas europeas de vanguardia*, Guadarrama (Madrid, 1965).
Videla, Gloria. *El ultraísmo: Estudios sobre movimientos poéticos de vanguardia en España*, Gredos (Madrid, 1971).

6. Other

Ades, Dawn. *Photomontage*, World of Art Series, Thames and Hudson (London, 1986).
Cirlot, J. E. *Dictionary of Symbols*, Routledge and Kegan Paul (London, 1971).
Culler, J. *The Pursuit of Signs*, Routledge and Kegan Paul (London, 1981).
Derrida, Jacques. "Structure, Sign and Play in the Discourses of the Human Sciences", in *Writing and Difference*, Routledge (London, 1978).
Ginestier, Paul. *The Poet and the Machine*, Chapel Hill (University of North Carolina, 1961).
Jameson, Frederic. *The Political Unconscious. Narrative as a socially symbolic act*, Methuen (Cornell University, 1981).
Jung, C. J. *Selected Writings*, ed. Anthony Storr, Fontana (London, 1986).
Keats, John. *The poems of John Keats*, ed. Jack Stillinger, Heinnemann (London, 1978).
Lewis, C. S. *The Allegory of Love: A Study in Medieval Tradition*, Oxford University Press, (Oxford, 1973).
Steiner, George. *Real Presences*, Faber (London/Boston, 1989).
Williams, Raymond. *What I Came To Say (1921-88)*, Hutchinson Radius (London, 1990).
_____. *The Politics of Modernism*, Verso (London, 1989).

Index